The Public Sector's Guide to
Skill-based Pay

System Development & Implementation

Targeting the Essential Techniques, Tips, and
Pitfalls in Skill-based Pay System Design

TABLE OF CONTENTS

ABOUT *THE GUIDE*: MESSAGE FROM THE AUTHOR

		Page Number
❋ Symbols Used in the Guide	....	2
❋ Definitions	....	3
❋ Introduction	....	7

CHAPTER ONE – BUILDING THE FOUNDATION

		Page Number
❋ Traditional VS. Skill Based	....	13
❋ Perception is Reality	....	16
❋ Organizational Readiness	....	19
❋ Summary of Appendices	....	29

CHAPTER TWO – DEFINING AND CONSTRUCTING

		Page Number
❋ Skill Hierarchy Identification	....	33
❋ Summary of Appendices	....	50

CHAPTER 3 – FORMATTING

		Page Number
❋ Skill Summary	....	53
❋ Learning Approaches	....	55
❋ Tying it All Together	....	60
❋ Summary of Appendices	....	62

CHAPTER 4 – REFINING

		Page Number
• Moving into Skill Tracks	....	71
• Skill Hierarchy and Sub Zones	....	74
• Summary of Appendices	....	79

CHAPTER 5 – OBJECTIVES AND CERTIFICATION MANUAL

		Page Number
• The Certification Manual	....	81
• Writing Skill Objectives	....	82
• Six Questions	....	84
• Summary of Appendices	....	93

CHAPTER 6 – FINALIZING YOUR MANUAL

		Page Number
• Requesting Additional Feedback	....	95
• Summary of Appendices	....	100

CHAPTER 7 – BEGINNING IMPLEMENTATION

		Page Number
• Assessing Current Employees	....	102
• Employee Skill Assessment	....	104
• Assessing New Hires	....	105
• Summary of Appendices	....	110

CHAPTER 8 – LINKING PAY TO YOUR SYSTEM

	Page Number
• Position Evaluation	113
• Broadbanding	113
• The Benefits of Broadbanding	116
• Examples of Broadbanding	120
• Reward Strategies	126
• Salary Survey Issues	127
• Design Issues	128
• Input	129
• Updating the Structure	129
• Summary of Appendices	131

CHAPTER 9 – CONTINUING IMPLEMENTATION AND ADMINISTRATION

	Page Number
• Skill Certification/Demonstration	133
• Current Employees	135
• New Employees	137
• Training Opportunities	138
• Movement Through Zones	139
• Summary of Appendices	140
• Closing Comments	141
• Index	143

APPENDICES

		Appendix
Organizational Readiness	....	A
Strategy Development	....	B
Skill Hierarchy	....	C
Skill Rating Tools	....	D
Category and Zone Table	....	E
Certification Training Methods	....	F
Skill Hierarchy Table	....	G
Skill Objectives Table	....	H
Inventory Scale	....	I
Sample Position Questionnaire	....	J
Broadbanded Job Descriptions	....	K
Sample Pay Structures	....	L
Policy and Administration	....	M
Certification Manual	....	N
Skill Lists and Ratings	....	O
Sample Skill Objectives	....	P
Visuals and Presentations	....	Q

The Public Sector's Guide to Skill-based Pay

ABOUT *THE GUIDE*: MESSAGE FROM THE AUTHOR

Welcome to *The Public Sector's Guide to Skill-based Pay (The Guide)*. Whether you are considering the implementation of Skill-based Pay or updating your current system, the practical examples and experience-based information provided here are sure to help. Written in a 9-chapter, step-wise format, *The Guide* provides a systematic methodology for design and implementation. As you progress further into this collection of hands-on materials and thought-provoking ideas, you will discover how *The Guide* can assist in designing and implementing a new approach toward people and pay in the public sector work environment.

As you begin your journey, understand that designing and implementing any pay plan is an ongoing process. The effort to assimilate a Skill-based Pay plan into your organization's culture will require a great deal of commitment, attention to detail and ability to adapt, both pre- and post-implementation. The intent of *The Guide* is to provide direction on how to approach this process during the development and implementation stages. These suggestions are based on the most current research available as well as our work experience in the design and implementation of Skill-based Pay plans for numerous organizations in a multitude of environments. Furthermore, *The Guide* will provide a strong foundation for your Skill-based Pay system and will greatly increase the probability of your program's success.

The Public Sector's Guide to Skill-based Pay

SYMBOLS USED IN *THE GUIDE*

Throughout you will see items, graphs, diagrams or sections of text marked with helpful symbols. These symbols represent tools and tips we want to emphasize in order to aid in the development and implementation process.

📖 NARRATIVE EXPLANATION

A Narrative Explanation is provided at each key step of the design and implementation process and is designated with the 📖 symbol. The narrative is intended to provide a more comprehensive description of each key step. These narratives are taken from direct experience. (For those of you that prefer charts and graphs to narratives, there will be plenty of these too.)

⚒ TOOLS

The tools symbol will be placed next to tables, charts, diagrams, etc. that will help you develop your Skill-based Pay system, communicate its features to others and save time. Use items marked with the ⚒ symbol as handouts for employees; illustrations for group presentations; communication sessions, etc. To make things even easier, review our comprehensive appendix section for the tools described in *The Guide*. The appendix has been designed as your personal, step-by-step, handbook for you to use in the development of your Skill-based Pay system.

🕯 HOT TIP

Due to the particular importance of some information contained in *The Guide*, we want to make certain we have your attention. The Hot Tip symbol, (🕯), is an alert for information in which you should pay special attention. These are tips that are particularly important in order for you to avoid potential pitfalls.

DEFINITIONS

Certification: The process of evaluating an employee's skill level and progress within a skill hierarchy. Certification may involve supervisory observation of performance, written tests, completion of formal training, or other pre-determined means.

Certification Manual: These manuals serve to specify how demonstration of the mastery of skills is achieved. It answers the questions…
- Which skills are important for each position within the plan?
- Which skills need to be learned first?
- Which skills need to be learned next as part of a long-term career strategy?
- What are the important conditions or constraints under which each employee must perform?
- What is the documentation needed in order to demonstrate that the employee has attained the required skill and how well must employees perform for certification or re-certification?

Gate: Requirements to be met before an employee is allowed to move from one Skill-based Pay zone or sub-zone, into the next higher zone or sub-zone (see below). Gates assist in cost containment and return on investment (ROI) for the implementing organization in a Skill-based Pay system through requirements such as a minimum time prerequisite in a zone, successful performance appraisal scores, and demonstration of mastery of all skills required within a zone.

Foundation Skills: These skills are not typically part of the skill hierarchy or Skill-based Pay system, but they still need to be learned and practiced by the employee on an ongoing basis. Foundation skills are essential for the successful performance of the job, but are not necessarily directly related to skills required to perform the task(s). For example, keeping work areas clean; opening and closing a facility, maintaining customer contact, safety, etc. would be considered Foundation Skills.

Skill: A broad term used in *The Guide* to describe any ability, knowledge-base, skill, certification, work task, etc. that is necessary for a particular job (or position) or group of jobs (or positions) that needs training to master.

Skill Hierarchy: The organized, structured listing of all skills for a particular job or skill group. The skills are typically arranged by zone and sub-zone (see below), from those skills to be learned first in a career through those skills learned later in a career.

Skill Mastery: When an employee demonstrates his or her ability to perform or use a particular skill in the skill hierarchy as defined by the plan in the Certification Manual (see above).

Skill Zone: A grouping of skills that are relatively equivalent in their level of difficulty and importance as well as when they should be learned in the progression of a particular job/position/group.

Sub-zone: A grouping of skills within a skill zone. As with skill zones, sub-zones are skills or sets of skills that have similar difficulty and importance, or skills that need to be learned at a particular point within an employee's career. Sub-zones allow for faster learning and result in rewards managed through policy decisions.

Subject Matter Experts (Subject Matter Expert): Those employees with detailed knowledge of a job included in the Skill-based Pay system. Most often, subject matter experts include current job incumbents, direct supervisors and human resource professionals. Subject Matter Expert Teams are groups of these employees working in the development of the Skill-based Pay system.

Tracks: Multiple skill hierarchies contained within the same Skill-based Pay family of jobs or job groupings. Tracks are often interrelated and used to encourage the identification of cross-training needs and opportunities.

In order to get the most from *The Guide*, we suggest taking notes as you read, with a particular emphasis on how the information provided herein might apply to <u>your specific situation</u>. You will also find *The Guide* useful in providing your project participants with the steps and work papers needed in developing your tailored Skill-based Pay system. Use this information as a design catalyst rather than as a set of inflexible steps. There is not one perfect Skill-based Pay system – only the one which is perfect for your organization and its needs.

The Public Sector's Guide to Skill-based Pay

Also note, at the end of each Chapter, we have provided a space for your personal notes as shown below…

✎ *My Chapter Notes:*

The Public Sector's Guide to Skill-based Pay

INTRODUCTION

Skill-based Pay (SBP) varies from traditional compensation methodologies in that it is a <u>person-based</u> rather than a <u>job-based</u> form of compensation. In a traditional, job-based compensation system, the nature of the work and the value of the job is the focus of determining pay decisions for individual employees. The amount of pay an employee receives is a function of the value of the job, not necessarily the value of the employee. However, in a Skill-based plan, employees are encouraged, developed, and rewarded for increasing their knowledge, skills, competencies, and their ability to contribute to the attainment of organizational and/or department goals. In this situation, the amount of pay an employee receives is a function of their individual value to the organization, as measured by the quantity and quality of the skills measured.

Just as if you were using a basic blueprint to build a house, *The Guide* serves as a blueprint for building a Skill-based Pay system. As you begin to build your house, you will find you may want to add a wing, or modify part of the kitchen. Likewise, you will find the need to remain flexible when constructing your Skill-based Pay plan. We encourage you to take these ideas and modify them to suit your needs. Moreover, every organization is unique, which means every system will be unique. *The Guide* provides a solid development process that, if followed closely, will result in the creation of an operational system.

The Public Sector's Guide to Skill-based Pay

📖 *Introduction continued...*

The City of Blue Skies is a fictitious city used in *The Guide* in order to provide practical examples of a working Skill-based Pay Plan. This is their story...

Last year, the City of Blue Skies decided to implement a Skill-based Pay system within its Water Utilities Department, with the goal of increasing cross-training and rewarding employees for skill attainment. Cross-training and skill development were viewed as a way to increase the productive capacity of the Department's overall workforce. Blue Skies' Water Utility Department was also faced with a significant budget shortfall. As an initial step to address the budget challenges, the Department Director made the decision to permanently eliminate all vacant positions. This resulted in the elimination of approximately 10% of all position titles and was a significant factor in reducing the Department's budget deficit. Skill-based Pay was presented to the employee group as a method to encourage their commitment to increasing productivity and their earning capacity during difficult times.

The Department had two major divisions: Water Distribution and Wastewater Collection. These two divisions had two major work groups in the technical field: Water Distribution Operator and Wastewater Collection Technician. These two work groups accounted for the majority of the Department's workforce. Prior to Skill-based Pay, the two divisions operated autonomously. After the Skill-based Pay system was installed, the divisions were merged and employees were cross-trained between the two in order to provide maximum productivity with minimum staffing levels.

During the development phase of the Skill-based Pay system, management decided each employee would focus on one of two primary career tracks: Water Distribution or Wastewater Collection. Additionally, each employee would be required to complete a core track which focused on overall career goals and department strategies.

Introduction continued...

The core track included skill development in areas such as safety, customer service and policy issues. The Skill-based Pay Project Team as well as Management and Subject Matter Expert teams worked over a six month period to create the resulting Skill-based Pay plan composed of the three tracks: 1) Foundation & Development, 2) Water Distribution, and 3) Wastewater Collection. An example is provided below in TABLE 1 and a more complete illustration may be found in TABLE 18 on page 73. When the program was introduced, two of the three tracks were assigned to each employee. The tracks assigned included a Foundation and Development track and one of the other two primary tracks, either Water Distribution or Wastewater Collection. The primary track to which an employee was assigned was dependent upon the employee's experience and the needs of the organization. For example, if an employee was more skilled in Water Distribution, then this was their primary track and they would have the opportunity to cross-train in Wastewater Collection. ∎

TABLE 1

	Track 1 Foundation and Development Skill Blocks (Completion of this track is required for all employees.)	Track 2 Water Distribution Technical Skill Blocks	Track 3 Wastewater Collection Technical Skill Blocks
Skill Zone 1: 6 Months. All minimum requirements for position must be met within 6 months of employment.	1. City Policy Review 2. Defensive Driving 3. First Aid/CPR 4. Basic Haz-mat 5. Confined Space Entry 6. Two-way Radio Protocol	1. Water Mainlines 2. Valves 3. Fire Hydrants 4. Service Connections 5. Disinfection/Sanitation 6. Basic Equipment Operation	1. Wastewater Mainlines 2. Manholes 3. Inflow/Infiltration 4. Service Connections 5. Disinfection/Sanitation 6. Basic Equipment Operation
Skill Zone 2: 1 Year. All certification in Skill Zone 1 has been completed for Tracks 1 and 2 or 3.	1. Operational Policies 2. Traffic Control 3. Basic Computer Skills/Work Orders 4. Customer Service 5. Plan and Map Reading 6. Teamwork	1. TNRCC Approved Basic Water 2. Water Mainlines 3. Valves 4. Fire Hydrants 5. Service Connections 6. Journey Level Equipment Operation	1. TNRCC Approved Basic Wastewater 2. Wastewater Mainlines 3. Manholes 4. Inflow/Infiltration 5. Service Connections 6. Journey Level Equipment Operation
Skill Zone 3: 1 Year. All certification in Skill Zone 2 has been completed. Tracks 1 and 2 or 3 have been completed in Skill Zone 2.	1. Operational Policies 2. Stress Awareness 3. Hazardous Materials 4. Trench Safety	1. TNRCC Approved Water Distribution 2. Electronic Detection 3. Disinfection Calculations 4. Water Mainlines/Appurtenances 5. Valves 6. Fire Hydrants 7. Service Connection	1. TNRCC Approved Wastewater Collection Class 2. Electronic Detection 3. SSO Reports/Disinfection/I&I 4. Wastewater Mainlines 5. Manholes
Skill Zone 4: 1 Year. All certification in Skill Zone 3 has been completed for Tracks 1 and 2 or 3.	1. System Mapping/GIS 2. Customer Service "D" 3. Leadership	1. Selected TNRCC Approved Class "C" Certification from TNRCC 2. Water Mainlines 3. Valves 4. Fire Hydrants 5. Service Connections 6. Disinfection/Sampling 7. Equipment Operation	1. Selected TNRCC Approved Class Class "II" Certification from TNRCC 2. Wastewater Mainlines 3. Manholes 4. Disinfection/Sampling 5. Equipment Operation

The Public Sector's Guide to Skill-based Pay

📖 *Introduction continued...*

We will focus on the technical classifications of Water Distribution Operators and the Wastewater Collection Technicians and the resultant position title of Water Operator (see diagram below) throughout *The Guide* in order to explain the development and implementation process. However, the action plan can be applied to any group of jobs targeted for Skill-based Pay.

DIAGRAM 1

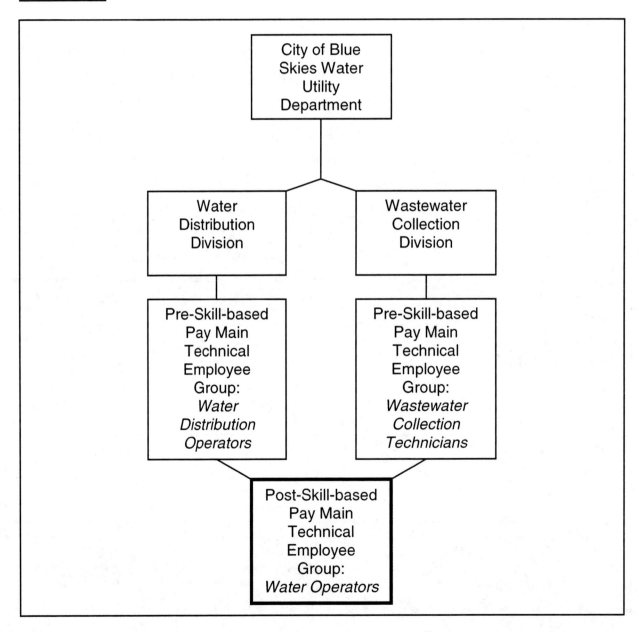

The Public Sector's Guide to Skill-based Pay

Let's get started...

✎ My Chapter Notes:

CHAPTER 1
Building the Foundation of your Skill-based Pay System through Effective Communication

> *There is nothing more difficult to plan, more doubtful of success, nor more dangerous to manage than the creation of a new system.*
>
> *- Machiavelli (1469-1527)*

The implementation of a Skill-based Pay system is a major undertaking that will impact the entire organization. It is important to approach the decision to implement Skill-based Pay from a strategic perspective. The question that needs to be answered is how this type of developmental and reward system can contribute to the accomplishment of goals and to the performance of desired employee behaviors in your specific culture.

As in our opening statements about the City of Blue Skies' Water Utility Department, the goal to integrate two divisions into one efficiently performing department was the focus during the development of the program. Once you determine your strategic business goals, your Skill-based Pay plan will be much easier to shape and customize to your employee's growth and compensation needs.

Our research and experience has proven that Skill-based Pay can create a motivational climate that encourages employees to learn and develop new and meaningful skills. Therefore, it is important to determine what skills and what type of learning is desired and beneficial as the first step in plan development. The proper alignment of the Skill-based Pay system with an organization's strategy and objectives is one of the strongest predictors for the success or failure of the overall program.

TRADITIONAL PAY VERSUS SKILL-BASED PAY

As mentioned above, in a traditional, job-based compensation system, increased pay is linked to higher-level jobs. This assumes the aspect of career promotion – which is then associated with more income – will motivate all employees. But what happens when there are only so many position titles in which to promote employees? In Skill-based Pay systems, the organization can strategically target the types of learning it wants employees to acquire based upon its business needs and future plans; then design a monetary reward associated with skill development and output measures. Skill-based Pay systems can result in highly talented, more productive and flexible workforces. Moreover, research and experience has shown that increased flexibility will not only lead to productivity increases, but also to greater employee satisfaction, lower staffing levels, fewer lost-time accidents, less absenteeism, and turnover[1].

How the program is managed greatly impacts an organization's ability to recruit, retain, develop, reward and motivate employees at all levels. If the system is purposefully developed and implemented, it can facilitate the attraction and retention of top performers, which can serve to enhance the success of the organization in both the short and long term.

---

[1] Higher levels of job satisfaction (Pulakos & Schmitt, 1983; Swaney & Prediger, 1985); Productivity increases (Iaffaldano & Muchinsky, 1985 and Petty, McGee, & Cavender, 1984); Less absenteeism (Hackett, 1989); Lower voluntary termination (Michaels & Spector, 1982).

The Public Sector's Guide to Skill-based Pay

> In addition to careful and deliberate development, employee acceptance of the new plan is a must. Thoroughly explaining why such a change is necessary and the positive impact on both the work team and the individual helps to facilitate the acceptance of the plan by employees. Having employees as Subject Matter Experts in the development of a new Skill-based Pay Plan is not only effective, but also efficient. Subject Matter Experts serve to assist in fully documenting key skills as well as promoting the new plan to other employees.

It is advisable to explore the long-term impact of Skill-based Pay with employees prior to plan development. One successful approach is to describe the advantages of Skill-based Pay and ask for employee input. The goal is to reach an agreement regarding the benefits of a Skill-based Pay system before the system development begins. If the concept of Skill-based Pay is generally accepted by employees and viewed as a positive opportunity, the chance of success increases dramatically. However, if employees are not allowed to participate in this initial phase then the probability of success decreases dramatically.

In today's environment the abilities, knowledge, and skills of employees is one of the few sustainable sources of a competitive advantage. For an organization to excel, it must utilize the full potential of this human capital, through as many different avenues as possible. The traditional approach to pay structure development by placement and assignment to specific job duties has forced employees into limited roles in many cases. Stated policy may strongly imply people are an important asset, but the design of day-to-day human resource practices typically do not realize the full value of employee talents. The assignment of employees to positions with defined responsibilities, but with little room for development personal and contribution in other arenas not specified by the job description, is shortsighted at best. Likewise, traditional compensation systems tend to focus more on the job than on the individual employee. Skill-based Pay is one means of attempting to realize the full value of employees by focusing on individual skill development and demonstrated performance coupled with sound compensation policy.

The Public Sector's Guide to Skill-based Pay

PERCEPTION IS REALITY

Perception is reality and one factor that will impact the system's potential for success is the organization's and management team's perspective towards work and employees.

In the picture below, do you see a sunrise or a sunset? That is, unless you were told that this picture was taken on the west coast or east coast, you would not know for sure. You would rely on your memories of sunrises and sunsets, then make a decision based on those events. The same holds true for introducing a new pay plan to employees. Unless you are fully equipped to explain the pros and cons of Skill-based Pay including all elements of development and implementation, employees will perceive the overhaul of the current compensation program as either negative or positive based on their past "memories" of such events.

DIAGRAM 2

DIAGRAM 3

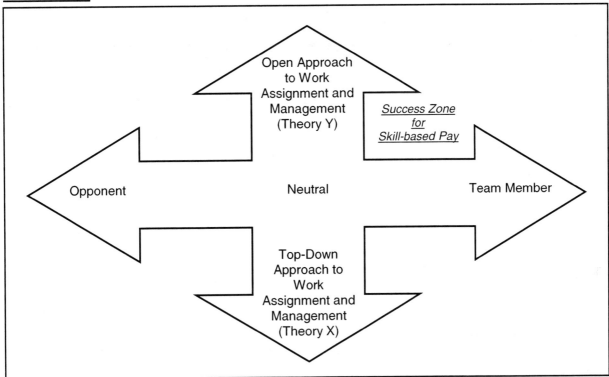

The view and philosophy of management in regard to employees and pay are key design considerations for a successful Skill-based Pay system. The illustration above shows a range of management views regarding work and employees. The horizontal axis in the illustration above (DIAGRAM 3) represents the possible perspectives toward employees that management may adopt – Opponent/Neutral/Team Member. When employees are viewed and treated as the Opponent instead of a Team Member, they typically respond by living up to this perception – a self-fulfilling prophecy. Conversely, viewing employees as Team Members implies a situation in which management and employees work together to achieve agreed-upon, achievable objectives. Skill-based Pay systems demand a team-focused approach to management. If a "me versus them" attitude toward people is currently in place in an organization, Skill-based Pay will not remedy this – and in fact, will most likely fail miserably.

The Public Sector's Guide to Skill-based Pay

The vertical axis in DIAGRAM 3 represents how work is conducted and organized. It could be a highly structured, bureaucratic organization where orders are given and expected to be followed without question, or it could be structured as a more open system, with overlapping job duties and an expectation of employee input and contribution. Skill-based Pay thrives in an open and participative organization where employee input, continuous learning and participation is encouraged.

> Skill-based Pay is most likely to succeed in an organization that practices open management and is one in which employees are viewed as team members whose goals of career success and personal development are shared by management.

In addition, employees in a Skill-based Pay system must be open to accepting the decision-making power relevant to their jobs, including process improvements and work assignments. A long-term perspective needs to be adopted by management and employees about their relationship and both must be willing to make sacrifices and share the responsibilities and challenges of the design and implementation of a Skill-based Pay system.

Realizing and acting upon a belief system that people want to contribute to the success of the group increases the probability of success for such a system. In our knowledge-based society, employees want to grow and develop, to become better equipped with skills and knowledge, and to contribute more efficiently and effectively to the success of their team. Greater productivity and effectiveness on the part of employees often leads to more recognition by the group. Moreover, this recognition often leads to greater feelings of satisfaction and commitment to the team, which often manifests itself in greater performance.

> *The benefits of Skill-based Pay are sometimes more personal than one might think...*
>
> The payback of an effectively designed and implemented system is limited only by the team's desire to grow and learn. In addition, Skill-based Pay can create an environment that encourages employees to grow personally, as well as professionally. For example, while facilitating a post-study focus group for one of our Skill-based Pay clients, we posed the question, "How has Skill-based Pay affected you?" A senior employee stood up and replied, "It has meant me getting my GED! Now I can tell my grandchildren that I have my high school diploma."
>
> Skill-based Pay can provide the drive for change not only throughout an organization, but also in an employee's personal life goals. ∎

UTILIZING AN ORGANIZATIONAL READINESS SURVEY

To help understand if the current culture is ready for Skill-based Pay, the design and distribution of an organizational readiness assessment is highly recommended. As discussed, one means for assessing organizational readiness is through meetings and discussions. An additional method is through the use of a formalized Organizational Readiness Survey (OR Survey). OR Surveys are used to isolate potential problem areas that might hinder the development of the Skill-based Pay system and that need to be addressed before the process begins.

A sample OR Survey is provided in the Appendix Section (Appendix A) of *The Guide*.

The Public Sector's Guide to Skill-based Pay

However, each organization's OR Survey should be designed based on the goals and needs of the employees as well as the long-term strategy of the entire work team.

The development and distribution process of your unique OR Survey should include the following key steps at a minimum:

1. The development of key questions in relation to acceptance and satisfaction with the current approach to training and development, willingness to participate in the work unit's decision making process, interest in training and learning and the overall trust relationship between employees, management and the organization at large.

2. The distribution of the OR Survey to all impacted employees during organized group presentations and/or through mailings – both methods should be designed to protect individual employee's identity in order to achieve maximum candid feedback.

3. Timely analysis of responses in order to quickly and accurately identify areas for added focus, group intervention and further clarification. If the organization is large enough, the demographics of this analysis should also be divided into work groups, departmental levels, race, gender, age, length of service and any other relevant group in order to identify any pockets of employee uncertainty or resistance toward Skill-based Pay.

The OR Survey should at the minimum address the issues outlined below, plus other topics that may impact the success of a Skill-based Pay system in your particular situation. Typical OR Survey topics and issues in a question format are provided below. As mentioned above, a sample OR Survey is included in the Appendix Section.

⚒ TOOL 1

Topic Area: Innovation and Change

Sample Questions:

1. Does your work environment encourage and support change? If so, how?
2. Does your department support suggestions that improve work processes?
3. Is experimentation with different work procedures encouraged in your department?

Topic Area: Training and Development

Sample Questions:

4. What type of opportunities do you have to attend training for professional development?
5. Do you think the organization is willing to make training and development a priority for Skill-based Pay success?
6. Does your department encourage training in the area of new technology or advances in the field?
7. Are you provided with adequate opportunities for career development within the organization?

Topic Area: Performance Management

Sample Questions:

8. How are reviews of employee performance currently delivered?
9. Do you view the current performance appraisal process as fair?
10. Do you view the current performance appraisal system as a positive experience?
11. Do you think the current performance appraisal process measures performance well?
12. Do your performance reviews include action plans for your continued development?

The Public Sector's Guide to Skill-based Pay

Topic Area: Communication

Sample Questions:

13. Is communication within your department open and effective? Why or why not?
14. In your opinion, is communication between co-workers open and team oriented? Why or why not?
15. In your opinion, is communication between employees and management open and team oriented? Why or why not?

Topic Area: Supervisory Practices

Sample Questions:

16. How do the employees perceive the management team?
17. Do you think employees are viewed as team members and partners in your department or just workers?
18. Do you think employees are viewed as team members and partners in your organization or just workers?

Topic Area: Relationships between Management and Employees

Sample Questions:

19. Do you think the management team treats employees well and with respect?
20. Do you think the relationship between management and employees is positive?
21. Generally speaking, do you think employees have professional respect for the management team?
22. Within your department, do you think management is generally respected?
23. Within your department, do employees and supervisors work in a team-based relationship?

> If the employees view any of these areas in a negative fashion, the issue needs to be adequately addressed before the project moves forward. Often, it is possible to address these issues by determining a course of action and adapting policy to properly address the concern. For instance, if management is viewed as non-supportive of training, then it will be necessary to begin discussions with your management team as to how things will be different under Skill-based Pay and communicate this positive resolution to the employee group(s). You may want to include Subject Matter Experts at this point.

Once you have all issues satisfactorily addressed, it is time to move forward through further communication of the goals and strategy of the new Skill-based Pay system.

It may sound overly simplistic, but open communication and employee involvement during all phases of Skill-based Pay is a must (see DIAGRAM 4 below). In particular, this is important during the initial stages of Skill-based Pay design and development.

The Public Sector's Guide to Skill-based Pay

DIAGRAM 4

Illustration of a recommended communication strategy flow chart

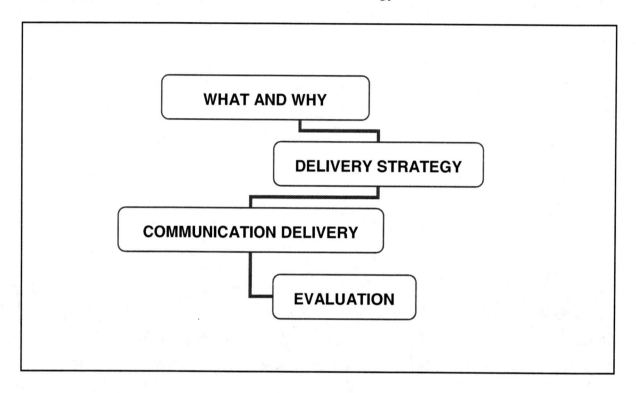

Decide WHAT you are communicating and WHY you are communicating it.

The first step of developing an effective communication strategy is to decide exactly what you want and need to communicate and to whom. For these sessions, a good rule of thumb is to prepare more information than might be necessary. The more organized and prepared you are in the communication phase, the more accepting employees will be of the change. Make your presentation with facts and not feelings for optimal success. Remember, compensation and advancement opportunities are often very emotional topics – so be equipped with solid facts and sound judgment.

As part of the communication process, it is important to explain why this change is being initiated. What are the advantages to the employees of moving to a Skill-based Pay system? What are the disadvantages if the organization does not move to a Skill-based pay system?

It is important to note that the majority of the employees will not have had access to this information until you provide it. Therefore, it is important that you explain the thought process and rationale behind the decision to implement a Skill-based Pay system.

Develop a STRATEGY to deliver the communication.

Some possibilities include:

- Organization-wide meetings and presentations
- Departmental/Divisional meetings and presentations
- Group e-mails
- Organizational newsletters
- Individual mailings
- Open phone lines
- E-mail questions/answers
- Suggestion boxes posted throughout the facility
- Answer "Hot Line" where employees can dial in to hear the latest updates and/or to leave messages with questions and inquiries

You may use some or all of the suggestions provided above. However, remember that communication is not a one-time occurrence. It is a collaborative process that needs to continue throughout the development, implementation and management process of a Skill-based Pay system.

DELIVER the communication

This seems obvious, but we have all been part of projects where great plans were made but then never implemented. It is essential that follow-through on the communication strategy occurs. It is often helpful to assign responsibility to a specified individual or group of individuals, with that person or team held accountable for communications delivery.

The Public Sector's Guide to Skill-based Pay

EVALUATE the effectiveness of your communications.

Communication is a two-way process. It is important for you to make sure employees have received and understood the messages sent. As you implement the communication strategy, you can assess whether or not your communications are being understood correctly by various means:

- One-on-one conversations with employees
- Focus groups where feedback is given and questions asked
- Organizational surveys
- Open meetings that include a question and answer session
- Open phones lines
- E-mails
- Suggestion boxes

Effective communication takes time and effort. Let's examine how the Blue Skies Water Utility Department developed the communication strategy for their Skill-based Pay project.

For the first step of the Skill-based Pay development process, the Blue Skies Project Team (consisting of the Department Director, key managers, the consulting team and various members of the Human Resources Department) held meetings with all managers and supervisors in the Water and Wastewater Divisions. At the first meeting, members of the Project Team made a presentation in which they described Skill-based Pay and the potential advantages and disadvantages associated with such a system. After the presentation, the Project Team asked the management team to spend two weeks discussing amongst themselves the potential benefits and challenges of moving to a Skill-based Pay system.

📖 *continued...*

Two weeks after the initial presentation, a second meeting was held. At this meeting, the management teams from Water and Wastewater discussed what was appealing about Skill-based Pay as well as their reservations. One of the primary concerns was a fear of not being able to return to the "old way of doing business" if the Skill-based system proved ineffective. The Project Team assured the mangers that nothing would be imposed upon them and made a recommendation to discuss the project further as a "pilot" for a specified period of time.

The Project Team also discussed how the goal was to create a system for the two divisions that emphasized the strengths of Skill-based Pay and how such a system could improve operations in and between those work groups. In addition, the system would be developed by and for the employees of each division, incorporating their specifications. The only way the Skill-based Pay system had a chance to succeed, the Project Team stated, was if the two divisions shaped the system to fit their needs. By the end of this second meeting, it was decided that the process for developing a Skill-based Pay system would begin as a Pilot Project.

The next step was to conduct an Organizational Readiness Survey. The Project Team was placed in charge of survey development and distribution. The managers of the Water and Wastewater divisions were in charge of encouraging employees to participate. When the surveys were returned, the results were largely positive, indicating a favorable environment in which to attempt a Skill-based Pay system. In addition, the Project Team communicated regularly throughout the development and distribution process with the Water and Wastewater management team to ensure the inclusion of appropriate items on the survey. Once the results had been analyzed, focus groups were held with those employees involved in the Skill-based Pay process.

The Public Sector's Guide to Skill-based Pay

> 📖 *continued...*
>
> The Project Team and the Department Management Team had also, at this second meeting, designated a Team that was to be responsible for the ongoing communications process. The Project Team met for strategy and preparation meetings as the survey was being distributed and analyzed. After the survey results were revealed as favorable, focus group meetings were held, and the Project Team moved forward with their plan and presented the results to all employees in the Department. The process began by conducting orientation sessions for those employees who would be in the Skill-based Pay system. Special efforts were made to describe the process and the potential advantages of moving to such a system in the Water Department and Wastewater Divisions.
>
> The Communications Team also placed a bulletin board in the cafeteria that was dedicated to the Skill-based Pay development process. The Team explained that throughout the process, notices, articles, updates, and requests related to Skill-based Pay could be placed on the bulletin board. A suggestion box was placed next to the bulletin board and employees were told that they could place anonymous comments, concerns, and suggestions. In addition, the Project Team established a group e-mail list that contained all of those employees effected by or involved in the Skill-based Pay development process. Weekly updates were to be sent via the group e-mail list throughout the project. Finally, a section of the *Blue Skies Employee Newsletter* was dedicated to the Water Utility Department's Skill-based Pilot Project. This provided exposure, excitement and support citywide. ∎

Any time change to an existing compensation structure or process is initiated, there will be anxiety associated with that change. A well-prepared and delivered communication strategy as described can facilitate relieving this inevitable anxiety. It is well understood that effective communication increases the acceptance, and subsequent success, of the change initiative.

Once the communication strategy was in place and operating and the OR Survey had been acted upon, it was time to move to Step Two of the development process; development of the skill hierarchy.

SUMMARY OF APPENDICES FOR CHAPTER 1

In the Appendix Section, you will find samples of the following tools for your use:
- Appendix A – Sample Organizational Readiness Survey
- Appendix B – Communication Strategy Development Worksheet

My Chapter Notes:

The Public Sector's Guide to Skill-based Pay

✏️ *My Chapter Notes:*

CHAPTER 2
Defining and Constructing your Skill-based Pay System's Hierarchy of Skills

Men habitually use only a small part of the powers they actually possess.
— William James (1842-1910)

If you "survived" the initial communication phase in Chapter 1, you are now well equipped to move to the first technical step of constructing your new Skill-based Pay System. The key message here is to remain flexible and expect the unexpected.

In order to implement an effective Skill-based Pay plan, the organization must work toward defining the skills it wants to reward employees. This is accomplished through the development of comprehensive skills lists as well as identifying the level of mastery needed for each skill.

The portion of the development process is comprised of three core steps:

Core Step 1 (Detailed in this Chapter): Skill Hierarchy Identification – where the skills are developed and initially organized by the Subject Matter Expert (Subject Matter Expert) Committees.

Core Step 2 (Detailed in Chapter 3): Skill Hierarchy Formatting – where the skills are further organized and then reviewed by management team members for preliminary approval

The Public Sector's Guide to Skill-based Pay

Core Step 3 (Detailed in Chapter 4): Skill Hierarchy Refinement – where the certification manual is written and the skill hierarchy is finalized

The Public Sector's Guide to Skill-based Pay

SKILL HIERARCHY IDENTIFICATION

The Core Step 1 of Skill Hierarchy Identification consists of four Sub-steps. Sub-steps include the development of the:

- **Sub-step 1A:** Development of Skill Lists;
- **Sub-step 1B:** Development of Skill Categories;
- **Sub-step 1C:** Development of Skill Ratings; and
- **Sub-step 1D:** Development of Skill Zones.

Sub-step 1A – Skill List Development: To begin developing the system, it is necessary to develop a complete inventory of all important and necessary skills, knowledge, and abilities (SKAs) for each position included in the system. The list will include all SKAs necessary for work at any level of the identified positions, from basic to advanced, from new employee to 20-year veteran.

As system development continues, the skill list will be refined more than once, so it is best to begin with the most comprehensive list possible. During this process, classic brainstorming rules apply – where there is no such thing as a bad idea – or in this case, a bad skill. If the skill seems even remotely plausible for the position, it should be documented.

At the City of Blue Skies, one member of the Subject Matter Expert Committee stated that "dog taming", like lion taming, was a necessary skill. In his experience, he had faced more than one unruly pooch while trying to install a new water meter and had learned to carry snacks to divert potentially hostile canines. This skill was not a department standard, but he used it in order to make hasty escapes on more than one occasion. While the Subject Matter Expert's recommendation received a few good laughs and almost instant jibes of not being a <u>real</u> skill, it was added to the list.

> *continued...*
>
> Later, during the refinement stage, the skill was included under "knowledge and practice of department-standard safety practices and policies". The actual policy in regard to animal contact calls for any worker to phone animal control experts and not attempt to "tame the lion". ∎

Again, the refinement process will be the time to review all skills in greater detail. This stage should be reserved for open communication and the development of a comprehensive list of skills for each effected position.

If you are developing a skill list for multiple positions, such as in the case of the City of Blue Skies, the list development process will vary somewhat. To illustrate one approach, we will examine the Blue Skies Water Distribution Operator positions, which will cross-train in skills for the Wastewater Collection Technician positions.

In the case of Blue Skies, a comprehensive list of skills was developed for all individual positions to be included. This Skill-based Pay group would eventually be called "Water Operator" under the final plan. The skill lists were combined into one master inventory of skills and then reviewed in order to eliminate obvious redundancies. Blue Skies began by developing skill lists for each of the Water Distribution Operator titles (Water Distribution Operator I, II, and III). That is, the skills of each title were listed and inventoried as one single skill group of the job family of Water Distribution Operator. This list represented not only all the relevant skills, but also associated abilities, tasks, duties, and knowledge requirements of the Water Distribution Operator positions.

The Public Sector's Guide to Skill-based Pay

In Blue Skies, Subject Matter Expert Teams, including both management and employee representatives from each of the two major technical work groups independently developed the skill lists for the positions they were combining into a single Skill-based Pay title. Initially, they met as one committee and combined their two independent lists. (Editor's Note: Later the teams decided that this was a false start and they reverted to three tracks, but the process was growth oriented and therefore we included it here.) In the combined list below (TABLE 2), any redundancies in skills listed under both Water Distribution and Wastewater Collection were eliminated. ■

TABLE 2

Water Distribution Skills	Wastewater Collection Skills	Combined List of Skills
Policy and Procedures Water Mainlines Valves Fire Hydrants Service Connections Disinfection/Sanitation Basic Equip. Operation Confined Space Entry	Policy and Procedures First Aid/CPR Wastewater Mainlines Manholes Electronic Detection Service Connections Basic Equip. Operation Disinfection Calculations Confined Space Entry	1. Policy and Procedures 2. Water Mainlines 3. Valves 4. Fire Hydrants 5. Service Connections 6. Disinfection Calculations 7. Basic Equip. Operation 8. First Aid/CPR 9. Wastewater Mainlines 10. Manholes 11. Electronic Detection 12. Confined Space Entry

The Public Sector's
Guide to Skill-based Pay

> If the two groups in Blue Skies would have met as one group initially, the process would have been altered slightly, but the outcome would have been essentially the same. The two Subject Matter Expert teams - Water Distribution and Wastewater Collection - would have met and developed the skill list for the positions they were combining into the single Skill-based Pay position. As you can see below, the management teams and Subject Matter Experts developed their lists of SKAs for both of their positions simultaneously and created one master inventory. As before, any redundancies in skills, those skills suggested in the meeting as necessary for Water and Wastewater, were eliminated and only listed once. ■

The table below (TABLE 3) represents a sampling of the skill inventory created for the Water Operator position by the two Subject Matter Expert groups. (For a complete list of the skills for Water Operator, please refer to Appendix C of *The Guide*.)

TABLE 3

Combined List of Skills for Water Operator (Created all at once by one combined Subject Matter Expert Committee)
1. City Policy Review
2. Water Mainlines
3. Valves
4. Fire Hydrants
5. Service Connections
6. Disinfection Calculations
7. Basic Equipment Operation
8. First Aid/CPR
9. Wastewater Mainlines
10. Manholes
11. Electronic Detection
12. Confined Space Entry

Which approach decided upon in the development of a skill list will be a function of your particular situation. If you have only a few positions being combined into a single Skill-based Pay group, and are familiar with the duties and requirements of each of the positions, it is appropriate to develop one master inventory list without making independent lists and then combining them together. However, if you have multiple positions, positions you are not familiar with, or positions in different geographical locations, you are urged to develop lists for each individual position first, and then combine the lists into one master skill list. A summary of the appropriate conditions for the different approaches is provided in the table below (TABLE 4).

TABLE 4

Conditions for Skill List Development Approaches	
Separate Meetings of Subject Matter Expert Committees followed by one Combined Meeting of both Subject Matter Expert Committees	**One Combined Meeting with both Subject Matter Expert Committees in Attendance**
1. Multiple Positions	1. Limited number of positions
2. Committee has a lack of familiarity with all positions	2. Committee has strong familiarity with all positions
3. Positions located at various geographic locations	3. All positions are in the same geographic location
4. Large number of SKAs	4. Small number of SKAs

Whatever your approach, it is important to account for any and all relevant skills, tasks, abilities, and knowledge necessary to complete the work assignments included in your Skill-based Pay system. At the end of this sub-step, you should have your initial skill list for each of the skill position(s) or group(s).

TOOL 2 (on the following page) is offered to facilitate the development of the complete skill list. Use the questions listed as prompts to begin outlining the items for inclusion in the skill list.

Appendix J shows a Sample Skill-based Pay Position Questionnaire that can be used to compile information for the Subject Matter Expert committees.

TOOL 2
Skill List Development Form

Position Title:	
1. List as many skills as you can think of that are required for this position. (You may want to refer to the current position description as a guide during this process.)	
What knowledge must an employee in this position(s) possess?	
What abilities are required of this position(s)?	
What are some common tasks or duties required of this position(s)?	

Sub-step 1B – Skill Category Development:

After developing the Skill List, you should now have a comprehensive list of SKAs necessary for the position or group of positions involved in your Skill-based Pay system. Sometimes, the size of the list can seem overwhelming. These next sub-steps, skill categories and skill ratings/zones, are used to help conceptualize and organize your skill list. By grouping and categorizing the skill list, it will make the establishment of your skill hierarchy more concise and accurate.

First, the items identified in your skill list should be placed into general skill categories. (See TABLE 5.) Group the items based upon the key functions or roles of each activity. Grouping SKAs by major category, rather than by existing position description titles, helps to develop a broad set of skills rather than specialized groups. It also helps everyone involved in the process to begin to think beyond the traditional organizational boundaries, particularly if you are combining multiple positions into one Skill-based Pay position. For example, when combining the Water Distribution Operators I, II and III into the single Skill-based Pay position of Water Operator along with the Wastewater Collection Technicians, you will need to make sure that all positions are adequately represented and their relative skills are specified. More specifically, all items in your skill list now apply to all positions being combined into the Skill-based Pay position.

Some systems will have more or less Skill Categories depending upon the size and complexity of the position(s) included in the Skill-based Pay system.

The Public Sector's Guide to Skill-based Pay

Common skill categories are provided below in TABLE 5.

TABLE 5

Major Skill Category Examples
1. Administrative
2. Customer/Client Services
3. General Support
4. Maintenance
5. Operations
6. Policies and Procedures
7. Safety
8. Technical Support
9. Skilled Technical/Electrical Services
10. Skilled Technical/Accounting Services

How you categorize the inventoried skills will vary based on your organization's unique needs. At this stage, it is best to thoroughly review your list for your particular situation and determine how items should be grouped or categorized. Clearly label each group in a way that communicates under that heading what SKAs are and/or how they will be used within the organization.

Grouping your skill list into categories will greatly facilitate the overall conceptualization and organization of this step. While these skill categories will be divided into more specific sets of individual items later, it is at this point that you will begin to divide the list into different formats. This will help in the decision process of where and how to place skills in the final zones and hierarchy.

In categorizing the skills for the City of Blue Skies Water Operator, the Subject Matter Expert Teams reviewed their combined list and decided upon three major categories: Water Distribution Skills, Wastewater Collection Skills and Foundation & Development Skills. Notice that during the process, initially the team decided that Water Distribution skills and Wastewater Collection skills should remain separate major categories. They discussed dividing the items into more than three categories, that they called "tracks", because the Skill-based Pay development teams wanted to be sure that they weren't limiting themselves or the employees by grouping skills along non-traditional lines. In the end, it was decided three categories were appropriate and would actually make it simpler to develop, explain and administer the system. Furthermore, the three categories enabled a manageable approach to cross training. This decision neutralized a concern that there wouldn't be enough opportunity to cross train across the Water Distribution Division and the Wastewater Collection Division. A portion of the finalized skill categories for the Blue Skies Water Operator position is provided below (TABLE 6). The entire list is included in Appendix C. ∎

TABLE 6

Skill Categories (Tracks) Table for Water Operator		
Foundation and Development Skills Track	**Water Distribution Skills Track**	**Wastewater Collection Skills Track**
City Policy Review Confined Space Entry First Aid/CPR	Water Mainlines Valves Fire Hydrants Service Connections Disinfection/Sanitation Basic Equipment Operation	Wastewater Mainlines Manholes Electronic Detection Service Connections Disinfection Calculations Basic Equipment Operation

The Public Sector's Guide to Skill-based Pay

Sub-step 1C – Skill Rating Development:

The basis for movement through a Skill-based Pay system is displayed as a hierarchical listing of the significant tasks and skills associated with a position. All relevant skills to a particular Skill-based Pay position are placed in order of difficulty and timing (learning sequence). The purpose of this sub-step is to rate each of the skills with a combination of the degree of difficulty and time in which it should be learned in the career path. "Difficulty" refers to how complex the task and skill are to perform and/or learn. "Timing" refers to the estimated time employees should be with the organization before they are required to learn and master a particular skill.

> This process for rating skills is included as a guide for how to place the list into a preliminary hierarchical order. For this step, initial ratings on each skill developed in the list will be performed. These ratings will then be used to make initial placements of each task into a hierarchical list.

Each skill from the list will be rated on two dimensions using the following two scales (TABLE 7 and TABLE 8).

TABLE 7

Skill Difficulty Scale
(Select a measurement from lowest to highest level of difficulty.)

How complicated/complex is this task to perform, learn, and/or master?
1. Very simple - requires limited instruction and can be mastered quickly
2. Requires some work and learning above one training session
3. Above average level of difficulty to learn/master
4. Difficult to learn/master
5. Very difficult to learn/master
6. Extremely difficult - requires repeated and ongoing training and experience

The Public Sector's Guide to Skill-based Pay

TABLE 8

Skill Timing Scale
(Note, time intervals will vary based on organization needs and practices.)

When should this skill be learned in an employee's career?

❶ At the very beginning – should be one of the first skills an employee learns

❷ <6 months – This skill should be learned within the first 6 months of an employee's career

❸ 6 months-1 year – This skill should be learned between the first 6 months and 1 year of service and experience

❹ 1-3 years – This skill should be learned between 1 and 3 years of service and experience

❺ 3-6 years – This skill should be learned between 3 and 6 years of service and experience

❻ 6 or greater years – This skill should be learned only after a majority of all other skills have been learned, after much experience and after much time in the position

---

Before beginning the rating process, discuss the meaning of each of the ratings. You should develop your own definitions, which will accurately reflect the culture of your organization. This discussion should help to develop a common understanding of how to use the rating scale for the skill evaluation.

The ratings you develop will help by placing the tasks/skills into a set order. Using the scales above as a guide, skills will be placed in order based upon how quickly they need to be learned in an individual's skill progression and how quickly and easily they can be learned. In other words, some skills will be more appropriate to be learned in the beginning of employees' career, whereas others are only appropriate for more experienced employees to possess.

The Public Sector's Guide to Skill-based Pay

During this process, you may find that some skills, though given a high rating of difficulty, need to be learned at the beginning of a skill progression and placed in an early skill zone. This will be discussed further in the next section.

The ratings provided in this step should be considered as a means of <u>beginning</u> to place skills in an order and are subject to open dialogue. Ultimately, regardless of what ratings they receive, each skill needs to be placed in the order that makes the most practical sense and is most effective for the organization. In other words, if you place skills in order based upon the ratings you initially assign, and the order doesn't fit your situation after a secondary review, move the skills to where they are suitable.

> In the Blue Skies Water Utility Department, the Subject Matter Expert Committee used the master skill list developed for the new combined position of Water Operator Position and assigned a rating for each skill's difficulty and timing. It is important to note that the group defined each skill in detail. After this was completed, the group decided upon the rating assignment in area of difficulty and timing. Next, they combined the two ratings to obtain one "score" for each skill. ∎

Below in TABLE 9 is a portion of a ranked skill list for the position of Blue Skies' Water Operator. Additional tools can be found in Appendix D.

TABLE 9

Skill Rating List Table						
Skill List for Water Operator	Difficulty		Timing			Overall Rating
1. City Policy Review	1	+	1	=		2
2. Water Mainlines	2	+	4	=		6
3. Valves	2	+	2	=		4
4. Fire Hydrants	5	+	6	=		11
5. Service Connections	3	+	3	=		6
6. Disinfection Calculations	5	+	5	=		10
7. Basic Equipment Operation – Water & WW	2	+	1	=		3
8. First Aid/CPR	1	+	1	=		2
9. Wastewater Mainlines	2	+	4	=		6
10. Electronic Detection	6	+	4	=		10
11. Confined Space Entry	1	+	1	=		1
12. Manholes	1	+	2	=		3

An optional approach the City of Blue Skies considered involved using a multiple rater methodology in order to facilitate the group consensus session. A rating form was developed and even though they did not use this approach, it is a good example to share.

This approach requires that each Subject Matter Expert Committee Member assign ratings on the two scales for each skill independently. Next, the group reviews the overall ratings for each skill and averages the scores together. To accomplish this for each task, the overall ratings are added and then divided by the total number of raters. This would provide a mean overall rating for each skill, across all of the raters. Then differences of opinions are explored and agreement is reached on the ratings. Using the same skill list as above, the process for using multiple raters would appear as follows in TABLE 10. ∎

The Public Sector's Guide to Skill-based Pay

TABLE 10

Skill Rating List Table for Multiple Raters – Difficulty/Timing Ratings					
	Multi-Rater Results				
	Rater 1	Rater 2	Rater 3	Rater 4	Mean
1. City Policy Review	2	3	2	3	2.50
2. Water Mainlines	4	7	4	7	5.50
3. Valves	4	5	4	3	4.00
4. Fire Hydrants	11	11	11	11	11.00
5. Service Connections	7	5	6	6	6.00
6. Disinfection Calculations	11	12	9	8	10.00
7. Basic Equipment Operation – Water & WW	3	3	3	3	3.00
8. First Aid/CPR	2	1	2	3	2.00
9. Wastewater Mainlines	7	6	7	5	7.75
10. Electronic Detection	10	10	9	10	9.75
11. Confined Space Entry	1	2	1	1	1.25
12. Manholes	3	3	4	2	3.00

Whether you choose to utilize the consensus-meeting approach or the multi-rater approach followed by a consensus-meeting to skill rating, at the end of the process you will be prepared to order the skills lowest to highest, based on the overall ratings assigned. This list will be used extensively in the next step, during which you will divide the skills in the list into a number of skill zones.

Please note that the ratings you have made are useful to help you decide on the initial placement of skills into zones. From this point forward, any changes made in the structure and order of skills in the hierarchy should be made based upon position and organizational requirements.

The Public Sector's Guide to Skill-based Pay

At this stage of the Skill-based Pay plan development in the Blue Skies Water Utility Department, the skill-rating list was placed in order from lowest to highest score for the position of Water Operator. The skill-rating list is provided below in TABLE 11. ■

TABLE 11

Skill List for Water Operator	Overall Rating
1. Confined Space Entry	1
2. City Policy Review	2
3. First Aid/CPR	2
4. Manholes	3
5. Basic Equipment Operation – Water & WW	3
6. Valves	4
7. Water Mainlines	6
8. Service Connections	6
9. Wastewater Mainlines	6
10. Disinfection Calculations	10
11. Electronic Detection	10
12. Fire Hydrants	11

Sub-step 1D – Skill Zone Development:

The Skill Rating list will now be used to refine the process of grouping the skills into zones according to their increasing difficulty *and* according to when they will be learned in an employee's career. For this exercise, we will place the skills into three skill zones. (See TABLE 12.) Zone 1 is for tasks/skills deemed least important (relatively speaking), simplest to learn, and/or that should be learned early in an employee's career. Zone 3 is for tasks/skills deemed most important, most difficult to learn, and/or that are more appropriately learned later in an employee's career. Zone 2 is reserved for skills between Zone 1 and Zone 3. Please note that this is intended as an initial zone placement. As your Skill-based Pay system develops, you may find you have a need for more or less than three zones. The City of Blue Skies developed eight zones.

The Public Sector's Guide to Skill-based Pay

The skill ratings developed in the previous step are now placed into the three zones by identifying natural breaks in their mean overall rating scores as an initial guide. The next step is to refine the skill zones by moving skill statements between the three zones as appropriate to meet the organization's needs and culture.

TABLE 12

Skill List for Water Operator	Overall Rating	Skill Zone
1. Confined Space Entry	1	1
2. City Policy Review	2	1
3. Manholes	3	1
4. First Aid/CPR	2	1
5. Basic Equipment Operation – Water & WW	3	1
6. Valves	4	2
7. Water Mainlines	6	2
8. Service Connections	6	2
9. Wastewater Mainlines	6	2
10. Disinfection Calculations	10	3
11. Electronic Detection	10	3
12. Fire Hydrants	11	3

In our example in TABLE 12, the resulting skill zones for Water Operator are:

- **Zone 1** = Skills 1 – 5
- **Zone 2** = Skills 6 – 9
- **Zone 3** = Skills 10 – 12

The ranges for zones may be different for each Skill-based position or group. There is no one right way to group the skills into skill zones. Review the overall ratings for each skill, but also ensure that each skill zone placement makes intuitive and practical sense for the particular position or skill group and make sure that training time is taken into consideration. If it will take two years to learn a discipline, do not group that skill or series of skills with another of equal or greater difficulty.

These zones may be further divided at your discretion, but this initial placement will facilitate decisions and processes in the Skill-based Pay system development process.

The Public Sector's Guide to Skill-based Pay

SUMMARY OF APPENDICES FOR CHAPTER 2

In the Appendix Section, you will find samples of the following tools for your use:

- Appendix C – Sample Skill Hierarchy
- Appendix D – Skill Rating Tools
- Appendix J – Sample Skill-based Pay Position Questionnaire

✎ *My Chapter Notes:*

My Chapter Notes:

CHAPTER 3
Formatting your Skill-based Pay System's Hierarchy of Skills

> *If people knew how hard I worked to get my mastery, it wouldn't seem so wonderful after all.*
>
> *- Michelangelo (1475-1564)*

Let's review. You should now have three different lists for your skills:

1. Tasks/skills grouped into skill categories (TABLE 6)
2. The Skill Rating list of all relevant position tasks/skills in hierarchical order (TABLE 11)
3. The tasks/skills grouped into skill zones (TABLE 12)

For a systematic description of all position skills, it is necessary to format the skill information you have created. During this phase in the process, you will place all information gathered thus far into two different formats:

- Skill Summary by Category and Zone Table
- Skills by Learning Approaches Table

Let's now move to **Core Step 2 – Skill Hierarchy Formatting** which is defined in greater detail in this Chapter.

The Public Sector's Guide to Skill-based Pay

SKILL SUMMARY BY CATEGORY AND ZONE TABLE

Your Skill Summary by Category and Zone Table may have more than the three skill categories shown in the sample template below. In fact, it can have as many skill categories as you created in Chapter 2 - Defining and Constructing your Skill-based Pay System's Hierarchy of Skills. The process of summarizing by category and zone assists in viewing the overall skill placement in the Skill-based Pay system and provides further opportunity to investigate revisions to or replacements of skills.

> Format your skill lists in a method that works best for your organization. Use the outline recommended here or alter the suggestions to fit your needs. The important thing to remember is that your goal during this step is to begin organizing lists in order to make them more manageable to facilitate decisions you will make about your Skill-based Pay system later on in the development process.

To develop the Skill Summary by Category and Zone Table:
1. Place all of tasks/skills into one list, grouping them by their skill category.
2. Next to each individual task/skill, indicate in which zone you have preliminarily placed the task/skill.

Your list will probably be much longer than the example on the following page in TABLE 13, but this example provides a general overview of the information presented. In addition, it is intended to offer insight into formatting the information acquired in this step.

The Public Sector's Guide to Skill-based Pay

TABLE 13

Combined Skill List by Category and Zone			
Water Operator		Zone 1	Zone 2	Zone 3
Category: Foundation and Development	Confined Space Entry	✓		
	City Policy Review	✓		
	First Aid/CPR	✓		
Category: Water Distribution	Basic Equipment Operation – Water	✓		
	Valves		✓	
	Water Mainlines		✓	
	Service Connections		✓	
	Fire Hydrants			✓
Category: Wastewater Collection	Basic Equipment Operation – Wastewater	✓		
	Disinfection Calculations			✓
	Electronic Detection			✓
	Wastewater Mainlines		✓	

> To work through the process, the Blue Skies Water Utility Department held a Subject Matter Expert Committee Meeting and included management. They presented the three lists developed to date: the Skill Category List, the Skill Ratings List and the Skill Zone List.
>
> During the meeting, the Subject Matter Expert Teams and the management team placed the skills into the Skill Summary by Category and Zone Table, grouping first by skill category and then by zone as indicated in the far right columns of TABLE 13. The resulting table was then sent to each division for review purposes. In addition, a focus group meeting was held with all affected employees requesting their feedback in regard to the initial placement of skills within categories and zones. This was to help encourage open communication and to help secure the system's overall success in the final implementation process. ■

LEARNING APPROACHES TABLE

During the development of the Learning Approaches TABLE 16 (below), the skill list will be further refined and organized to assist in the identification of appropriate training methods and certification standards for each of the skills.

It is understood that each skill used in the system will need to be learned and mastery demonstrated by the employee in order for his or her progression to take place. Now it is necessary to begin assessing the means available to the employees for this to take place.

During this step, some questions to ask include:

1. Are there training courses available through which an employee can learn skills? Are they internal or external?
2. Are there vendor-sponsored programs available?
3. Will paid classroom training be more appropriate?
4. Can the skills be learned on-the-job with training by qualified supervisors or employees?

The Learning Approaches Table helps to compile information that will aid you to answer these and other questions in regard to training and development.

In order to get started with this phase, it is recommended that you continue to work through a committee approach. For this process, you will begin by listing each of the skills by zones first – this is different from all other exercises up to this point. The reason we recommend assigning the required training and learning to skills by zone is so that you can better see the natural career path of the entire Skill-based Pay plan for the position and the timelines that are involved to progress through the zone. You may move some skills to a different zone placement after this exercise.

It is important to note that training methods and certification standards will vary by position. Based on our experience, TABLE 14 and TABLE 15 below shows definitions of the most commonly used types of training and development. These methods of training will be dependent upon your organization's ability to supply the courses using the methods identified.

TABLE 14

Training Method Legend			
OJT	**VS**	**C/V**	**OT**
On-the-Job Training	Vendor Sponsored Training	College/Vocational Courses	Organizational (Internal) Training

TABLE 15

Certification Standards Legend			
TC	**DS**	**WT**	**CC**
Trade Certification	Demonstrated Skill and Observation by Supervisor	Written Test	Class/Training Certificate

Now that you have established the methods for Training and Certification, assignment of skills to the proper method is in order. Each skill may have multiple training methods available as well as multiple certification standards. In TABLE 16 provided on the following page, we have checked each box for our Water Operator in the Blue Skies Water Utility Department.

When you complete this step for your positions, you should also note that like Blue Skies, this table is considered a draft which is subject to future refinement.

The Public Sector's Guide to Skill-based Pay

TABLE 16 **Learning Approaches Table**	Training Method				Certification Standards			
	OJT	VS	C/V	OT	TC	DS	WT	CC
Skill Zone 1 – Water Operator								
Foundation and Development Category								
Confined Space Entry	✓			✓		✓		✓
City Policy Review	✓			✓			✓	✓
First Aid/CPR			✓	✓				✓
Water Distribution								
Basic Equipment Operation - Water	✓	✓		✓	✓	✓		✓
Wastewater Collection								
Basic Equipment Operation - WW	✓	✓		✓	✓	✓		✓
Skill Zone 2 – Water Operator								
Water Distribution								
Valves	✓	✓		✓	✓	✓		✓
Water Mainlines	✓	✓		✓	✓	✓		✓
Service Connections	✓	✓		✓	✓	✓		✓
Wastewater Collection								
Wastewater Mainlines	✓	✓		✓	✓	✓		✓
Skill Zone 3 – Water Operator								
Water Distribution								
Fire Hydrants	✓	✓		✓		✓	✓	✓
Wastewater Collection								
Disinfection Calculations	✓	✓		✓		✓	✓	✓
Electronic Detection	✓	✓		✓		✓	✓	✓

Please note that some skills have multiple boxes checked in TABLE 16. The purpose of this phase is to begin to assess the options available to your organization for training and certifying your employees on those skills placed into the Skill-based Pay system. It is important to remember that for each skill, we recommend the use of a committee of Subject Matter Experts to determine the following information:

1. Training Methods Available: What avenues for training are available for employees wishing to learn a particular skill? How will the employee go about learning or developing a particular skill listed in the skill hierarchy?
2. Certification Standards: How will it be determined that the employee has attained the requisite skill? How will skill mastery be demonstrated and proven?
3. Re-certification Standards: Will re-certification be required? If so, how often?

The Subject Matter Expert Committee for the Blue Skies Water Utility Department held a meeting dedicated to the creation of the Learning Approaches Table. Before the meeting, three team members were assigned the task of creating a preliminary table with all skills assigned to zones. This table was used as the master work sheet for this Committee meeting.

Additionally, the Subject Matter Expert Teams decided it was important to have management representation at this meeting – since the level of training and certification assigned would impact departmental workflow as well as the training budget. For each skill, team members reached a consensus and entered information into the box that was appropriate. In only one case was the group not able to reach a consensus opinion and that was in regard to Customer Service training. Half of the group felt that in-house training was sufficient and half of the group felt that it should be outsourced to a professional training firm since the City's organization-wide classes were often full and did not focus on their specific department's needs.

> 📖 *continued...*
>
> The group agreed to disagree and decided to revisit the issue after a two-week period. One member was assigned to find an outsourcing alternative to present and another member was assigned to speak to the City's training director in order to determine if an in-house program could be affordably and effectively developed – specifically addressing the needs of the Water Utility Department.
>
> In the final analysis, the Department recommended to outsource the training to a third-party company with a train-the-trainer approach incorporated for the Department to take over training internally within a one-year period. ∎

TYING IT ALL TOGETHER

At this point in the process, four different lists and tables have been developed for your skills:

1. The skill-rating list in hierarchical order starting from the lowest rated skill to the highest rated skill (TABLE 11)
2. The tasks/skills grouped by skill zone (TABLE 12)
3. A Skill Summary by Category and Zone (TABLE 13)
4. The Learning Approaches Table (TABLE 16)

> Now it's time to review each of these lists and tables to ensure completeness. Make certain each of the skills from the initial list is accounted for in each of the other forms. If skills from the initial list are not included in other forms, or new skills have been added, make sure to account for these changes. In addition, you may have eliminated or combined some skills from your initial list.

Once each of these lists and tables are in place, you are ready to move on to the next part of the development process. In the next steps, you will begin to systematically assess each skill listed for completeness and then write an objective measurement for each skill. This objective will specify how employees must demonstrate mastery of a skill, the conditions under which this demonstration must occur, and the means by which mastery of the skill is assessed and recorded. You will then further refine the placement of skills into skill zones and sub-zones (if needed). Moreover, you will now begin to combine and divide the skills into a system that meets your organization's unique needs and goals.

The Public Sector's Guide to Skill-based Pay

SUMMARY OF APPENDICES FOR CHAPTER 3

In the Appendix Section, you will find samples of the following tools for your use:

- Appendix E – Category and Zone Table – Template
- Appendix F – Sample Certification Training Methods

My Chapter Notes:

The Public Sector's Guide to Skill-based Pay

My Chapter Notes:

CHAPTER 4
Refining your Skill-based Pay System's Hierarchy of Skills

> *Never discourage anyone... who continually makes progress, no matter how slow.*
>
> *- Plato (427 BC – 347 BC)*

At this point in the development process, you now have made significant progress. You have created a large list of skills, tasks, and abilities. In addition, you have placed this list into skill categories and skill zones and formatted the skill lists into the Category and Zone and Learning Approaches Table (TABLE 16). However, now it becomes necessary to make sure that these skills are listed in the most effective, efficient, and prudent way possible. To do this, you need to ensure that each item in the list is assigned to a distinct skill or skill set. Each item on the list should be one set that can be assessed in terms of mastery resulting in the opportunity for continued growth and additional compensation.

Let's now move to **Core Step 3 – Skill Hierarchy Refinement** which is defined in greater detail in this Chapter.

The simplest way to do this is to take each item in the list and ask the question "What skill does this particular item concern?" You may find you have multiple items that all refer to the same specific skill. If so, multiple items should be combined into one set.

In the following simple example, you may have the following items in your skill list:

1. Hang sheet rock and repair holes
2. Tape and float sheet rock
3. Texture walls

As you look at each of those items, you realize that each are just individual tasks all referring to the same skill of sheet rock installation and finishing. Therefore, you should combine these items on your list into the single skill title of sheet rock installation and finishing. The charts on the following page (DIAGRAM 5) illustrate this point.

The Public Sector's Guide to Skill-based Pay

DIAGRAM 5

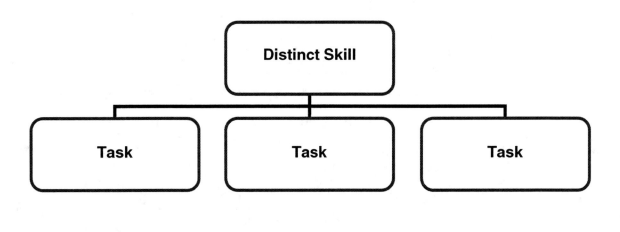

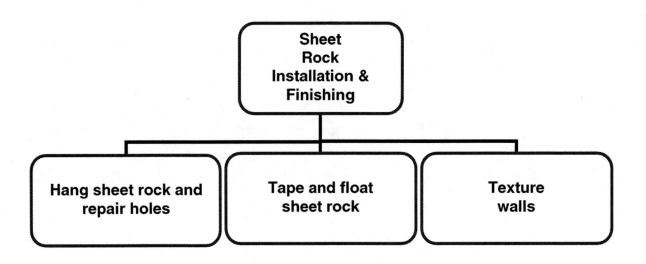

The goal is to combine individual tasks into distinct skills as necessary. Usually, the more technical a position, the more skills will be listed.

Additionally, you will have items that are already distinct and do not require any consolidation or combination. Do not feel required to combine every item on the list with other item(s). You may also find that some skills have tasks that should be placed in different skill zones. For example, the first two tasks under the skill of sheet rock installation and finishing could be placed into a skill zone one and the third task could be moved to a skill zone two. It is important to note that all of the tasks that fit into one particular skill do not have to be placed into a single zone.

TABLE 17 contains simple examples of task items on a skill list for a grounds employee working in the zoo. Originally, each of the items listed below had been developed and placed into a general skill list.

However, upon a closer inspection, it was determined that some of the items should be combined into one skill or skill set, as illustrated below.

TABLE 17

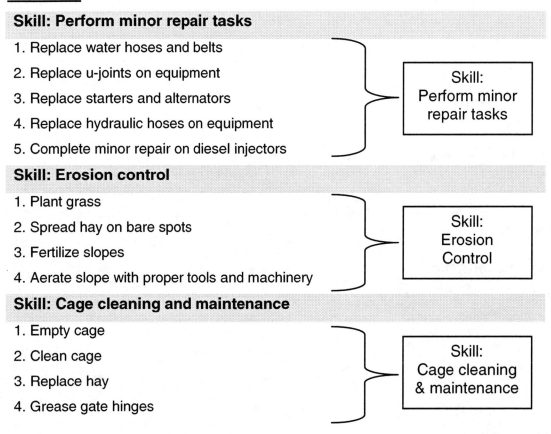

📖

The Blue Skies Utility Department Project Team met with the Subject Matter Expert teams to determine if there were any items in their skill lists that could be combined into a single skill set. At the meeting, the Subject Matter Expert teams reviewed each item and determined the skill to which each item was related. As they found multiple items that related to the same skill, they combined those items into a single skill. Once they had reviewed the entire list, the teams then revisited the new hierarchy that had been created and gave the skill sets a new, descriptive title. ■

📖 *continued...*

For example, while reviewing the skills in zone one, the Subject Matter Expert teams found four different items that all seemed to refer to valve installation. They combined the four skill items into a single skill set and re-named it as "Valves".

Original items:
- Locate and mark valves
- Conduct basic valve operations
- Adjust top section of valve to grade
- Clean out valve

New title of four combined skill items:
- Valves

During this same meeting, the Subject Matter Expert teams found other instances where multiple items could be combined into a single skill. However, the items had been placed into different skill zones. It was decided that only those tasks located in the same skill zone would be combined, and all combined skills would have the same title. To differentiate, the title would simply state which zone those skills belonged. An example is provided below.

Original items:
- Identify components
- ID three types of water mainline pipe
- Install and repair clamp and coupling
- Use water system map to identify three appurtenances

New title of combined skill items:
- Water Mainlines – Zone One

Original items:
- Transfer service to new mainline
- Schedule and excavation
- Install mainline fittings: bends, tees, s-bends, grade locks

The Public Sector's Guide to Skill-based Pay

New skill title of combined items: -Water Mainlines – Zone Two

MOVING INTO SKILL TRACKS

In most cases, you will be designing a Skill-based Pay system so that there is one skill hierarchy. However, what happens if you find that all of the skills in your skill hierarchy are not compatible? It then becomes necessary to explore the possibility that your system may require multiple skill hierarchies – or tracks – within the same position or position group. This challenge does have a solution! In fact, the development process presented thus far is designed to complement this scenario.

Let's focus on an example of multiple tracks by reviewing the Water Operator example.

Tracks are individual skill hierarchies within the same Skill-based Pay position. You are more likely to use tracks when combining positions with differing tasks in order to facilitate more extensive cross training. There may also be a need to use tracks when a list contains distinct sets of skills that are not typically found in an individual employee. The following narrative along with TABLE 18 helps to illustrate the use of multiple tracks in the Water Operator position. Remember, it was decided early in the process that the Water and Wastewater employees would be combined into the single position of Water Operator.

> The Blue Skies Water Utility Department decided it did not need all employees to learn each skill in the hierarchy. Although it would seem to be an ideal goal to have every employee cross-trained in all skills, the internal training budget, the work process and the number of employee training hours deemed this impractical.

The Public Sector's Guide to Skill-based Pay

> 📖 *continued...*
>
> As mentioned earlier, the Department divided its skill list into three tracks:
>
> 1. The Foundation & Development Track – Knowledge that all employees must possess
> 2. The Water Distribution Track – Skills that employees with a strong background in Water Distribution must possess
> 3. The Wastewater Collection Track – Skills that employees with a strong background in Wastewater Collection must possess
>
> It was decided that all employees would be required to learn the items in Track 1: Foundation and Development. Then, each employee would be placed into one of the two base tracks of either Water Distribution or Wastewater Collection. Each of the two base tracks contained some overlap in skill development while also emphasizing one particular area of expertise. Blue Skies hoped to develop a workforce that shared a common foundation of skills, with strong expertise in one area. Moreover, the workforce would be required to develop a skill set in a second general area so that cross-functionality of employee talent would occur. ∎

TABLE 18 on the following page demonstrates all skill lists combined to create the Skill Hierarchy for the Blue Skies Water Operator position.

The Public Sector's Guide to Skill-based Pay

TABLE 18

	Track 1 Foundation and Development Skill Blocks (Completion of this track is required for all employees.)	Track 2 Water Distribution Technical Skill Blocks	Track 3 Wastewater Collection Technical Skill Blocks
Skill Zone 1: 6 Months. All minimum requirements for position must be met within 6 months of employment.	1. City Policy Review 2. Defensive Driving 3. First Aid/CPR 4. Basic Haz-mat 5. Confined Space Entry 6. Two-way Radio Protocol	1. Water Mainlines 2. Valves 3. Fire Hydrants 4. Service Connections 5. Disinfection/Sanitation 6. Basic Equipment Operation	1. Wastewater Mainlines 2. Manholes 3. Inflow/Infiltration 4. Service Connections 5. Disinfection/Sanitation 6. Basic Equipment Operation
Skill Zone 2: 1 Year. All certification in Skill Zone 1 has been completed for Tracks 1 and 2 or 3.	1. Operational Policies 2. Traffic Control 3. Basic Computer Skills/Work Orders 4. Customer Service 5. Plan and Map Reading 6. Teamwork	1. Approved Basic Water 2. Water Mainlines 3. Valves 4. Fire Hydrants 5. Service Connections 6. Journey Level Equipment Operation	1. Approved Basic Wastewater 2. Wastewater Mainlines 3. Manholes 4. Inflow/Infiltration 5. Service Connections 6. Journey Level Equipment Operation
Skill Zone 3: 1 Year. All certification in Skill Zone 2 has been completed. Tracks 1 and 2 or 3 have been completed in Skill Zone 2.	1. Operational Policies 2. Stress Awareness 3. Hazardous Materials 4. Trench Safety	1. Approved Water Distribution 2. Electronic Detection 3. Disinfection Calculations 4. Water Mainlines/Appurtenances 5. Valves 6. Fire Hydrants 7. Service Connection	1. Approved Wastewater Collection Class 2. Electronic Detection 3. SSO Reports/Disinfection/I&I 4. Wastewater Mainlines 5. Manholes
Skill Zone 4: 1 Year. All certification in Skill Zone 3 has been completed for Tracks 1 and 2 or 3.	1. System Mapping/GIS 2. Customer Service "D" 3. Leadership	1. Selected Approved Class 2. "C" Certification 3. Water Mainlines 4. Valves 5. Fire Hydrants 6. Service Connections 7. Disinfection/Sampling 8. Equipment Operation	1. Selected Approved Class 2. Class "II" Certification 3. Wastewater Mainlines 4. Manholes 5. Disinfection/Sampling 6. Equipment Operation
Skill Zone 5: 1 Year. *Base Track certification in Skill Zone 4 has been completed. **Alternate Tracks in Skill Zone 2 have been completed.	1. Coaching 2. Customer Service "C" 3. Introduction to Supervision	1. Selected Water Class 2. Review/Critique Construction Plans 3. Pressure, Valving, Pump, Storage 4. Cross Connection Control 5. Water Mainlines 6. Valves 7. Fire Hydrants 8. Equipment Operation	1. Selected Wastewater Class 2. Review/Critique Construction Plans 3. Lift Stations, Pumps 4. Clean Water Act/SSO Regulations 5. Equipment Operation
Skill Zone 6: 1 Year. *Base Track certification in Skill Zone 5 has been completed. **Alternate Tracks in Skill Zone 3 and 4 has been completed.	1. Advanced Computer Skills 2. Customer Service "B" 3. Communications 4. Selected Supervisory Development- 2 classes	1. Customer Service Inspection 2. Water System Operation and Control 3. Customer Service/Dispatch 4. PR/Boil Water Notice 5. Equipment Operation	1. Flow Metering 2. I&I Investigations 3. SSO Sampling 4. Equipment Operation
Skill Zone 7: 2 Years. *Base Track certification in Skill Zone 6 has been completed. **Alternate Tracks in Skill Zone 5 and 6 has been completed.	1. Water Utility System Trainer 2. Customer Service "A" 3. Water Utility Codes and Ordinances 4. Selected Supervisory Development- 4 classes	1. Backflow Prevention Certification 2. Basic Instrumentation 3. Basic Treatment Plant Operation 4. Basic Laboratory	
Skill Zone 8: All prior required certifications have been completed.	1. Water Utility System Operator/Trainer/Leader 2. Selected Supervisory Development to Maintain Skills	Employees reaching this Skill Zone will be granted annual raises based on their performance review scores and maintenance of skills. Employees must demonstrate complete operational control and competency in all areas of water utility operations at all times.	

Page 73
©Copyright 2003, 2004 - All rights reserved - The Waters Consulting Group, Inc.

The Public Sector's Guide to Skill-based Pay

Once you have placed skills into tracks, employees move through the system by demonstrating mastery of skills in much the same way as employees in a single-track system. Although the precise method in which employees move through differs, the basic mechanics of development, administration and maintenance remain the same.

SKILL HIERARCHY AND SUB-ZONES

At this point you should have:

- Refined the items in your lists into distinct skills
- Finalized the number of tracks for your skill groups and
- Compiled the information into a Skill-based Table (See TABLE 18 on the previous page.)

It is now time to finalize your skill hierarchy. Remember that the Skill Hierarchy is an ordered listing of all skills. As stated, TABLE 18 is an excellent example of a completed skill hierarchy. The hierarchy should list all of the final skills and skill sets in the order in which the skills should be learned.

At this point, let's return to your sample skill hierarchy that is divided into only three zones. If left this way, your options for pay and administration of the system would seem to be only two:

1. Give increases in pay for each individual skill learned, as the employee learns it, *or*
2. Give increases only after the employee has demonstrated mastery for all of the skills within a zone.

You may decide that neither of these are attractive options by themselves. The first option would potentially increase the administrative portion of the system.

If the first option is chosen, employees would be receiving consistent and frequent pay increases after each skill learned, which is potentially a strong motivator, however, the burden placed upon your compensation/HR services would be increased. The second option is more manageable, in that employees would receive a pay increase after demonstrating mastery of all skills within a zone. However, this approach could decrease the motivational potential of the system to encourage employees to learn new skills because of the amount of time involved to complete the learning phase in a defined zone.

Dividing your skill hierarchy into sub-zones is one means for balancing the advantages of the two options described above. Think of sub-zones as items that have similar difficulty and importance and/or have a need to be learned at a particular point within an employee's career. Sub-zones are used as guideposts for learning, recognition and salary increases and are driven by policy. They are sometimes referred to as pay blocks. Sub-zones allow you to group small numbers of skills (usually 4-8) together and then offer increases in pay to employees as they complete all or a percentage of the skills within the created sub-zone. This addresses the need for ongoing pay increases in a timely fashion while also easing the administrative/compensation burden by offering certification and pay increases in a consistent and more uniform fashion.

Each organization must determine the exact number of sub-zones for its skill hierarchy. When making this decision, it is important to realize that the number of sub-zones and the time constraints placed on the movement within the system will dictate how quickly an employee may advance through the pay range. Most organizations also establish "time gates" for each zone or sub-zone. A "time gate" is a set amount of time that an employee must remain in a particular zone or sub-zone before moving on to the next learning opportunity. That is, you may require an employee to remain in a particular zone or sub-zone for a set amount of time, usually 3-12 months (though it can be more/less), before advancing to the next learning level (zone or sub-zone).

The Public Sector's Guide to Skill-based Pay

In this way, the sub-zones may be designed as means of cost containment or control in relation to skill-based to pay increases.

In the example provided below, there are sub-zones within each of the three zones. In this example, an employee will not need to wait for long periods between movement and pay increases, as they would if increases were granted only when entire skill zones were completed.

Additionally, sub-zones provide the ability to measure individual growth as employees acquire distinct sets of additional skills. This structure also provides an opportunity to more carefully organize and administer the order in which employees learn skills. TABLE 19 on the following page illustrates a skill hierarchy divided into sub-zones. This particular skill hierarchy contained the skill categories of:

- Maintenance Skills
- Computer Skills
- Water Operations Skills
- Wastewater Skills
- Lab Skills

Each of these categories contained a number of skills that had been distributed across all three zones. Within each zone, a determination was made as to how many sub-zones were appropriate and which skills would be placed into each sub-zone. Moving forward, employees received pay increases only after they demonstrated mastery of all skills within a particular sub-zone.

TABLE 19

		Skill Hierarchy with Sub-Zones Sample	
Action Item	Skill Zone	Skills Attained	Skill Sub-Zone
$	1	Maintenance Skills 1-4, Computer Skills 1-2	Sub-Zone 1.0
$		Water Operations Skills 1-4	Sub-Zone 1.1
$		Wastewater Skills 1–3	Sub-Zone 1.2
⚑		Lab Skills 1-5	Sub-Zone 2.0
$	2	Maintenance Skills 5-6	Sub-Zone 2.1
$		Computer Skills 3-5	Sub-Zone 2.2
$		Water Operations Skills 5-6	Sub-Zone 2.3
$		Water Operations Skills 7-8	Sub-Zone 2.4
$		Wastewater Skills 4-7	Sub-Zone 2.5
⚑		Lab Skills 6-10	Sub-Zone 3.0
$	3	Maintenance Skills 7-10, Computer Skills 6-9	Sub-Zone 3.1
$		Water Operations Skills 9-14	Sub-Zone 3.2
$		Wastewater Skills 8-11	Sub-Zone 3.3
⚑		Lab Skills 11-14	Sub-Zone 3.4

$ Pay Increase
⚑ Performance Milestone

The Public Sector's Guide to Skill-based Pay

> In the Blue Skies Water Utility Department, there was much debate and discussion during this particular phase regarding whether to create sub-zones. It was decided that instead of dividing the hierarchy into sub-zones, there would be multiple zones and tracks with a compensation policy assigned to reinforce movement and cross training. The result was similar to creating sub-zones, however the movement was more vertical than horizontal. (See TABLE 18)
>
> An alternative would have been to label each block of skills in the Skill-based Table as a sub-zone. For example, skills 1-6 in Track 1 and Skill Zone 1 could have been labeled Skill Sub-zone 1.1. However, for Blue Skies' purposes, it was more appropriate to designate each block of skills based upon the defining track skill zone. ∎

SUMMARY OF APPENDICES FOR CHAPTER 4

In the Appendix Section, you will find samples of the following tools for your use:

- Appendix G – Skill Hierarchy Table – Sample Template

My Chapter Notes:

The Public Sector's Guide to Skill-based Pay

My Chapter Notes:

The Public Sector's Guide to Skill-based Pay

CHAPTER 5
Writing your Skill-based Pay System's Objectives and Certification Manual

> *The greatest thing in this world is not so much where we are, but in what direction we are moving.*
>
> *- Oliver Wendell Holmes (1841-1935)*

THE CERTIFICATION MANUAL

By now, a complete list has been developed for those skills that have been placed into a hierarchy, indicating the order in which the skills must be learned. It is now time to develop the Certification Manual.

The Certification Manual contains clear, precise information on how employees move through the skill hierarchy. The Manual will help employees determine:

- Their skill position in the overall hierarchy
- Skills in order of importance in the learning and development process
- The method in which they will need to acquire the skills as well as demonstrating the required level of competency

In order to satisfy the above criteria, the Certification Manual should contain at a minimum:

- The complete skill list
- The skill hierarchy
- Skill objectives for each item in the hierarchy

The Public Sector's Guide to Skill-based Pay

For maximum success, it is essential that all employees and managers involved have a clear and distinct set of terms and tools which specifically define progression through the system. The Certification Manual is but one tool in this process, but it serves to provide the most comprehensive procedural plan for system support.

WRITING SKILL OBJECTIVES

For each distinct skill set developed, the Certification Manual will need to contain an objective. The purpose is to communicate exactly how one moves through the hierarchy in terms of necessary skill attainment and demonstration of skills.

Advantages of developing clear and meaningful skill objectives include:

- **Clarity of Communication** – To ensure all employees involved in the Skill-based Pay system have an explicit understanding of what is required in order to advance through the system

- **Recognizing Appropriate Levels of Performance** – To ensure supervisors assessing the achievement of mastered skills (or lack thereof) have a clear understanding of the required skills.

- **Consistency and Fairness** – All employees must be treated in the same manner. In any pay or performance program, there is no room for inconsistencies in terms of following set policy. The Certification Manual should be viewed as the unbiased, objective "measuring stick" by which skill mastery is determined.

- **Measurable Results** – One reason for writing specific skill objectives for each item is to ensure skill mastery is assessed objectively and is measurable in finite terms. Making sure skills are quantifiable is a fundamental trait in successful Skill-based Pay.

A skill objective is a specific, observable, and measurable statement that describes in specific terms what must be provided as "proof" that a skill has been achieved. Essentially, a well-written objective is the same thing as a well-written goal.

The two examples below of skill objectives in TABLE 20 are provided for your consideration. Ask yourself if each is specific, observable, and measurable.

TABLE 20

> 1. Understand where safety shutoff is located within the wastewater plant and know how to turn it on and off.
> 2. Complete the approved certification course in the proper operation of the emergency wastewater treatment valve and demonstrate the skills learned to immediate supervisor within 72 hours of course completion.

The first skill objective is not very specific; therefore, it is difficult to measure. How will a supervisor fully know if the employee truly understands where the safety valve is located? The skill objective should be written so there is a specific action to be performed that indicates mastery of a particular skill.

In this first example, the intent of the skill is to ensure that the employee knows where the safety valve is located. How could you assess whether or not an employee knows this? The options are varied, but two examples are: 1) On a map of the plant, circle where the safety equipment is located or 2) With a list of the safety equipment, walk with a supervisor to where each safety valve is located.

The second example is much better in its stated objective. It lists requirements that are observable and measurable. Did the employee go to the session? Did they turn in a certificate of completion? In addition, it is focused on the performance to be accomplished in order to demonstrate the skill.

The Public Sector's Guide to Skill-based Pay

You may find that training or other class/course work is an appropriate way for an employee to demonstrate mastery of a skill. However, you need to ensure that the training you have chosen addresses the skill in the appropriate manner.

SIX QUESTIONS IN WRITING EFFECTIVE SKILL OBJECTIVES

To write a skill objective, answer these six questions:

1. What is the *skill*?
2. What *action* will the employee take to demonstrate mastery of this skill?
3. What is the *proof* or *measurement* that indicates successful demonstration and how well must the skill be performed?
4. Are there any *standards* to be observed when demonstrating mastery and under what situation(s) should the employee be able to demonstrate mastery?
5. Are there any *safety criteria* for skill demonstration that must be considered?
6. Is there any *equipment needed* for skill demonstration?

Each of these six questions is explored in greater detail on the following pages.

Question 1. What is the <u>skill</u>?

This is simply the title of the Skill or Skill Group for which you are writing a Skill Objective. The way the Skill is labeled is also how it should appear in the Skill Hierarchy. This makes it easier to look up a particular skill in the Certification Manual.

Question 2: What _action_ will the employee take to demonstrate mastery of this skill?

What is the specific act or task that should be occurring when skill mastery is being demonstrated? If you want an employee to be able to safely change a tire on one of the organization's work vehicles, simply state, "following safety procedures, change tire on work truck". Remember to state the main intent of the skill as an observable, measurable performance.

Question 3: What is the _proof_ or _measurement_ that indicates successful demonstration and how well must the skill be performed?

Will you require the certification from a course with a certain passing score or will the skill be demonstrated with an in-house checklist? There are questions you will need to answer. Another consideration should be the level of performance. For example, did the employee change the tire, but forget to properly tighten two lug nuts and check the tire pressure? Did the employee follow the proper safety procedures? Make certain you specify the level it takes to obtain successful demonstration – not just the completion of the task at a mediocre level. Additionally, you will need to consider how will you record the successful skill demonstration. For example, when developing a Skill-based System for Lifeguards, one of the skills is treading water. Is it enough for an individual to simply tread water, or should the individual be capable of treading water for a set amount of time? Lifeguards should also know pool safety rules. Is it enough that the lifeguards know most of the rules, or should they have all of the safety rules committed to memory? Skill demonstration should represent the use of the skill at an appropriate level and manner in which it will be used during work activities.

When assessing the proof and/or measurement component of the Skill Objective, there are four primary items for additional consideration.

- **Speed** – Does the performance need to occur at a certain rate (50 words per minute), for a certain amount of time (for 20 minutes), within a set time frame (in less than 5 minutes), etc?

- **Accuracy** – How precise does the performance need to be – 50%, 80%, 100%? Ensure the MEASUREMENT you set is realistic and applicable to actual position requirements.

- **Effectiveness** – Is there a manual or training guide that describes or outlines what effective performance should be within your organization? For example, maybe the skill is "Changing the Oil on the Forklift." If there is an operation manual which outlines the appropriate steps for changing the oil in the forklift, then state this (i.e. "Change the oil on the forklift according to the Forklift Operator's Manual, pages 33-35.").

- **Proof** – What is the proof that the employee successfully demonstrated the skill? Does a supervisor need to approve the demonstration of skill mastery in writing? Does the employee need to present a certificate indicating they completed the training with a passing score? Again, an important consideration during the development of Certification Manual.

Question 4: Are there any _standards_ to be observed when demonstrating mastery and under what situation(s) should the employee be able to demonstrate mastery?

The purpose of addressing the standards is to identify the setting and conditions under which demonstration of skill mastery must occur. For example, are there certain tools that an employee will or will not have access to when demonstrating skill mastery such as a calculator or measuring tape? What will use of the skill being demonstrated look like in the real world and is it a realistic expectation? Is there anything the employee needs to request in preparation for demonstrating skill mastery? When writing the standards for your skill objective, address the following items:

- **A. Resources Given?** – Are there items, lists, tools, maps, etc. that the employee will have access to when demonstrating mastery of the skill?
  - On a spreadsheet
  - Without a calculator
  - Given a standard set of tools
  - On a blank block diagram

- **B. Resources Excluded?** – Are there items, lists, tools, maps, etc. that the employee will not have access to when demonstrating mastery of the skill?
  - Without the Policy Manual
  - With only a screwdriver and role of duct tape
  - Without a map

- **C. Setting/Conditions?** – Is there a particular location that the skill demonstration should occur? Are there certain conditions under which the demonstration should occur?
  - On a hill
  - Given a broken pump, submerged in water
  - In the presence of a supervisor

- **Other Considerations?** – Are there other issues that should be accounted for when demonstrating mastery of the skill?

Question 5: Are there any *SAFETY CRITERIA* for skill demonstration that must be considered?

If there is safety equipment to be worn or procedures to be followed during demonstration? If so, make sure to be specific. It is important that Skill Mastery demonstration be performed in as "life-like" a way as possible. This means safety procedures that should be observed in real-world use of the skill should be observed during skill demonstration, as well. For example, "able to change a valve while submerged in waste-deep water" would be appropriate, but adding the condition of "during a driving hail storm and under hurricane conditions" might be too much.

Question 6: Is there any *EQUIPMENT NEEDED* for skill demonstration?

Is there any EQUIPMENT needed for skill demonstration, outside of the resources addressed in the Standards section of your Skill Objective? For example, will the person need to come prepared with their Haz-Mat gear in order to demonstrate a chemical spill situation?

Once these six key questions have been answered, you will have written a complete Skill Objective. It will take some practice to excel at writing Skill Objectives. Allow about 30-45 minutes to write each one when you first begin. With practice, it does become easier and quicker and should take approximately 10-15 minutes per objective.

Below is a sample of a formatted table that will facilitate the writing of skill objectives, followed by an illustration of this process using our Water Operator example.

The Public Sector's Guide to Skill-based Pay

🛠 TOOL 3

Skill Objectives Table/Template

SKILL:

Action: What should the employee be able to do?

Proof/Measurement: How well must it be done?

Speed/Time	Accuracy	According To...	Proof {Sign-Off? Certificate? Other?}

Standards: Under what conditions do you want the employee to be able to do it?

Items Given	Items Excluded	Setting/Conditions	Other

Safety Criteria

Equipment Needed

Location of Skill Mastery Demonstration: (check all that apply)	☐ Field (on-the-job)	☐ Lab Set-up/Training	☐ Classroom instruction
Estimated Time requirement to complete demonstration:			

Page 89
©Copyright 2003, 2004 - All rights reserved - The Waters Consulting Group, Inc.

The Public Sector's Guide to Skill-based Pay

In the Blue Skies Water Utility Department, the Skill-based Pay Project Team decided once again to ask for the participation of the Subject Matter Expert Teams. The Subject Matter Expert teams were asked to attend a brief training session on the principles of writing Skill Objectives. During this training, the importance of writing solid and complete Skill Objectives was discussed. Additionally, the Subject Matter Expert Teams were allowed time to begin writing Skill Objectives for the items in their inventoried lists. Feedback on the initial objectives written was given to the Subject Matter Expert Teams during this meeting to help refine the approach to writing.

At the close of the meeting, each Subject Matter Expert Team agreed to have all of their Skill Objectives written within a month's period. The Skill-based Pay Project Team offered to provide feedback to the Subject Matter Expert Teams as they were writing the Objectives.

Once the Skill Objectives were written, the Skill-based Pay Development Team reviewed the objectives for completeness. Some Skill Objectives were deemed incomplete and returned to the Subject Matter Expert Teams for further work. The amount of time for the additional work and edits was one week.

Two examples of completed Skill Objectives for the position of Water Operator are provided on the following pages with TABLE 21 and TABLE 22. ∎

TABLE 21

Skill Objectives Table/Example			
SKILL POSITION: Water Operator			
Skill ID: 1.1.4	*Basic Haz-Mat*		
Action: What should the employee be able to do?			
Attend an approved 1-day training class on Basic Haz-Mat.			
Proof/Measurement: How well must it be done?			
Speed/Time	Accuracy	According To…	Proof
Must occur within 45 days of employment	*N/A*	*N/A*	*Give Certificate of completion of class to Supervisor*
Standards: Under what conditions do you want the employee to be able to do it?			
Items Given	Items Excluded	Setting/Conditions	Other
N/A	*N/A*	*Approved training course*	*N/A*
Safety Criteria:			
None			
Equipment Needed:			
Equipment to be provided by course instructor			
Location of Skill Mastery Demonstration: (check all that apply)	☐ Field (on-the-job)	☐ Lab Set-up/Training	☑ Classroom instruction
Estimated Time requirement to complete demonstration: *1 day*			

The Public Sector's Guide to Skill-based Pay

TABLE 22

Skill Objectives Table/Example			
SKILL POSITION: Water Operator			
Skill ID: 2.2.5	*Service Connections*		
Action: What should the employee be able to do?			
Install a water meter.			
Proof/Measurement: How well must it be done?			
Speed/Time	Accuracy	According To…	Proof
N/A	N/A	City specifications	Give Certificate of completion of class to Supervisor
Standards: Under what conditions do you want the employee to be able to do it?			
Items Given	Items Excluded	Setting/Conditions	Other
Standard set of tools	Without assistance	Field Setting	Meter must be in operating condition after installation
Safety Criteria:			
Standard Safety Equipment			
Equipment Needed:			
Standard Tool Set			
Location of Skill Mastery Demonstration: (check all that apply)	☑ Field (on-the-job)	☐ Lab Set-up/Training	☐ Classroom instruction
Estimated Time requirement to complete demonstration: *2 Hours*			

The Public Sector's Guide to Skill-based Pay

SUMMARY OF APPENDICES FOR CHAPTER 5

In the Appendix Section, you will find samples of the following tools for your use:

- Appendix H – Skill Objectives Table

My Chapter Notes:

The Public Sector's Guide to Skill-based Pay

My Chapter Notes:

CHAPTER 6
Finalizing Your Skill-based Pay System's Hierarchy and Certification Manual

> *The achievements of an organization are the results of the combined effort of each individual.*
>
> *- Vince Lombardi (1913-1970)*

This Chapter is dedicated to finalizing and reassessing the program you have developed so far. The goal during this review phase is to make certain your program is still aligned with the organization's overall goals and strategic mission while complementing the climate and culture of your organization. It is easy to become so absorbed in the creation and placement of skills, the writing of objectives and the management of the process that the original goal is lost. One method in verifying that you are still on track with creating a Skill-based Pay system that focuses on organizational goals, and individual expectations is to solicit the opinions of participating employees.

REQUESTING ADDITIONAL FEEDBACK

As stated in Chapter 1, employee communication and involvement is key to the success of a Skill-based Pay system. This is important at all stages of development and particularly during the finalization process. Gaining additional employee feedback can be effectively accomplished through one-on-one and/or group focus sessions. An organization's size and culture will dictate which method of communication is the most feasible.

Assuming you have involved all employees at some stage during the development process, this step will be relatively easy to accomplish since a participatory environment has already been established. Take this opportunity to ask for input from employees who have been actively involved in the process thus far. Ask for final recommendations, thoughts and suggestions regarding the current arrangement of the program.

> Caution is advised at this point in garnering feedback from employees that have not participated – for whatever reason – in the development of the program. It would take a significant amount of education regarding the program in order to gain meaningful advice – whether it is positive or negative. Of course it is important that all employees be heard during the entire development process, but make certain you are asking for suggestions from those that can provide solid feedback based on fact – this way, you can make consequential alterations to the program as necessary.

Employee involvement and their ability to provide feedback is consistently linked to employee satisfaction and commitment to new systems.

Means by which you can gather and incorporate the closing series of employee comments include, but are not limited to, the following:

- **Focus Groups** – Focus groups are meetings with small numbers of employees (5-7 employees per group), conducted by members of the Skill-based Pay Development Team or other individuals closely familiar with the Skill-based Pay system and its development process. A set list of questions should be created before the meetings by the Skill-based Pay Development Team.

These questions should probe for information relevant to the system structure and format from the employees. Even though focus groups require a substantial time investment it is not as time intensive as the one-on-one interview approach described below. Focus groups provide an environment conducive to giving and receiving quality input on the Skill-based Pay system from the perspective of the end-user – the employee.

- **Town-Hall Meetings** – Town Hall meetings are large, open sessions in which many, or all, employees are present when the basic structure of the Skill-based Pay system is presented. This presentation should be conducted by members of the Skill-based Pay Development Team. A controlled question and answer session usually follows with a moderator and a set number of audience questions allowed in order to maintain order and the timeline. Typically there are members of the audience that have been asked prior to the session to prepare several questions and to be prepared to be called upon by the moderator. This format allows for the maximum amount of downward communication in a short amount of time, but is the poorest environment for receiving feedback since the number of questions from the audience is limited based on time constraints.

- **One-on-One Interviews** – One-on-One Interviews are meetings conducted on an individual basis with a sampling of affected employees. As with the focus groups, these discussions should be conducted by members of the Skill-based Pay Development Team or other individuals closely familiar with the Skill-based Pay System and its development process. A set list of questions should be created by the Skill-based Pay Development Team that probes for information relevant to the Skill-based Pay system structure and format from the employees.

These interviews should be conducted with only two individuals in the room: the employee and the Skill-based Pay Development Team representative in order to allow for the most conducive environment to receive candid feedback. This format requires the largest amount of time and resource investment. However, this is typically the best environment for receiving quality and candid employee input.

The more employee input included during the entire process…
- The more commitment to the program from employees
- The less resistance you will experience when implementing the system
- The more effective and applicable to "real-world" situations the program will be
- The more satisfaction employees will feel as the system is implemented
- The more likely the program will be to succeed

Once you feel you have involved all of those who will be affected by the new Skill-based Pay system, then you are ready to move towards implementation. The Skill-based Pay system you are developing is a dynamic initiative that should adapt to changing organizational issues. Such programs are often referred to as "living systems".

The Skill-based Pay Development Team for the City of Blue Skies wanted to gain a thorough perspective on the program developed. They decided first to return to other projects other than Skill-based Pay for a period of one week. After one week, they reviewed their process with a fresh outlook.

When they met, they began by reviewing their efforts involving their communication plans. They asked themselves if they had incorporated all the employees that should be included in the process and if they had made a significant effort to gain the input and expertise of the affected groups. They agreed that their communication strategy had been more than adequate with the inclusion of the OR Survey, various committees, numerous communication sessions and focus groups. Additionally, they had utilized employees as Subject Matter Experts and posted the results of the various meetings at key project stages on the Skill-based Pay Bulletin Board. Finally, they had worked to include updates in the Citywide newsletter.

However, to ensure that employees were afforded every available opportunity to provide their input, the Skill-based Pay Development Team decided to hold one last informational meeting, prior to proceeding with the implementation phase. This was an open meeting to all employees and was conducted in a town hall meeting format. At the open meeting, there was a PowerPoint™ presentation made which outlined the varying stages of program development, employee involvement, timelines and next steps. The remainder of the meeting was reserved for an informal question and answer period which was moderated by a member of the Skill-based Pay Development Team. The meeting was held open until all employees had their questions addressed.

After the meeting, the Skill-based Pay Team compiled the comments and suggestions received and incorporated these into the finalization of the system as appropriate. ■

The Public Sector's Guide to Skill-based Pay

Once your system is in place, with the Skill Hierarchy finalized and all of the necessary materials developed, it is time to implement Skill-based Pay.

SUMMARY OF APPENDICES FOR CHAPTER 6

- Appendix A – Sample Organizational Readiness Survey
- Appendix B – Communication Strategy Development
- Appendix Q – Sample Visuals and Presentations

My Chapter Notes:

CHAPTER 7
Beginning the Implementation Process with Employee Skill Assessments

> *There is no man living who isn't capable of doing more than he thinks he can do.*
> *- Henry Ford (1863-1947)*

Some of the most frequently asked questions to our consultants during Skill-based Pay System design involves the placement of employees into the new system. For example…

1. How do you determine the skill level of current employees?
2. Is length of time in the position a factor?
3. What about new employees – those that have been with the organization for less than six months or those that you want to hire but are unsure of their skills?
4. What if someone is in a senior position, but their skills are at a lower position?
5. Who gets to decide the skill level of the employee? Does the employee have any input?
6. Won't employees get mad and quit if you rate their skills lower than they think they should be?

Certainly, one of the most difficult aspects of implementation is placing employees into the new system. The following pages outline some recommended approaches toward this phase.

The Public Sector's Guide to Skill-based Pay

> Before we proceed, we want to issue a warning: we strongly advise against any pay decreases as a result of Skill-based Pay implementation.

A Skill-based Pay system should be viewed as an opportunity for employees to:

- Increase their professional skill base
- Have a clearer picture of how their compensation system works
- Have greater control over their movement through the compensation system
- Achieve a greater sense of professional achievement through the systematic achievement of skills

> In Chapter 8, we will address the development of the compensation structure. It is important to develop the Skill-based system <u>first</u> – including the assessment of individual employees and their skills - prior to linking any participant to pay ranges. This is particularly important in order to allow the organization to produce a non-biased system that is based on actual skill assessment and not pay. In Chapter 9, we will review in detail recommended policies for governing the placement of employees in relation to pay and skill level and objectively evaluating the skills of affected employees.

ASSESSING CURRENT EMPLOYEES

A complete assessment of the employee's current skill base by an evaluation team consisting of direct supervisors and/or senior employees and the incumbant is an integral first step in the implementation process. By allowing the employee to participate, it helps to reduce objections in the final determination of their placement within the Skill-based hierarchy.

The use of an Evaluation Committee is also particularly helpful since it allows for group consensus coupled with an approach focusing on objective employee evaluation. Remember, this hierarchy will be linked to a pay structure and the skill evaluation process will be a sensitive issue for most employees.

The Public Sector's Guide to Skill-based Pay

STEPS FOR CURRENT EMPLOYEE SKILL ASSESSMENT

Working together, the employee, their direct supervisor and the Evaluation Committee will examine the list of skills in the hierarchy and agree upon which skills the employee does or does not currently possess. This occurs in three main steps:

1. **Employee/Supervisor Independent Assessments:** The employee and their direct supervisor meet and review the skill list. The employee is asked to rate themselves on each skill by using a set scale (such as the sample provided below in TOOL 4). The employee is usually given five days to complete this process and return the rating sheet to the supervisor. During the same period, the supervisor also rates the employee on the skills they feel the employee possesses. They then meet and review the results. The goal is to attempt to reach resolution on the skill level assessment. On all areas where consensus is achieved, a notation is made indicating the outcome (either skill attained or not). On all areas in which they do not concur, the Evaluation Committee is notified. Again, the goal during this phase is for the employee and supervisor to resolve as many discrepancies as possible before reaching the Evaluation Committee level of review.

2. **Evaluation Committee Assessment:** The resultant assessment, complete with the supervisor's and employee's original and edited scores, are forwarded to the Evaluation Committee. The Committee reserves the right to question any of the scores – even the ones in which both the employee and supervisor agreed upon.

3. **Final Consensus Meeting:** Based on the Evaluation Committee's review, the employee and supervisor are called upon for a final review of the resulting assessment scores. All skills in which the Committee, supervisor and employee agree are reviewed first, followed by all areas in which the Committee and/or supervisor rated the employee higher than the employee rated him or herself. All skills for which the employee rated themselves higher than the Committee or supervisor are reviewed last. An attempt is made during this meeting to reach consensus with the employee (and supervisor if necessary). During this meeting, employees are given the opportunity to present any facts that may change the Committee's opinion in regard to ratings. It is during this time that an employee may also request to validate a particular skill during a scheduled demonstration. If a consensus of opinion cannot be reached, the final decision of the rating score is made by the senior manager or department director. Employees have the right to appeal these ratings with another office, such as a Human Resources Department. Typically, line management has the final authority in such cases.

The following is an excerpt from the Skill Inventory Assessment form developed and used by the Blue Skies Water Utility Department.

ASSESSING NEW HIRES

The placement of new hires into the Skill-based Pay system occurs in a similar fashion. Skills of the new employee are assessed based on documentation they produce. The employee is given a reasonable amount of time to prove or demonstrate the skills and then is allowed to progress through the program just as all other employees. The key difference here is that new employees are on a modified honor system for a short period of time because they are paid for skills before the point of demonstration. New employees should be placed at or near the bottom of the zone or sub-zone in which they are assessed during this initial probationary period. Of course they should be presented with a copy of the Certification Manual explaining the entire program prior to the job offer and be required to pass the necessary skill requirements during their probationary evaluation period. Specific policies should be developed to address this process.

The Public Sector's Guide to Skill-based Pay

Please note the following key points when designing your assessment process…

City of Blue Skies Water Utility Department - Skill Inventory Assessment Key Points

1. For each skill, both the employee and the employee's supervisor, independently, should assign a rating, based on the employee's current level of ability, using the scale provided on the following page (TABLE 23).

2. Average the two scores for each skill, placing the average score next to the appropriate skill.

3. Based upon organizational Skill-based Pay policies, determine if the score achieved is adequate for "passing" a skill or skill group. The level for a "Passing" score would be determined by the organization.

4. Where a "passing" score occurs, the employee would be given credit for that skill as though Skill Mastery demonstration had already occurred. Where a "passing" score does not occur, the employee would need to demonstrate mastery of those skills according to the Skill-based Pay System Policy and Administration Guidelines in place.

5. For new employees starting above the minimum level of the skill hierarchy - The employee should be placed in the Zone and Track that is at the highest level "passed." For instance, if an employee "passes" Track 2.2 of Skill Zone 2, but does not "pass" Track 2.3 of Skill Zone 2, the employee would be placed into Track 2.2 of Skill Zone 2, so that they may then begin to attain the skills in the next Track which they do not currently possess.

Scoring Option – If desired, the averaging of scores may be skipped. Instead of averaging scores, the employee and supervisor would focus only on those skills where there is disagreement or where both parties placed a rating of "2." If a rating of two is given, it must be agreed upon by the supervisor and employee whether the level of skill the employee possesses is adequate or inadequate as outlined in the Skill Objective.

The Public Sector's Guide to Skill-based Pay

TABLE 23

	Blue Skies Water Utility Department Employee Skill Inventory Analysis Scale
1	**Cannot** perform the Skill in question. Can only perform skill with detailed and thorough supervision.
2	**Can perform some** aspects of the skill. May require general supervision and feedback.
3	**Can** perform the Skill in question, completely and without supervision (unless specifically required by the Skill Objective).
0	**N/A** – This skill is not applicable to this position at this time. A score of zero does not have a negative impact on the overall score.

✗ TOOL 4

Blue Skies Water Utility Department Employee Skill Inventory Rating Sheet (Partial)	
Skill Zone 1	
Track 1 – Foundation and Development Skill Blocks	**Score ↓**
1.1.1 City Policy Review	_____
1.1.2 Defensive Driving	_____
1.1.3 First Aid/CPR	_____
1.1.4 Basic Haz-mat	_____
1.1.5 Confined Space Entry	_____
1.1.6 Two-way Radio Protocol	_____
Average Score for Track 1	
Track 2 – Water Distribution	**Score ↓**
1.2.1 Water Mainlines	
Identify Components	_____
Identify three types of mainline water pipe	_____
Install repair clamp and compression coupling	_____
Use water system maps to ID at least three appurtenances	_____
1.2.2 Valves	
Locate and mark	_____
Basic operations	_____
Adjust top section to grade	_____
Clean out valve	_____
1.2.3 Fire Hydrants	
ID three brands by manufacturer; determine mainline size	_____
ID major components from mainline to private service line	_____
Demonstrate proper operation	_____
Clean and paint	_____
Average Score for Track 2	

The Public Sector's Guide to Skill-based Pay

The City of Blue Skies Water Utility Department had approximately 200 employees to assess in the area of skill attainment. Supervisors involved in the new Skill-based Pay system were assigned the task of completing a Skill Inventory for each of their employees in the Skill-based Pay system as well as working with their employees in one-on-one sessions in order to gain consensus in the rating process. Each of the ten supervisors had approximately 20 employees. There were given one month to complete this phase of the assessment.

Before this process began, group meetings were held for the Skill-based Pay employees during which the Skill Assessment form was distributed and the scale for scoring was explained. Time was allowed for questions and their candid feedback in regard to their personal level of skill achievement.

During the next month, supervisors scheduled one-hour meetings for each of their employees. During the meeting, the supervisor and employee compared scores they had given in the following order: 1) both agreed; 2) supervisor rated higher than employee; and 3) employee rated higher than supervisor. The goal during the meeting was to reach consensus or resolution on how skills in dispute would be demonstrated.

Results of the assessment and meetings were then forwarded to the Evaluation Committee for further review and final approval. ■

The Public Sector's Guide to Skill-based Pay

SUMMARY OF APPENDICES FOR CHAPTER 7

In the Appendix Section, you will find samples of the following tools for your use:

- Appendix I – Skill Inventory Scale and Form - Template

My Chapter Notes:

✏️ *My Chapter Notes:*

CHAPTER 8
Linking Pay to your Skill-based System

> *Folks who never do any more than they are paid for, never get paid for more than they do.*
>
> *- Elbert Hubbard (1856-1915)*

You have now established your Skill-based progression and employee assignments! You now have to make some serious decisions regarding the attachment of pay to your system. It is strongly recommended that you do this in conjunction with a compensation expert, whether it is your in-house compensation staff or an outside consultant. You may even want to include this compensation expert throughout the entire experience – depending on your time, budget and organizational constraints.

Though much of *The Guide* has focused on the project development end of a Skill-based Pay system, the pay portion of this system can make or break its success if it lacks internal or external equity. The involvement of compensation expertise in this development process will greatly increase your chances of success. Most organizations have compensation professionals assigned to their Human Resources Department. Our advice would be to seek out these individuals for guidance in the structure development. This Chapter will explore the basic compensation practices used to support a Skill-based Pay environment.

The Public Sector's Guide to Skill-based Pay

POSITION EVALUATION

One step for moving to a Skill-based Pay system is transitioning from the current traditional pay structure. This is typically accomplished by collapsing the current structure into bands that contain families of positions or positions in the same career ladder. While organizations that currently have a point factor position evaluation system must begin to look at valuing jobs differently, they can use their current system to transition to a structure that supports Skill-based Pay by slotting jobs into pay zones based on the benchmarks salaries surveyed.

However, organizations that use point factor position evaluation systems will typically discontinue their current job evaluation system and move directly to a salary survey process using market data as the guide for structure development. This is our recommended approach. Regardless of which system is currently used by the organization, the first step is to identify the job title (and skill necessary) of the positions that have been selected for the Skill-based Pay system. Once that information is identified, the transition begins.

BROADBANDING IN CONJUNCTION WITH SKILL-BASED PAY

All public sector organizations strive to meet the needs of its customers. However, the way these needs are being met is changing as technology and outsourcing affect the way employees complete their job tasks. In the process of requiring more skills and licensing requirements, some tasks are being combined while in some cases higher-level duties are added. The work culture is constantly changing based on the needs of both management, employees and customers. Compensation programs are vital ingredients to those changes. As priorities within organizations shift in support of the efficient application of customer service excellence, the traditional methods of pay and rewards are no longer effective in supporting these strategies.

The Public Sector's
Guide to Skill-based Pay

Broadbanding and Skill-based Pay, alternative approaches to pay and rewards, support the new organizational philosophy of a more customer and employee oriented organization. Specifically, broadbands support today's more dynamic and less hierarchical organizations by breaking down the functional barriers created by traditional organizational structures. Broadbands also foster horizontal skill development and lateral mobility.

Broadbanding commonly refers to the collapsing of many salary grades into a few wide bands for numerous purposes such as improving overall organizational effectiveness by managing career development and overseeing pay. For this reason, broadbanding is commonly paired with Skill-based Pay systems. In addition, broadbanding reduces much of the hierarchy associated with a traditional pay structure (see DIAGRAM 6) to support a flatter, leaner, more customer-focused organization.

The Public Sector's Guide to Skill-based Pay

DIAGRAM 6

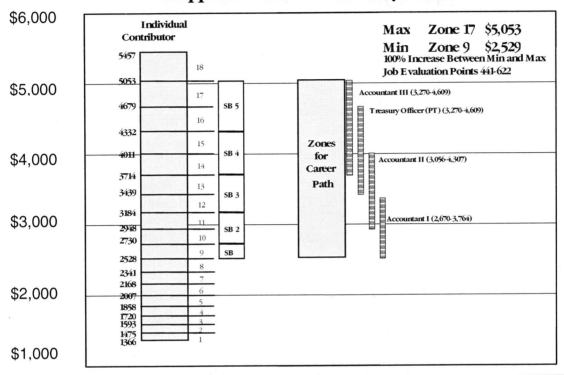

Accountant Support Career Path
Support Services Provider Pay Zones

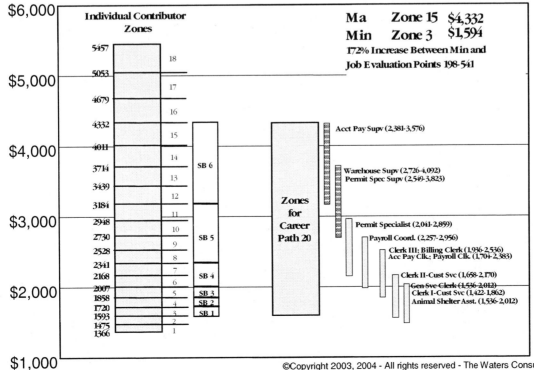

Customer Service Support Career Path
Support Services Provider Pay Zones

Page 115
©Copyright 2003, 2004 - All rights reserved - The Waters Consulting Group, Inc.

The Public Sector's Guide to Skill-based Pay

THE BENEFITS OF BROADBANDING

Broadbanding aids in the elimination of "empty" pay grades and excessive job titles while facilitating employee movement through defined career paths ultimately allowing employees to build their skills. The Skill-based Pay approach focuses on building individual employee flexibility. Instead of compensating an employee for retaining a certain job position for a number of years, the employee will be rewarded for acquiring specific groups of skills. When employees demonstrate competence in a skill zone, they are certified in that zone and are then able to progress to the next zone. This movement is linked to pay within set guidelines established by policy.

Employees in the Skill-based Pay system will become more versatile (i.e. capable of performing many different tasks within the team) or more specialized (i.e. capable of applying advanced technology to customer problems).

The following are potential benefits of broadbanding in organizations:

- Supports a flexible and fluid organization by making it easier to restructure work and reorganize work teams;
- Encourages lateral employee movement and development by flattening or eliminating the pyramid driven job family career ladders;
- Supports teamwork by de-emphasizing differences in level and status;
- Promotes internal equity by reducing the number of salary grades and position description distinctions;
- Supports employee and line management empowerment and individual pay fairness by giving line management more control over pay decisions; and
- Reduces the need for an elaborate job evaluation process – reevaluating only the most significant changes in job responsibilities.

The Public Sector's Guide to Skill-based Pay

An example of broadbanding lies in the practices of one of our client cities who was practicing the concepts of Total Quality Management (TQM) in 1993. Broadbanding and Skill-based Pay were introduced in late 1996 almost three years after the management change had begun. The City spent more than twelve months identifying competencies, developing progress review evaluation tools and designing employee development programs and processes. In addition, they began modeling new career paths to support the TQM organization. Broadbanding and Skill-based Pay were used properly as tools to support this vast organizational change; not as a lead to this change. Sample groupings of transition City positions under Broadbanding can be seen on the following pages.

There are alternative compensation strategies for employees who achieve many of the same objectives as broadbands. For example, gainsharing also encourages employees to broaden their skills.

Contrary to popular belief, broadbands do not represent a laissez-faire approach to managing salaries. Most organizations using broadbands replace old controls with guidelines that provide line managers greater flexibility. For example:

- Instead of creating separate budgets for merit, promotional, cost of living, or market adjustments, they often combine these separate pools into a single budget, which increases managers' flexibility while using these same dollars.

- Instead of using market pay as a control point like a midpoint, data is used as reference points to help managers make informed decisions. These market pay data points are often used with other pay guidelines that aid in managing competitive pay within the broadbands.

- Broadbands can change how human resource and compensation professionals work with line managers to control compensation costs. In lieu of publishing guidelines and monitoring compliance, compensation professionals spend more time ensuring that line managers have the information and skills they need to manage employee salaries at a competitive level.

Employee reactions to broadbands vary by organization based on the culture and the role pay grades served in that culture. Employees may view broadbands as a take-away in organizations where grades and titles determine status.

In these cultures, employees who have earned their "stripes" may resent the loss of prestige if the organization eliminates these grade or title distinctions. In addition, employees who are now striving to earn their "stripes" may become unmotivated because the organization has taken away something in which they have been working towards.

Besides this loss of status, employees may also be concerned about broadbands because they have relied on grades to monitor how they are progressing in their careers. Without grades, employees have a more difficult time judging whether their careers are "on track." This concern stems from the paradigm we have all experienced: career advancement means moving to a higher grade. These issues also stress the need for open communications as we have discussed throughout *The Guide*.

Due to their apparent simplicity, organizations often underestimate the amount of education and training needed to support the change to broadbands. Managers typically need more training because broadbands give them more information and flexibility than traditional salary administration programs.

Training is also critical because many of the concepts organizations have taught managers and many of the methods managers have used to sidestep the compensation program, no longer work with broadbands. Managers need to "unlearn" the old way before they can support the new program that is strongly linked to measured learning.

The success of broadbands depends on managers' commitment to this concept. To build this commitment:

- Managers need to understand the organization's total compensation strategy and the role the base salary program serves in supporting the organization's goals and human capital objectives.

This often means developing a new total compensation philosophy.

- Managers also need to be proficient at coaching employees about performance and careers. This means educating management on concepts and developing skills that extend well beyond salary administration. They need to become proficient at employee development, coaching and giving feedback.

- Managers need to be comfortable using the market data as a guide and not an absolute. Traditional systems treat salary grades as "law." The career path approach gets us in the ballpark and allows managers to make the decisions they need to ensure internal and external equity.

The Public Sector's Guide to Skill-based Pay

SAMPLES OF BROADBANDING IN CITY GOVERNMENT

TABLE 24

Broadbanded Title	Current Titles	
Managing Director	Chief Civil Engineer Director of Engineering Director of Planning Director of Public Works Police Chief	Director of Finance Director of Personnel Director of Public Health District Fire Chief
Engineering Administration	City Engineer	Civil Engineer
Operations Administration	Engineering Construction Supt Facility Maintenance Supt Streets and Drainage Supt Landfill Manager	Equipment Services Supt Parks Supt Waste/Wastewater Supt.
Municipal Services Director	Building Official Director of Emergency Mgmt Director of Libraries	Director of Aviation Director of Leisure Services Director of Management Services
Program Manager	Accounting Supervisor Mammal/Zoo Curator Emergency Program Manager	Computer Operations Supervisor Recycling Coordinator Support Service Manager
Technical Administrator	Systems Administrator Tax Assessor Collector	Water Treatment Superintendent
Inspection Supervisor	Code Enforcement Supervisor	Environmental Health Supervisor
Program Administrator	Systems Administration Asst. Director of Personnel Recreation Superintendent Zoo Superintendent	Asst. Director of Community Services Traffic Operations Manager
Custodian	Custodian	Sr. Custodian

The Public Sector's Guide to Skill-based Pay

Broadbanded Title	Current Titles	
Medical Coordinator	Case Management Supervisor Nutrition Manager Public Health Nurse Manager	Dental Clinic Supervisor HIV/STD Manager OCC Health Nurse Coordinator
Program Supervisor	Customer Service Supervisor Records Supervisor	Personnel Office Supervisor
Operations Supervisor	Airport Operations Supervisor Street Maintenance Supervisor Water Service Supervisor	Convention Facilities Supervisor Traffic Maintenance Supervisor Water Utility System Supervisor
Program Coordinator	Athletic Supervisor	Public Service Supervisor
Field Supervisor	Asst. Sanitation Collection Supervisor Maintenance Crew Supervisor Maintenance Crew Supervisor-Streets Maintenance Crew Supervisor II-DOT	Equipment Maint. Crew Supervisor Maintenance Crew Supervisor-DOT Maintenance Crew Supervisor II Sanitation Collection Supervisor
Operations Coordinator	Athletic Facilities Coordinator Convention Facilities Coordinator Crewleader of Parks-DOT Crewleader of Streets-DOT Crewleader of Utilities Crewleader of Utilities II Plant Maintenance Coordinator Sr. Water Service Technician	Construction Coordinator Crewleader of Parks Crewleader of Sanitation Crewleader of Sanitation-DOT Crewleader II Maintenance Coordinator Sr. Water Utility System Operator
Planner	Metropolitan Planner Urban Planner II	Urban Planner I
Meter Reader	Water Service Technician	Water Meter Technician

The Public Sector's Guide to Skill-based Pay

Broadbanded Title	Current Titles	
Community Relations Specialist	Community Development Coordinator Convention Promotions Coordinator Tourism Clerk Visitor Services Manager	Convention & Visitors Specialist Education Curator Sr. Tourism Clerk Tourism Coordinator Volunteer Coordinator
Senior Planner	Engineering Planner	Sr. Urban Planner
Assistant City Attorney	Assistant City Attorney I	Assistant City Attorney II
HR Generalist	Compensation Coordinator	Recruiting & Staffing Coordinator
Financial Analyst	Accountant Internal Auditor	Budget Analyst
Librarian	Librarian I	Sr. Librarian
Financial Analyst – Sr.	Budget Officer Sr. Internal Auditor	Sr. Consultant
Project Analyst	Sr. Project Analyst	Utility Office Analyst
Nurse	Advanced Nurse Practitioner Public Health Nurse I	Health Nurse Public Health Nurse II
Management Analyst	Administrative Analyst	Economic Research Analyst
Health Aide	Dental Assistant Crisis Team Counselor Victim Service Coordinator	Nutrition Aide Sr. Victim Service Coordinator
Information Specialist	Municipal Information Officer Tourist Info Center Coordinator	Sr. Municipal Information Officer
Welder	Sr. Welder	Welder
Service Helper	Collection Station Monitor Collection Station Monitor-DOT	Scales Operator Sr. Concession Worker

The Public Sector's Guide to Skill-based Pay

Broadbanded Title	Current Titles	
Buyer	Buyer Purchasing Agent Sr. Buyer	Buyer II Purchasing Assistant
Health Specialist	Public Health Technician Sanitary Inspector	Sanitarium I Sanitarium II
Admin. Services Coordinator	Executive Secretary to ACM	Executive Secretary to CM
Crime Technician	Photo Lab Technician Police Service Technician	Police Fingerprinting Technician
Project Funds Specialist	Community Initiative Associate Public Health Coordinator	Sr. Community Initiatives Associate
Case Worker	Case Management Aide Nutrition Specialist	Case Worker Outreach Worker
Communication Specialist	Police Dispatcher	Police Dispatcher Technician
Assistant City Secretary	Assistant City Secretary	Records Management Officer
Deputy Court Clerk	Court Clerk	Deputy Court Clerk
Curator	Manager/Curator Hall of Fame Curator	General Curator Reptile Curator
Customer Service Rep. - Sr.	Asst. Water Collection Supervisor Sr. Administrative Clerk	Customer Service Rep. II Sr. Customer Service Rep
Secretary - Sr.	Executive Secretary Secretary II	Personnel Technician
Recreation Specialist	Community Outreach Specialist Recreation Coordinator Sr. Museum Coordinator	Convention Center Service Rep. Recreation Program Coordinator
Park Ranger	Park Ranger I Park Ranger II	Sr. Park Ranger

The Public Sector's Guide to Skill-based Pay

Broadbanded Title	Current Titles	
Customer Service Rep	Administrative Clerk II Customer Service Orator	Customer Service Advisor
Center Aide	Concession/Catering Coordinator Center Aide	Event Coordinator Rental Clerk
Computer Operator	Computer Operator I Data Analyst I Data Entry Operator	Computer Operator II Data Analyst II
Secretary	Administrative Assistant-Intern	Secretary I
Plant Operator	Plant Operator I	Plant Operator II Field Utility Locator
Inventory Clerk	ID and Property Technician Clerk I	Inventory Inventory Clerk II
Jet Truck Operator	Line Inspection Technician	Sr. Line Inspection Technician
Environmental Investigator	Environmental Coordinator Pre-Treatment Coordinator Plans Examiner/Chief Inspector	Environmental Inspector Sr. Environmental Inspector
Inspector	Commercial Inspector II Construction Inspector II Residential Inspector I	Commercial Inspector I Rehabilitation Inspector Residential Inspector II
Traffic Signal Technician	Signal Technician I Signal Technician III	Signal Technician II Senior Signal Technician
Water Systems Operator	Water Utility System Operator II	Water Utility System Operator I
Water Quality Technician	Sr. Water Quality Analyst	Water Quality Analyst
Planning Technician	Civil Design Technician	Property Agent

The Public Sector's Guide to Skill-based Pay

Broadbanded Title	Current Titles	
Lab Technician I	Laboratory Technician I Medical Lab Technologist	Laboratory Technician II Sr. Lab Technician
Communication Technician	Electronic Technician II Sr. Electronic Technician	Electronic Technician I
Survey Technician	Survey Technician I Senior Survey Technician	Survey Technician II
Traffic Checker	Sr. Traffic Analyst	Traffic Analyst I
Plant Mechanic	Plant Maintenance Mechanic Sr. Plant Mechanic	Plant Mechanic-Utilities
Mechanic	Mechanic I	Sr. Mechanic
Tradesworker	HVAC Mechanic Electrician I Building Repairer of Leisure Services Sr. Building Repairer-DOT	Sr. Building Repairer-CC Sr. Electrician Sr. Plant Maintenance Mechanic Utilities Electrician
Service Technician	Building Maintenance Parks Maintenance Worker II Sr. Building Rep Maintenance Sr. Zookeeper	Sr. Service Provider Horticulturist Parks Maintenance Worker II Sr. Parks Maintenance Worker
Service Provider	Equipment Operator I-Parks Equipment Operator I-Streets Equipment Operator I-Utilities Maintenance Worker I-Parks	Maintenance Worker-Streets Maintenance Worker-Utilities Zookeeper Zookeeper II
Equipment Operator	Heavy Equipment Operator-General Heavy Equipment Operator-Utilities	Heavy Equipment Operator-DOT Heavy Equipment Operator - Streets
Transport Driver	Equipment Operator II-General Equipment Operator II-DOT Collection Station Monitor-DOT	Equipment Operator II-Streets Equipment Operator-Utilities Sr. Concession Worker

The Public Sector's Guide to Skill-based Pay

How do you match positions in a Broadbanded/Skill-based Pay system, when three or more career ladders become one series of pay zones? Positions as we know them disappear (broadbanding), so compensation practitioners will have to address issues such as:

- How do you use salary surveys when there are no positions (as we know them)?
- How do you match positions when there are no positions to match?
- How do you address internal and external equity when there are no positions?

These issues can be addressed in much the same way we currently perform salary surveys. First, let's review the different approaches to paying employees in an organization.

ORGANIZATIONAL REWARD STRATEGIES

A salary survey is a method to describe what organizations pay for – the measurements organizations use to value work when compared to the market. Traditionally, salary surveys have focused on throughputs, with jobs being the main focus.

For example, when conducting a survey, we learn what organizations pay employees in similar positions, as described by duties and responsibilities. Internally, we can place a value on the positions with an evaluation process, such as a point factor position evaluation system, resulting in a grade hierarchy or we can view the results of the salary survey to place positions in a market-based hierarchy.

The Public Sector's Guide to Skill-based Pay

SALARY SURVEY ISSUES

Organizations use salary surveys for two main purposes: to identify their relative position with respect to the chosen competition and, within that perspective, to serve as input for creating a salary structure and respective budget.

A common survey method for traditional work design is a benchmark survey, which focuses on a sample of benchmark positions and describes what organizations pay people for doing similar or comparable positions. Position matching is a key concern for organizations using these benchmark surveys. This is highly relevant to the issues mentioned above. When you create career paths with several jobs in a broadband, how do you use benchmarks to survey the market pay? If none of your target organizations have broadbands, then you may not get accurate information for developing a salary structure.

For example, let's use a Financial Analyst career path using the positions of Accountant I, Accountant II, Accountant III, and Treasury Officer instead of Water Operator. Which of these titles should you survey? Should you survey all of them? Are these positions unique to your organization? And once you have surveyed them, how should you combine the data mathematically – a simple average of all of the data, a weighted average, or some combination of the two? Remember how you combine the information can dramatically affect the outcomes.

When evaluating your options, the key issue to consider is "What is the purpose of conducting the salary survey?" In general terms, the purpose is to ensure that your organization's employees are paid fairly compared to the marketplace. In the traditional mode, the salary survey serves to define a range of pay opportunities for jobs in the organization. In the world of broadbands, the salary survey is a guide in defining a minimum and a maximum for a pay range.

The Public Sector's Guide to Skill-based Pay

Therefore, when conducting a salary survey in a Skill-based system, our goal is to make sure that the minimum starting salaries are high enough relative to the market to attract entry-level employees, and that the maximum of the pay range enables us to reward skilled, long-term employees comparably to what the market says they deserve. In a Skill-based Pay system, the maximum must allow adequate room for advanced learning to be compensated. Collect as much data on the traditional job titles assigned to the broadbands as well as the skills and duties associated with these positions. See TABLE 24 for a sample of job titles assigned to broadbanded titles. Match the skills to those titles and ensure the broadband compensates at least at market values (see Diagram 6).

This approach should function effectively for the majority of your Broadbands. However, in some cases, such as professional or upper level managerial broadbands, you may have only two or three traditional job titles in the band so more detailed matching of skills, knowledge and abilities to the market place will be necessary.

DESIGN ISSUES

In a broadband system, the salary ranges (from minimum to maximum) of a grade are considerably wider than traditional salary ranges of forty to sixty percent (40-60%). A range of eighty to one hundred percent (80-100%) is common for most broadbands, and spreads of two hundred to three hundred percent (200% or 300%) are not unheard of. When determining how wide to set the range, it is key to consider the ranges of the positions that merged to form the broadband. As mentioned previously, the new minimum should not dip below the old starting salary for the position at the bottom of the career ladder. The top of the range should not be so low that high-level, well-trained employees are lost to the outside because they are limited in their earning potential. In some cases, the ranges may be narrowed or widened to alleviate one or the other of these concerns; in other cases, the range control points may require upward adjustments to ensure equity on these issues.

Overlap of Bands:

Broadbanding reduces the number of grades found in a traditional salary structure, and the creation of skill-based career paths in such a system means that it is not necessary to have a close overlap between bands for promotional opportunities. However, salary ranges under a broadbanding system are also considerably wider than in a traditional pay system, allowing for more room for overlap in the bands. In this case, the degree of overlap will depend more on the width of the grades than the typical control point progression found in standard pay systems.

INPUT FROM A VARIETY OF SOURCES

The final result is a structure that incorporates input from a variety of sources:

- Employees through position description questionnaires;
- Supervisors through review of position description questionnaires;
- Market comparisons from the salary survey data by compensation professionals;
- Management through review of the resulting salary structure;
- Department Heads through review of initial position description questionnaires, position descriptions and review of tentative findings;

UPDATING THE SALARY STRUCTURE

Each year, the salary structure may be updated by conducting a salary survey of the original survey participants. A full-scale survey of typical benchmark positions (duties and responsibilities) found in each band should be performed. As an optional process every other year, the organization may choose to conduct a telephone survey and ask survey participants by what percentage they have increased salaries over the previous year on banded positions. Regardless, a full-scale survey should be conducted every two to three years. Remember to monitor the duties of the top and bottom positions responsibilities and the surveyed range spreads!

SUMMARY OF APPENDICES FOR CHAPTER 8

- Appendix J – Sample Job Description Questionnaire
- Appendix L – Sample Pay Structures

My Chapter Notes:

The Public Sector's Guide to Skill-based Pay

✎ *My Chapter Notes:*

CHAPTER 9
Continuing the Implementation Process with Policy and Administration Guideline Development

For everything you must have a plan.

- Napoleon (1769-1821)

Consideration of transition issues related to Skill-based Pay policy and administration must begin in the earliest stages of the design and development process. Following are some primary issues to address when developing your organization's policy and administration guidelines for its new Skill-based Pay system. Final decisions regarding policy and administration should be made by the implementing organization, based upon its particular needs and situation.

Each section in this Chapter addresses a particular topic area that appropriate policy decisions should be made upon before full implementation of a Skill-based Pay system occurs.

CREATING A POLICY FOR SKILL CERTIFICATION/DEMONSTRATION OF SKILL MASTERY

Developing the policy which will govern precisely how employees' skills and competencies are certified and re-certified will be a critical and important task.

The Public Sector's Guide to Skill-based Pay

One or more methods for certification may be necessary for the demonstration of mastery of a skill such as: paper/pencil testing, completion of approved coursework or actual demonstration of competence. With formal training or education, completion of the course requirements typically satisfies certification requirements. For cross training, on-the-job-performance or other situations in which a demonstrated level of proficiency is required, a supervisor, a senior employee with advanced skills or, in some cases, peer reviews are an effective means for meeting certification requirements. Peers are usually in the best position to truly evaluate performance and the skill level of their co-workers. The organization should decide and document what limits, if any, to apply to an employee's unsuccessful attempts to certify for a higher skill level.

Many of these issues will be resolved as the Skill Objectives are written. However, it is important that resolution of these issues is captured within your organization's Policy and Administrative Guidelines. In particular, some of the issues that may not be resolved while writing skill objectives but need to be in the Policy Manual include:

1. A policy to address failed demonstration of skills – For example, if an employee does not demonstrate a skill to satisfaction, how long must he or she wait until allowed to make a second attempt? What will be the consequences for a second failed attempt? What will happen in the meantime? Reduction in pay? Reduction in duties? Paid leave of absence? Unpaid leave of absence?

2. A policy to address recertification of skills – For example, what are the skills in which an employee must be re-certified? How often should this occur? Which skills should not require re-certification and why?

3. A policy to address the appointment of Skill Assessors – For example, what are the requirements for acting as an objective assessor of skill mastery demonstration? What level of supervisor is allowed to sign off on skill completion? Will there need to be more than one level of sign off?

CREATING A POLICY FOR PLACEMENT OF CURRENT EMPLOYEES INTO THE NEW SKILL-BASED PAY SYSTEM

Employee placement in the system was addressed in detail in Chapter 7, but it is important to briefly revisit this topic.

Employees are placed into the new plan in the skill level that most closely corresponds to their current SKAs. They are then given a period of time to prove they are qualified to remain at this level.

A significant number of employees that are either paid lower or higher than their current skill level dictates can be a challenge during the implementation phase.

- **Green Circle** employees are defined as those employees that have a demonstrated and ranked skill level that is higher than they are currently paid.
- **Red Circle** employees are those employees that do not possess skills commensurate with their current rate of pay

Increasing the pay for large numbers of employees that are currently green circled can generate significant implementation costs and may cause difficulties in the control of budgets.

The Public Sector's Guide to Skill-based Pay

It has been our experience during implementation that most employees are paid at a level commensurate with their current skill level and approximately 2% to 4% fall in the green circle category. If you experience more than this percentage range (2% to 4%) within your organization, it is advised that the skills of these employees be strongly re-evaluated to ensure accuracy.

The challenge for red circled employees is often a greater obstacle in that the organization now must decide how to tell the employee that they are being paid too much given their current level of skills. Immediate attention should be given to the training and development of these individuals in order to make certain they do not lose their current rate of pay. As we have mentioned before, we do not advise a decrease in pay. After all, it is not the employee's fault that he or she is being paid more than their skill level indicates – and you will have a difficult time in convincing the employee otherwise. Further, the employee has created a lifestyle and personal financial budget around this rate of pay.

However, the organization has an obligation to protect and maintain a sensible approach to compensation. Balancing the two is the issue. One effective approach to this quandary is to provide the employee with the means to gain the skill, provide a reasonable amount of time and then re-evaluate the employee. Another consideration may be to "grandfather" employees in that are near retirement. This has to be approached and treated very carefully – and should only be a onetime event at program implementation.

> There is another approach that more and more of our clients are using: allowing current employees to opt out of the program if they wish. These employees would receive the benefit of the current pay system (cost of living adjustments, etc.). however, all new employees would be required to be in the system.

One of our Skill-based Pay clients dealt with red circled employees by developing a performance contract that specified the improvements in performance and skill level the employee was expected to make and the timeframe for the changes.

Employees who did not meet the expected skill level within the prescribed time faced either a freeze of salary or a reduction in salary. While this approach was tough, it was most certainly effective and allowed the organization to control costs while still maintaining a fair approach to managing employees that were paid higher than their skills dictated.

To control the budgetary impact of moving green circled employees to the appropriate level, you could also consider a cap on the first upward increase and then establish a schedule for moving the employee to the appropriate level. This approach also provides the organization the opportunity to evaluate the employee's skill level on more than one occasion before permanently increasing the salary of the employee.

CREATING A POLICY FOR PLACEMENT OF NEW EMPLOYEES INTO THE SKILL-BASED PAY SYSTEM

A policy should be established regarding the placement of newly hired employees in the Skill-based Pay system as well. Minimally qualified employees will normally be brought in to the system at the bottom of the pay range for Skill Zone 1. If a newly hired employee has certifiable skills that would qualify the employee for a higher rate of pay, the organization must decide how to manage the situation. Often the Skill-based Pay policy allows new employees to be placed at a pay rate above the minimum, with approval of higher authority, and with the understanding of what certification process will be used. This also helps the organization with a more competitive approach to

The Public Sector's Guide to Skill-based Pay

recruitment since hiring employees above the minimum is allowed. However, if the organization has "capped" current employees to control cost of implementation (see above) this will prove to be a very controversial policy.

CREATING A POLICY FOR TRAINING OPPORTUNITIES

Under a Skill-based Pay system, training is no longer an option or extra benefit for employees. Training becomes vital to career and salary progression. For this reason, it is important that the organization takes steps to ensure equal and fair access to training opportunities.

This concern generates the following main policy issues for the organization's consideration:

- How much money is available for the training budget?
- What kind of training is available?
- How are training opportunities distributed among employees?

The new Skill-based environment will probably require a higher level of training activity and organization than you have previously provided. Creativity should be used in identifying training resources both inside the organization and outside. On-the-job-training, cooperation between departments with varying needs, local college and university courses and various other opportunities for learning new skills should all be considered. Guidelines should be developed specifying the allowable training time per employee during the initial skill development cycle and employee equality in relation to training access should be monitored. In addition, the organization needs to consider the amount of time an employee will spend demonstrating the skill learned in the training session in order to receive a return on its investment (ROI).

CREATING A POLICY FOR MOVEMENT THROUGH SKILL ZONES

There are two primary questions an organization should answer regarding this issue before implementing its Skill-based Pay system.

- How does the employee qualify for increased pay within each skill zone?
- Does the employee have to complete certification for all skill blocks in a track or a sub-zone before earning the increase in pay, or does completion of part of the skill blocks in the zone qualify the employee for a portion of the pay for that skill zone?

Budgetary constraints, motivational concerns and ease of administration will all greatly impact this decision. Find a system for your situation that is easy to administer, provides consistent motivation to employees and is affordable.

The City of Blue Skies' Skill-based Pay Development Team worked with a team of consultants specializing in Skill-based Pay in order to develop and finalize the Policy and Administration Guidelines. This final document was sent to upper management for approval and coordinated with the organization's consultants. The consultants also assisted Blue Skies with the development of the pay structure which was linked to the new Skill-based system since this was outside of the area of Committee's expertise.

The Public Sector's Guide to Skill-based Pay

SUMMARY OF APPENDICES FOR CHAPTER 9

- Appendix M – Sample Policy and Administration Structures

✎ *My Chapter Notes:*

The Public Sector's Guide to Skill-based Pay

CLOSING COMMENTS

The Skill-based Pay System that you implement today will probably not look like or operate the same way two years from now. One of the most important stages of any organizational change initiative is the maintenance stage. What you have created is not written in stone. Your Skill-based Pay organizational change initiative should adapt as skills and knowledge requirements evolve. Administrative responsibility for maintaining a Skill-based Pay system most often falls to the line department(s) involved due to the need for tracking of employee records, and the system's relationship to budgets. Moreover, those departments where Skill-based Pay has been implemented need to play a large role in the system's administration. These systems are driven by education, personal growth and accountability. It has been our experience and observation that the line department that is implementing Skill-based Pay should be the center of the implementation and administration process.

Additionally, it is important to collect and implement employee thoughts and comments regarding the Skill-based Pay System. If you are receiving consistent feedback that one part of the system is not working correctly, or unfair, then modifications to the component of the Skill-based Pay system are likely in order. Employees are the ultimate end users of this system. If employees do not perceive benefits from the system, the system will not be accepted and will likely fail. Line departments need to be in a position to respond quickly.

Thank you for allowing us this opportunity to share with you our expertise in the arena of Skill-based Pay. We are confident that you will have found *The Guide* extremely useful in you Skill-based Pay initiative. Should you have any questions or ideas you would like to share, please feel free to contact us at any time. We wish you much success with you Skill-based Pay system.

The Public Sector's Guide to Skill-based Pay

✎ Closing Notes:

index

A

Accuracy	86
Action	84
Assessing Current Employees	102
Assessing New Hires	105

B

Benchmark Survey	127
Broadbanding	113
Broadbanding Examples	120
Building The Foundation	12

C

Career Paths	117, 127, 129
Certification	3
Certification Manual	3, 81
Certification Standards	59
Certification Standards Legend	57
Class/Training Certificate	57
Closing Comments	141
Closing Notes	142
Coaching	119
College/Vocational Courses	57
Combined Skill List By Category And Zone	54
Communication	23
Communication Strategy Flow Chart	24
Compensation Practices	112
Control Of Budgets	135
Control Point	117
Core Step 1	31
Core Step 2	31, 52
Core Step 3	32, 64
Core Steps	31
Core Track	8, 9

D

Defining And Constructing	31
Demonstrated Skill And Observation By Supervisor	57
Design Issues	128
Development Of Skill Categories	33
Development Of Skill Lists	33
Development Of Skill Ratings	33
Development Of Skill Zones	33
Diagram 1, Classifications	10
Diagram 2, Sunset	16

The Public Sector's
Guide to Skill-based Pay

Diagram 3, Range of Management Views 17
Diagram 4, Recommended Communication Strategy 23
Diagram 5, Combining Skills Sample 66
Diagram 6, Traditional Pay Structure 115
Distinct Skills 67, 74

E

Effective Communication 12
Effectiveness 86
Elbert Hubbard 112
Employee Feedback 95
Employee Skill Inventory Analysis Scale 108
Employee Skill Inventory Rating Sheet (Partial) 108
Employee/Supervisor Independent Assessments 104
Equipment 84
Equipment Needed 84
Evaluation Committee 102
Evaluation Committee Assessment 104

F

Feedback 95
Final Consensus Meeting 105
Finalizing 95
Focus Groups 96
Formatting 52
Foundation & Development 9
Foundation Skills 3
Freeze Of Salary 137

G

Gate 3
Grade Hierarchy 126

H

Henry Ford 101
Hierarchy Of Skills 31
Horizontal Skill Development 114
Hot Tip 2

I

Implementation 101
Implementation Costs 135
Independent Assessments 104

L

Ladder 113, 128

Learning Approaches Table	58
Learning Approaches Table	55
Linking Pay	112

M

Machiavelli	12
Major Skill Category Examples	40
Management Views	17
Master Inventory Of Skills	34
Mastery Of All Skills	3, 75, 76
Maximum	8, 20, 82, 97, 127, 128
Measurable	83
Measurement	84
Michelangelo	52
Midpoint	117
Minimum	3, 8, 20, 81, 107, 127, 128, 137
Movement Through Skill Zones	139
Multiple Raters	46
Multiple Skill Hierarchies	71
My Chapter Notes	6, 11

N

Napoleon	133
Narrative Explanation	2
New Title Of Combined Skill Items	69

O

Objectives And Certification Manual	81
Oliver Wendell Holmes	81
One-On-One Interviews	97
On-The-Job Training	57
OR Survey	19
Organizational (Internal) Training	57
Organizational Readiness Survey	19
Overlap Of Grades	129
Overpaid	135

P

Pay	112
Pay Decreases	102
Pay Grades	116, 118
Perception	16
Placement Of Current Employees Into The New Skill-Based Pay System	135
Placement Of New Employees Into The Skill-Based Pay System	137
Plato	64
Policy And Administive Guideline Development	133
Policy Manual	87, 134
Position Evaluation	113
Project Team	26
Proof	83, 84

The Public Sector's Guide to Skill-based Pay

R

Re-Certification Standards	59
Reduction In Salary	137
Refining	64
Retention	13
ROI	138

S

Safety Criteria	84
Salary Survey Issues	127
Salary Surveys	126, 127
Sample Or Survey	20
SBP Policy	133
Skill	4, 84
Skill Assessment	104
Skill Categories	52
Skill Categories (Tracks) Table For Water Operator	41
Skill Category Development	39
Skill Certification/Demonstration Of Skill Mastery	133
Skill Difficulty Scale	42
Skill Hierarchy	4
Skill Hierarchy Formatting	52
Skill Hierarchy Identification	33
Skill Hierarchy Refinement	64
Skill Hierarchy With Sub-Zones Sample	77
Skill Inventory Assessment Key Points	107
Skill List Development	33
Skill List Development Form	38
Skill List For Water Operator	47, 48
Skill Mastery	4
Skill Objective	83
Skill Objectives Table/Example	91
Skill Objectives Table/Template	89
Skill Rating Development	42
Skill Rating List	52
Skill Rating List Table	45
Skill Rating List Table For Multiple Raters – Difficulty/Timing Ratings	46
Skill Set	68
Skill Summary By Category And Zone Table	52, 53
Skill Timing Scale	43
Skill Zone	4
Skill Zone Development	47
Skill Zones	52
Skill-Based Pay	13
Skill-Based Table	74, 78
Skills By Learning Approaches Table	52
Speed	86
Standards	84
Subject Matter Expert	4
Subject Matter Experts	4
Subject Matter Experts (Subject Matter Expert):	4
Sub-Step 1a	33
Sub-Step 1b	33
Sub-Step 1c	33
Sub-Step 1d	33, 47

The Public Sector's Guide to Skill-based Pay

Sub-Zone 4
Sub-Zones 61, 75, 76, 78
Sub-Zones 4, 75

T

Table 1, Skill-based Pay System Tracks 9
Table 10, Skill List for Multiple Raters 46
Table 11, Skill Zone List for Water Operator 47
Table 12, Skill Zone List for Water Operator 48
Table 13, Combined Skill List by Category and Zone 54
Table 14, Definitions 57
Table 15, Definitions 57
Table 16, Learning Approaches Table 58
Table 17, Combining Skills 68
Table 18, Skill Hierarchy 72
Table 19, Skill Hierarchy with Sub-Zones Sample 77
Table 20, Objectives 83
Table 21, Skill Objectives 91
Table 22, Skill Objectives 92
Table 23, Employee Skill Inventory Analysis Scale 108
Table 24, Samples of Broadbanding 120
Table 2, Skill Lists 35
Table 3. Combined Skill List 36
Table 4, Skill List Development Approaches 37
Table 5, Major Skill Category Examples 40
Table 6, Skill Categories for Water Operator 41
Table 7, Skill Difficulty Scale 42
Table 8, Skill Timing Scale 43
Table 9, Skill Rating List Table 45
Tasks/Skills 52
The City Of Blue Skies 8
Tool 1, Sample Questions 21
Tool 2, Skill List Development Form 38
Tool 3, Skill Objectives Table 89
Tool 4, Employee Skill Inventory Rating Sheet 108
Tools 2
Total Quality Management 117
Town-Hall Meetings 97
TQM 117
Tracks 5, 8, 9, 35, 41, 71, 72, 74, 78
Trade Certification 57
Traditional Pay 13
Training Budget 138
Training Method Legend 57
Training Methods Available 59
Training Opportunities 138
Transitioning 113

U

Underpaid 135

V

Vendor Sponsored Training 57

The Public Sector's Guide to Skill-based Pay

Vince Lombardi 95

W

Wastewater Collection 8
Wastewater Collection Technician 8
Water Distribution 8
Water Distribution Operator 8
Weighted Average 127
William James 31
Writing Skill Objectives 82
Written Test 57

Z

Zone 3, 4, 44, 47, 48, 53, 55, 56, 60, 67, 69, 74, 75, 76, 78, 105, 116, 139
Zones 4, 39, 40, 46, 47, 48, 49, 55, 56, 59, 61, 64, 67, 69, 74, 75, 76, 78, 126, 139

Please note, Appendices may be found after this Index.

APPENDIX A
SAMPLE ORGANIZATIONAL READINESS SURVEY

Organizational Readiness Survey

Thank you for completing this survey. The information from this survey will only be used by the SBP Steering Committee to understand employee attitudes and knowledge about issues related to developing a skill-based pay system. Your responses will help determine how the Steering Committee communicates to employees as well as assist with other areas of the project. Your individual responses to this survey will be kept confidential, so please respond to each statement candidly.

Demographic Information: Please indicate your classification and department by checking the box next to the appropriate category.

Classification

Supervisory/Managerial ○   Non-supervisory/Non-managerial ○

Departments

Non-Civil Service Police	○	Transportation	○
Solid Waste	○	Public Works	○
Environmental Services	○	Parks	○
Building Inspection & Planning	○	Recreation	○
Library – Main Library	○	Facilities & Fleet	○
Manager's Office (Human Res., Secretary, Legal, CIO)	○	Golf	○
Finance	○		

Appendix A - Page 1

©Copyright 2003, 2004 - All rights reserved - The Waters Consulting Group, Inc.

Questionnaire Instructions – Part 1: The following list of statements concerns issues relating to <u>your department</u>. Please read each statement carefully. Using the following scale, determine the extent to which you agree with each statement. Your response should be recorded by filling in the appropriate bubble following the statement. For example, if you agree with statement #1, you would fill in circle "3" preceding this statement.

Example:

		Strongly Disagree	Disagree	Agree	Strongly Agree
1.	My organization is nice.	①	②	**③**	④

		Strongly Disagree	Disagree	Agree	Strongly Agree
1.	My department supports changes that will affect work processes.	①	②	③	④
2.	In my department, employees who strive to improve work processes are recognized and rewarded by management.	①	②	③	④
3.	In my department, experimenting with different work procedures is encouraged.	①	②	③	④
4.	If I identify a better way to complete a task, my co-workers are willing to try the suggestion.	①	②	③	④
5.	I am given the power to make decisions and solve problems on my own.	①	②	③	④
6.	Communication with co-workers is open.	①	②	③	④
7.	Management communicates changes that will affect me and/or my work.	①	②	③	④
8.	I receive the information I need to perform my job well.	①	②	③	④
9.	Communication with my supervisor is open and I am comfortable talking about problems with him/her.	①	②	③	④
10.	When decisions are being made that affect me, I am usually involved or asked for my ideas.	①	②	③	④
11.	I understand the "chain of command" within my department.	①	②	③	④
12.	My co-workers cooperate in order to work effectively.	①	②	③	④
13.	My department works well with other departments in the Organization.	①	②	③	④
14.	My co-workers have the skills needed to perform the job and they are well trained.	①	②	③	④
15.	There is little confusion as to who has what authority.	①	②	③	④
16.	I am satisfied with the opportunities for personal growth in my job.	①	②	③	④

	Strongly Disagree	Disagree	Agree	Strongly Agree
17. I know exactly what is expected of me in my job.	①	②	③	④
18. Employees and immediate supervisors respect each other.	①	②	③	④
19. I am comfortable asking my immediate supervisor for help.	①	②	③	④
20. I am encouraged to make suggestions or give ideas to my immediate supervisor.	①	②	③	④
21. Supervisors respond in a timely fashion to employee complaints and suggestions.	①	②	③	④
22. Supervisors make fair decision regarding employee complaints and suggestions.	①	②	③	④
23. No immediate supervisors assume more authority than they should.	①	②	③	④
24. Top management in my department demands that people give their best efforts.	①	②	③	④
25. Top management in my department provides clear expectations for performance to be at or above standards	①	②	③	④
26. Top management in my department emphasizes teamwork.	①	②	③	④
27. Top management in my department is fair with employees.	①	②	③	④
28. Top management in my department notices and shows appreciation when employees put in extra time and effort.	①	②	③	④
29. Training is part of the development plan established between my supervisor and myself.	①	②	③	④
30. My performance reviews are given on time.	①	②	③	④
31. My performance reviews are given often enough.	①	②	③	④
32. My performance reviews include specific action plans for my development.	①	②	③	④
33. I am encouraged to offer input during my performance reviews.	①	②	③	④
34. I am confident in departmental senior management's leadership.	①	②	③	④
35. Overall, I am satisfied with my job.	①	②	③	④

memorandum

To: All Employees of the Organization
From:
Re: Skill-based Pay Organizational Readiness Survey
Date:

Introduction: As you may know, our organization is moving towards the implementation of a Skill-based Pay System. At this time, we are asking for your assistance with the first step in this process. One of the best ways to identify specific needs and issues relating to Skill-based Pay is to ask employees. We plan to use your input concerning important project-related issues to ensure that the project will meet your needs and the needs of the Organization. To facilitate this process, we have designed an Organizational Readiness Survey. The survey contains questions relating to the following topics:

1. Change within the Organization and your department
2. Communication within the Organization and your department
3. Teamwork within your department
4. Training and development opportunities offered
5. The current performance evaluation process
6. Job Satisfaction and Pay
7. Employee/Supervisor Relationships
8. Top Management

Confidentiality: The questionnaire will be completely anonymous and will take approximately 20 minutes to finish. Once you have completed the questionnaire, you will be asked to seal it in an envelope and place it in a collection box supervised by the HR department. The collection box will then be returned to our offices so that we may tabulate the results. That is, no one will be able to identify individual employee ratings. Remember, this information is being collected to help us to understand the impact of your department's practices as well as the Organization's current management style in regard to the design of the new pay system.

Times and Locations: The questionnaire will be administered on Tuesday, March 9 at City Hall (Council Chambers) and on Wednesday, March 10 at the Central Service Center (Lunch Room). Below is a time schedule for the administration of the questionnaire. You will need to arrive promptly at one of the times and dates listed below.

Compensation Study Questionnaire Locations and Times			
Tuesday - March 9 City Hall - Council Chambers		Wednesday - March 10 Central Service Center - Lunch Room	
Morning Times	Afternoon Times	Morning Times	Afternoon Times
8:00 a.m.	1:00 p.m.	7:00 a.m.	1:00 p.m.
8:30 a.m.	1:30 p.m.	7:30 a.m.	1:30 p.m.
9:00 a.m.	2:00 p.m.	8:00 a.m.	2:00 p.m.
9:30 a.m.	2:30 p.m.	8:30 a.m.	2:30 p.m.
10:00 a.m.	3:00 p.m.	9:00 a.m.	3:00 p.m.
10:30 a.m.	3:30 p.m.	9:30 a.m.	3:30 p.m.
11:00 a.m.	4:00 p.m.	10:00 a.m.	4:00 p.m.
11:30 a.m.	4:30 p.m.	10:30 a.m.	4:30 p.m.

We look forward to working with you and appreciate your participation in this most important project.

Should you have any questions regarding this process, you may contact the HR Department.

Dear Organizational Readiness Survey Participant:

As you know, our organization is developing skill-based pay. During this process, we will address issues such as how best to communicate with staff and how department cultures differ. The enclosed confidential survey, "Organizational Readiness Survey", will help us plan how to address these types of issues.

The purpose for conducting this survey is to look for trends across the organization and within each department. We will not be looking at individual responses to survey items. Individual responses to this survey will be confidential, so please respond to each statement candidly.

Please read each statement carefully. Fill in the bubble that best represents your level of agreement with the statement. When finished, use the enclosed envelope to return your survey responses. Surveys must be returned by **DATE**. If you have questions regarding the questionnaire please contact the HR Department.

Thank you for your cooperation!

APPENDIX B

COMMUNICATION STRATEGY DEVELOPMENT WORKSHEET

The Public Sector's Guide to Skill-based Pay

COMMUNICATION STRATEGY DEVELOPMENT WORKSHEET

1a. WHAT – What, precisely, do you need to communicate?	Name everyone who needs to hear this communication.
1b. WHY – What will happen as a result of implementing this system?	**2. DELIVERY STRATEGY** – What methods will you use to deliver the communication?
What will happen if you don't implement this system?	**3. COMMUNICATION DELIVERY** – Who will be responsible for delivering the communication? What is the timeframe for delivery and who will the responsible parties report to?

4. EVALUATION – How will you determine if your communication strategy has succeeded?

Appendix B – Page 1
©Copyright 2003, 2004 - All rights reserved - The Waters Consulting Group, Inc.

APPENDIX C

SAMPLE SKILL HIERARCHIES

The Public Sector's Guide to Skill-based Pay

SKILL HIERARCHY FOR WATER OPERATOR

	Track 1 - Foundation & Development Skill Blocks (Completion of this track is required for all employees.)	Track 2 Water Distribution Technical Skill Blocks	Track 3 Wastewater Collection Technical Skill Blocks
Skill Zone 1: 6 months. All minimum requirements for position must be met within 6 months of employment.	1. Organization Policy Review 2. Defensive Driving 3. First Aid/CPR 4. Basic Haz-mat 5. Confined Space Entry 6. Two-way Radio Protocol	1. Water Mainlines 2. Valves 3. Fire Hydrants 4. Service Connections 5. Disinfection/Sanitation 6. Basic Equipment Operation	1. Wastewater Mainlines 2. Manholes 3. Inflow/Infiltration 4. Service Connections 5. Disinfection/Sanitation 6. Basic Equipment Operation
Skill Zone 2: 1 year. All certification in skill zone 1 has been completed for tracks 1 and 2 or 3.	1. Operational Policies 2. Traffic Control 3. Basic Computer Skills/Work Orders 4. Customer Service 5. Plan and Map Reading 6. Teamwork	1. TNRCC Approved Basic Water 2. Water Mainlines 3. Valves 4. Fire Hydrants 5. Service Connections 6. Journey Level Equipment Operation	1. TNRCC Approved Basic Wastewater 2. Wastewater Mainlines 3. Manholes 4. Inflow/Infiltration 5. Service Connections 6. Journey Level Equipment Operation
Skill Zone 3: 1 year. All certification in skill zone 2 has been completed. Tracks 1 and 2 or 3 have been completed in skill zone 2.	1. Operational Policies 2. Stress Awareness 3. Hazardous Materials 4. Trench Safety	1. TNRCC Approved Water Distribution 2. Electronic Detection 3. Disinfection Calculations 4. Water Mainlines/Appurtenances 5. Valves 6. Fire Hydrants 7. Service Connection	1. TNRCC Approved Wastewater Collection Class 2. Electronic Detection 3. SSO Reports/Disinfection/I&I 4. Wastewater Mainlines 5. Manholes
Skill Zone 4: 1 year. All certification in skill zone 3 has been completed for tracks 1 and 2 or 3.	1. System Mapping/GIS 2. Customer Service "D" 3. Leadership	1. Selected TNRCC Approved Class "C" Certification from TNRCC 2. Water Mainlines 3. Valves 4. Fire Hydrants 5. Service Connections 6. Disinfection/Sampling 7. Equipment Operation	1. Selected TNRCC Approved Class "II" Certification from TNRCC 2. Wastewater Mainlines 3. Manholes 4. Disinfection/Sampling 5. Equipment Operation

©Copyright 2003, 2004 - All rights reserved - The Waters Consulting Group, Inc.

The Public Sector's Guide to Skill-based Pay

SKILL HIERARCHY FOR WATER OPERATOR CONTINUED

	Track 1 - Foundation & Development Skill Blocks (Completion of this track is required for all employees.)	Track 2 Water Distribution Technical Skill Blocks	Track 3 Wastewater Collection Technical Skill Blocks
	1. Coaching 2. Customer Service "C" 3. Introduction to Supervision	1. Selected Water Class 2. Review/Critique Construction Plans 3. Pressure, Valving, Pump, Storage 4. Cross Connection Control 5. Water Mainlines 6. Valves 7. Fire Hydrants 8. Equipment Operation	1. Selected Wastewater Class 2. Review/Critique Construction Plans 3. Lift Stations, Pumps 4. Clean Water Act/SSO Regulations 5. Equipment Operation
	1. Advanced Computer Skills 2. Customer Service "B" 3. Communications 4. Selected Supervisory Development- two classes	1. Customer Service Inspection 2. Water System Operation and Control 3. Customer Service/Dispatch 4. PR/Boil Water Notice 5. Equipment Operation	1. Flow Metering 2. I&I Investigations 3. SSO Sampling 4. Equipment Operation
	1. Water Utility System Trainer 2. Customer Service "A" 3. Water Utility Codes and Ordinances 4. Selected Supervisory Development- 4 classes		1. Backflow Prevention Certification 2. Basic Instrumentation 3. Basic Treatment Plant Operation 4. Basic Laboratory
	1. Water Utility System Operator/Trainer/Leader 2. Selected Supervisory Development to Maintain Skills	Employees reaching this Skill Zone will be granted annual raises based on their performance review scores and maintenance of skills. Employees must demonstrate complete operational control and competency in all areas of water utility operations at all times.	

Skill Zone 5: 1 year.
*Base track certification in skill zone 4 has been completed.
**Alternate tracks in skill zone 2 have been completed.

Skill Zone 6: 1 year.
*Base track certification in skill zone 5 has been completed.
**Alternate tracks in skill zone 3 and 4 have been completed.

Skill Zone 7: 2 years.
*Base track certification in skill zone 6 has been completed.
**Alternate tracks in skill zone 5 and 6 have been completed.

Skill Zone 8:
All prior required certifications have been completed.

*Base Track is defined as the track the employee follows for which they were originally hired. (i.e. If hired for Water Distribution, employee follows track 2 as their base track.)
**Alternate Track is defined as the track the employee follows for cross-training purposes. (i.e. If hired for Water Distribution, employee follows track 3 as their alternate track

Skill Hierarchy
Nurse

Skill Zone One ⇨

Track I – LVN Skill Zones

General: Employee is hired with a 1 year vocational nursing degree and has passed the State Licensing Boards. The employee passes through X pay points in zone 1. It will take _____ to complete the skill zone.

Care Provision

- Takes client history using structured assessment tools and structured interviews
- Assists with performing basic assessments to identify health status, un-met client needs, and monitor for change
- Records and reports assessment data
- Administers medications and treatments following established protocols
- Contributes to the development of a teaching plan
- Implements aspects of an established teaching plan
- Assists in evaluating learning outcomes using structured evaluation tools
- Participates in modifying plan of care and/or expected outcomes
- Helps to develop discharge plans for clients
- Assists in modifying daily plan of care and/or expected outcomes
- Monitors compliance and efficiency of prescribed medications and treatments
- Establishes priorities for each client
- Provides basic initial intervention for emergencies
- Performs safe and appropriate activities that assist clients to meet basic physiological needs
- Accompanies the client, when appropriate, to scheduled appointments to ensure medical information is provided accurately

Documentation

- Documents all client data in the clinical record
- Completes lab, EKG and other forms for the psychiatrists

Skill Hierarchy
Nurse

General: Employee is hired with a 1 year vocational nursing degree and has passed the State Licensing Boards. The employee passes through X pay points in zone 1. It will take _____ to complete the skill zone.
Communication with/about Client
• Communicates client needs to family or significant others
• Reports client data to other staff and/or community health providers
• Discusses the plan of care and client needs with members of the team
• Identifies and communicates reasons for deviation from plan of care
Policies and Procedures
• Follows procedures to prevent the transmission of pathogens
• Ensures significant medical records are maintained according to protocol
Administration
▪ Ensures nursing coverage
▪ Schedules health care and ensures client receives health care on schedule
Technical Knowledge
▪ Completes one training module on age-specific health issues

Skill Hierarchy
Nurse

Skill Zone Two

Track I – LVN Skill Zones

General: Employee has completed all requirements in skill zone 1. The employee passes through X pay points in zone 2. It will take _____ to complete the skill zone.
Care Provision
• Identifies the level of competency of family/client
• Determines available support systems and resources
• Assesses learning outcomes of teaching plans
• Assesses the client's ability to self-administer medications
• Identifies common and overt actual and potential health care needs
• Identifies short-term/immediate goals and selects an intervention to meet client's goals
Documentation
• Documents responses to medications and treatments
Communication with/about Client
• Educates the staff on the impact of life-style preferences and health issues relevant to the client
Care Coordination
• Helps to identify others who can assist with client care
• Identifies major community resources that can assist the clients to meet their needs
Technical Knowledge
• Participates in implementing changes that lead to improvement in the work setting
• Participates in problem-solving activities with other team members
• Implements established cost containment measures in direct client care
• Uses a self evaluation process to improve nursing skills
• Completes one training module on age-specific health issues

Skill Hierarchy
Nurse

Skill Zone Three

Track I – LVN Skill Zones

General: Employee has completed all requirements in skill zone 2. The employee passes through X pay points in zone 3. It will take _____ to complete the skill zone.
Professional Development
• Acquires advanced clinical training in area of need
• Works in area of expertise (*must perform one of the following*)
1. works with clients in area of expertise
2. conducts research in area of need

Track II – ADN Skill Zones

General: Employee is hired with a 2 year degree in nursing and has passed the State Licensing Boards. The employee passes through X pay points in zone 3. It will take _____ to complete the skill zone.
Care Provision
• Takes client history using structured and unstructured data collection tools
• Performs assessment to identify health status and monitor for change
• Collects, validates, and reports assessment data using established assessment tools
• Performs activities that prevent exposure to and transmission of pathogens
• Administers medications and treatments safely
• Evaluates and documents responses to treatment
• Individualizes and implements established teaching plans
• Evaluates learning outcomes of the client or family members receiving instruction
• Identifies and communicates reasons and rationales for deviating from the daily plan of care to multi-disciplinary health care team
• Refers clients to appropriate individuals to promote continuity of care
• Modifies plan of care and/or expected outcomes

Skill Hierarchy
Nurse

General: Employee is hired with a 2 year degree in nursing and has passed the State Licensing Boards. The employee passes through X pay points in zone 3. It will take _____ to complete the skill zone.
• Identifies providers and resources to meet the needs of clients and their families
Training
• Identifies health related learning needs of clients and families
Technical Knowledge
• Collaborates with other health care providers and members of the organization to solve client care problems
• Uses current technology to enhance client care
• Uses knowledge and experience when delegating to other health care providers
• Assists other health care providers with treatments
• Reads and discusses relevant current nursing practice journal articles and applies information in practice
• Takes courses to earn BSN degree
• Completes one training module on age-specific health issues

Skill Hierarchy
Nurse

Skill Zone Four ↯

Track II – ADN Skill Zones

General: Employee has completed all requirements in skill zone 3. The employee passes through X pay points in zone 4. It will take _____ to complete the skill zone.
Care Provision
• Develops appropriate teaching methods to accommodate societal /cultural differences
• Identifies client's and family's unmet needs
Administration
• Monitors incidents surrounding staff health-related interventions and maintains an accurate record of such incidents
• Ensures schedules are completed by clinic support staff
• Communicates the results of the audit to nurses and maintains a log of the audit results
• Performs RN delegation
Technical Knowledge
• Provides consultation in area of expertise
• Identifies and participates in activities to improve health care delivery within the organization
• Completes BSN degree
• Conducts training in community in area of expertise
• Completes one training module on age-specific health issues

Skill Hierarchy
Nurse

Skill Zone Five

Track II – ADN Skill Zones

General: Employee has completed all requirements in skill zone 4. The employee passes through X pay points in zone 5. It will take _____ to complete the skill zone.
Professional Development
• Acquires advanced clinical training in area of need
• Works in area of expertise (*must perform one of the following*)
1. works with clients in area of expertise
2. conducts research in area of need
3. applies for grants

Track III – BSN Skill Zones

General: Employee is hired with a 4 year degree in nursing and has passed the State Licensing Boards. The employee passes through X pay points in zone 5. It will take _____ to complete the skill zone.
Care Provision
• Assesses factors impacting health status and health needs for individual families, clients, and community
• Uses a variety of data collection tools
• Analyzes and interprets health data for individual families, clients, and community
• Identifies nursing diagnoses for individual families, clients, and community
• Assumes responsibility for ensuring documentation is complete
• Evaluates and clarifies clients' understanding of health care rights
• Defines health-related learning needs for individual families, clients, and community
• Uses current literature or research findings in developing and modifying teaching plans
• Evaluates implementation of comprehensive teaching plans
• Modifies plan of care as needed for individual families, clients, and community

Skill Hierarchy
Nurse

General: Employee is hired with a 4 year degree in nursing and has passed the State Licensing Boards. The employee passes through X pay points in zone 5. It will take _____ to complete the skill zone.
• Assesses teaching skills of self and members of health care team and modifies as needed
• Identifies providers and resources to meet individual families, clients, and community health care needs
Administration
• Evaluates the skill level of the assigned staff through use of the nursing process and clinical supervision
• Assists staff to identify their on-going training and educational needs
• Schedules work flow and caseload assignments
• Performs periodic audits of a random sample of clinical records
• Establishes regular meetings with staff to review client cases
• Verifies current licensing of nursing staff
Technical Knowledge
• Completes one training module on age-specific health issues

Skill Hierarchy
Nurse

Skill Zone Six
Track III – BSN Skill Zones

General: Employee has completed all requirements in skill zone 5. The employee passes through X pay points in zone 6. It will take _____ to complete the skill zone.
Care Provision
• Evaluates the care provided by other health care providers
• Participates in multi-disciplinary health planning conferences
• Assesses the support systems in place for clients, families and the community and helps these groups communicate their needs
Technical Knowledge
• Works with clients, families, and the community to improve the quality of care provided
• Analyzes the management structure and nursing care delivery system in place within the organization
• Applies research findings and principles of research to improve the practice base for nursing
• Reviews and critiques research studies for use in care
• Completes one training module on age-specific health issues

Skill Hierarchy
Administrative Service Provider

Skill Zone One ⇨

Administrative Service Provider Skill Zones

General: Employee is hired with a high school diploma or the equivalent. The employee passes through X pay points in zone 1. It will take _____ to complete the skill zone.
Documentation/Records
• Enters correct information in spreadsheet with assistance
• Files relevant documentation with assistance
• Requests updated information from consumers at each visit
Administration
• Files/re-files charts in the appropriate location
• Follows and uses a tracking system for files checked out by staff
• Maintains files of completed contracts
• Requests, monitors and issues transportation passes
• Prints excel spreadsheets
• Delivers check requests and other items to Hulen and picks up checks
• Sorts and distributes mail and other correspondence
• Takes messages
• Photocopies documents
• Answers telephones
• Directs calls to the appropriate person
• Faxes documents
• Ensures that conference rooms are available
• Processes department correspondence
Inventory/Maintenance
• Stores and secures supplies
Client Services
• Checks consumers in for appointments
• Sets appointments

Skill Hierarchy
Administrative Service Provider

General: Employee is hired with a high school diploma or the equivalent. The employee passes through X pay points in zone 1. It will take _____ to complete the skill zone.
• Greets and directs staff and visitors to locations within the organization
Team Building
• Advises superiors of situations that require action and/or problem solving
Professional Development
• Develops basic word processing skills and familiarity with frequently used word processing software
• Completes records training successfully
• Completes orientation training provided by the organization

Skill Hierarchy
Administrative Service Provider

Skill Zone Two ↴

Administrative Service Provider Skill Zones

General: Employee has completed all requirements in skill zone 1. The employee passes through X pay points in zone 2. It will take _____ to complete the skill zone.
Documentation/Records
• Registers new consumers on-line and updates existing consumer records regularly
• Enters consumer information into CMHC
Administration
• Prepares cover letters and contracts for distribution to Service Providers
• Prepares and submits completed mobile phone responsibility forms for the Purchasing Dept
• Enters correct information in spreadsheet without assistance
• Files relevant documentation without assistance
• Demonstrates responsibility for P.O. mail by collecting mail from the post office
• Coordinates travel for groups and individuals
• Maintains active pager list for key staff and switchboard
Inventory/Maintenance
• Maintains, stocks, orders and shops for coffee supplies
• Coordinates building maintenance requests
Client Services
• Responds to questions, complaints, or requests for information
• Pulls files when consumers call with questions about medication
Processing
• Collects billing and phone payments, calculates expense information and submits with required documentation to Accounting
Professional Development
• Develops proficiency with spreadsheet software such as excel

Skill Hierarchy
Administrative Service Provider

Skill Zone Three ⇨

Administrative Service Provider Skill Zones

General: Employee has completed all requirements in skill zone 2. The employee passes through X pay points in zone 3. It will take _____ to complete the skill zone.
Documentation/Records
• Collects missing information from consumer records
• Transcribes dictated psychological reports
• Maintains service activity logs
• Completes forms with necessary information
• Maintains data file with current addresses and contacts
• Makes charts for new consumers
• Requests and transfers consumer records
• Enters consumer information into CARE
Administration
• Photocopies documents according to state regulations
• Faxes documentation, receives faxed documentation, tracks documentation and routes to appropriate service coordinator according to timeline
• Faxes confidential information per records procedures
• Takes and processes minutes for staff meetings
• Gathers data from CARE
• Keeps a log for mobile phones
• Collects and compiles monthly report data
• Uses formulas in spreadsheet to calculate due dates for PDP's and quarterlies
• Tracks consumer PDP meeting dates
• Maintains tracking system
• Compiles ERS/GRS reports from CMHC
• Creates and prints brochures for MRLA Unit
Inventory/Maintenance
• Coordinates office equipment repairs
• Orders building custodial supplies

Skill Hierarchy
Administrative Service Provider

General: Employee has completed all requirements in skill zone 2. The employee passes through X pay points in zone 3. It will take _____ to complete the skill zone.
• Ensures the repair or replacement of all pagers and procurements
• Coordinates vehicles for maintenance
Analysis
• Researches problems associated with consumer planning packets
Professional Development
• Demonstrates thorough understanding of word-processing software (e.g., develops forms)

Skill Zone Four ↪

Administrative Service Provider Skill Zones

General: Employee has completed all requirements in skill zone 3. The employee passes through X pay points in zone 4. It will take _____ to complete the skill zone.
Documentation/Records
• Maintains spreadsheet to track all names removed from the waiting list
• Enters SAL's data
Administration
• Maintains copier usage, meter readings and supplies
• Manages petty cash fund
Processing
• Submits inventory request forms
• Requisitions, monitors and issues standing PO's to the Service Coordinator for consumer use
• Maintains timesheet process
• Prepares scheduled weekly allowance checks
Training
• Trains staff to complete paperwork accurately
Team Building
• Provides appropriate supervisor with list of concerns obtained from audits

Skill Hierarchy
Administrative Service Provider

Skill Zone Five

Administrative Service Provider Skill Zones

General: Employee has completed all requirements in skill zone 4. The employee passes through X pay points in zone 5. It will take _____ to complete the skill zone.
Documentation/Records
• Completes paperwork to amend contracts
• Purges charts as needed
• Updates CMHC and Texas Medical Net
• Manages consumer charts (locations, purged, lost charts)
Inventory/Maintenance
• Follows-up/tracks purchases
Processing
• Prepares scheduled consumer trust fund checks and maintains accurate information
• Works with Business Manager to ensure reports are submitted in timely manner
• Processes accounts payable
Training
• Provides records training on chart room procedures
Professional Development
• Maintains current copies of licenses and professional insurance documentation for all contractors

Skill Hierarchy
Administrative Service Provider

Skill Zone Six

Administrative Service Provider Skill Zones

General: Employee has completed all requirements in skill zone 5. The employee passes through X pay points in zone 6. It will take _____ to complete the skill zone.
Documentation/Records
• Develops job descriptions
Client Services
• Communicates with consumers or guardians regarding enrollment and documents
Processing
• Reviews MAC forms with staff and MAC Coordinator for accuracy
Manages Others
• Disseminates information to unit staff
• Coordinates work flow for staff
Manages Unit Activities
• Manages keys to the facility
Training
• Trains staff to perform their job functions
Team Building
• Represents the program area on committees or special project teams

Skill Hierarchy
Administrative Service Provider

Skill Zone Seven

Administrative Service Provider Skill Zones

General: Employee has completed all requirements in skill zone 6. The employee passes through X pay points in zone 7. It will take _____ to complete the skill zone.
Analysis
• Ensures budget amount on P-78 does not exceed actual budget
• Reviews and signs off on all P-78's and P-34's
• Ensures accuracy of budget amounts and BPSS information
• Analyzes year-to-date costs to produce budget amounts for new year
• Combines budget information from units to create a division summary
• Maintains accurate PSS and distributes to department heads
• Maintains worksheet for contracts pending through completion with budget totals
• Reviews and balances the trust fund account on a timely basis
• Approves purchases
• Performs calculations for unit timesheets
• Develops and implements processes to review and insure that documentation is accurate and complete
Manages Others
• Mentors staff
• Interviews and selects candidates for hire to vacant positions
• Develops team goals and objectives
• Resolves staff performance problems through corrective action
• Establishes a development plan for individual employees based on performance evaluation
• Evaluates team and individual performance with outcome measures
• Provides back-up to duties for the Business Manager

APPENDIX D

SKILL RATING TOOLS

The Public Sector's Guide to Skill-based Pay

SKILL RATING TOOLS

Item Rating Scales – Difficulty and Timing

Skill Difficulty Scale

How complicated/complex is this task to perform, learn, and/or master?

1. Very simple - requires limited instruction and can mastered quickly
2. Requires some work and learning above one training session
3. Above average level of difficulty to learn/master
4. Difficult to learn/master
5. Very difficult to learn/master
6. Tremendous difficulty - requires repeated and ongoing training and experience

Skill Timing Scale
(Note: time intervals will vary based on skill sets.)
When should this skill be learned in an employee's career?

1. At the very beginning – should be one of the first skills an employee learns
2. <6 months – This skill should be learned within the first 6 months of an employee's career
3. 6 months-1 year – This skill should be learned between the first 6 months and 1 year of service and experience
4. 1-3 years – This skill should be learned between 1 and 3 years of service and experience
5. 3-6 years – This skill should be learned between 3 and 6 years of service and experience
6. 6 or greater years – This skill should be learned only after a majority of all other skills have been learned, after much experience and after much time in the position

Appendix D – Page 1

The Public Sector's Guide to Skill-based Pay

Skill Rating Table - Template

Skill List for: _____	Difficulty	Timing	Overall Rating
1.		+	=
2.		+	=
3.		+	=
4.		+	=
5.		+	=
6.		+	=
7.		+	=
8.		+	=
9.		+	=
10.		+	=

Skill Rating Table: Multiple Users - Template

Skill Difficulty/Timing Ratings	Multi-Rater Results				
	Rater 1	Rater 2	Rater 3	Rater 4	Mean
1.					
2.					
3.					
4.					
5.					
6.					
7.					
8.					
9.					
10.					
11.					

APPENDIX E

CATEGORY AND ZONE TABLE TEMPLATE

The Public Sector's Guide to Skill-based Pay

CATEGORY AND ZONE TABLE

Category and Zone Table - Template

SBP Group or Position: _____		Zone 1	Zone 2	Zone 3
Category:				
Category:				
Category:				
Category:				
Category:				

Appendix E – Page 1

APPENDIX F

SAMPLE CERTIFICATION TRAINING METHODS

Sample Skill Hierarchy Certification Training Methods
Classification: *Customer Service Representative*

A	C	Requirements for Skill Block 1	Type of Training						What method will be used to certify the skill/competency?
			On-the-Job	In-House Training	Coach	Job Rotation	Vendor School	College/ University	
		Administrative Support							
		Exhibits the ability to:							
		• make copies of documents and send faxes	✓						Observation
		• type correspondence	✓		✓				Observation
		• copy files for open records requests	✓						Observation
		• copy, send by interoffice mail and match invoices	✓		✓				Observation
		• file plats in plat room	✓						Observation
		• prepare payroll distributions, inter-departmental mailings	✓	✓	✓				Observation
		• proficiently perform basic data entry							
		• maintain filing systems							
		• operate basic office equipment							
		Documentation							

A – Applies to this position
C – Certified for this employee

Appendix F – Page 1

©Copyright 2003, 2004 - All rights reserved - The Waters Consulting Group, Inc

Sample Skill Hierarchy Certification Training Methods
Classification: *Customer Service Representative*

A	C	Requirements for Skill Block 1	Type of Training						What method will be used to certify the skill/competency?
			On-the-Job	In-House Training	Coach	Job Rotation	Vendor School	College/ University	
		Demonstrates the ability to:							
		• create and produce correspondence to accompany billings	✓						
		• send notices to departments when vendor invoices have become past due	✓						Observation
		Processing							
		Demonstrates the ability to:							
		• close out non-inspection permits	✓						Observation Evaluation
		• provide fuel keys to vehicles that come in the shop when their fuel system is not working	✓				✓		Observation
		• check fuel tank information					✓		Observation
		Customer Service							
		Exhibits the ability to:							
		• route calls and visitors to appropriate sources	✓						Observation
A	C	Requirements for Skill Block 1	Type of Training						Type of Training

A – Applies to this position
C – Certified for this employee

Sample Skill Hierarchy Certification Training Methods
Classification: *Customer Service Representative*

		On-the-Job	In-House Training	Coach	Job Rotation	Vendor School	College/ University	What method will be used to certify the skill/competency?
	• provide necessary forms for employees and customers	✓						Observation
	• create and mail reminder notice and application for permit	✓						Observation
	Teamwork							
	Demonstrates the ability to:							
	• assist with special events and activities	✓		✓				Observation

A – Applies to this position
C – Certified for this employee

Sample Skill Hierarchy Certification Training Methods
Classification: *Customer Service Representative*

A	C	Requirements for Skill Block 2	Type of Training						What method will be used to certify the skill/competency?
			On-the-Job	In-House Training	Coach	Job Rotation	Vendor School	College/ University	
		Administrative Support							
		Exhibits the ability to:							
		• maintain files on correspondence, records, reports and cards	✓						Observation Evaluation
		• prepare packets for new employees, special applications, etc	✓						Observation
		• collect all mortgage company requests for statements							
		• receive, sort, and distribute interdepartmental as well as incoming and outgoing mail	✓						Observation Evaluation
		• act as a notary					✓		Notary Certificate
		• complete DPO using correct codes							
		• comply with purchasing guidelines for all purchasing transactions							
		Documentation							
		Demonstrates the ability to:							

A – Applies to this position
C – Certified for this employee

Sample Skill Hierarchy Certification Training Methods
Classification: *Customer Service Representative*

A	C	Requirements for Skill Block 2	On-the-Job	In-House Training	Coach	Job Rotation	Vendor School	College/ University	What method will be used to certify the skill/competency?
								Type of Training	
		• determine correct posting dates on accounts							Observation
		• maintain log entries of transactions	✓		✓				
		• maintain plat maps	✓						Observation
		• enter company codes on accounts	✓						Observation
		• maintain monthly reports	✓						
		• assign codes to all mortgage company agents							
		• prepare documents using correct grammar and punctuation							
		• compose, design and print monthly newsletters		✓					Observation
		• use publications and professional manuals to assign code terminology/laws.							
		• assign procedure codes to EMS billing utilizing a basic knowledge of the ICD9 codes							
		Cash Box							
		Demonstrates the ability to:							
A	C	Requirements for Skill Block 2							Type of Training

A – Applies to this position
C – Certified for this employee

Sample Skill Hierarchy Certification Training Methods
Classification: *Customer Service Representative*

	On-the-Job	In-House Training	Coach	Job Rotation	Vendor School	College/University	What method will be used to certify the skill/competency?
• maintain petty cash fund or a supply of postage stamps	✓	✓					Observation
• process cash payments							
Processing							
Demonstrates the ability to:							
• issue certificates of occupancy	✓						Observation
• request and obtain funds from accounts payable	✓						
• process and write out refunds	✓	✓					Observation
• process collection notifications for returned checks			✓				Observation
• request DPO's from invoices	✓	✓	✓				Feedback-Purchasing & Accounts Payable Observation
• submit written requests to the appraisal district for address/name changes requested by the customer							
• perform accounts/receivable functions including data entry, balancing and processing reports							

A – Applies to this position
C – Certified for this employee

Appendix F – Page 6

©Copyright 2003, 2004 - All rights reserved - The Waters Consulting Group, Inc

Sample Skill Hierarchy Certification Training Methods
Classification: *Customer Service Representative*

A	C	Requirements for Skill Block 2	On-the-Job	In-House Training	Coach	Job Rotation	Vendor School	College/University	What method will be used to certify the skill/competency?
		• process large sums of revenue accurately							
		Inventory/Supplies							
		Demonstrates the ability to:							
		• maintain and track inventory							
		• determine or recommend material and/or equipment needs	✓		✓				Observation
		• take inventory and order supplies	✓		✓				Observation
		• receive, deliver and stock inventory							
		Customer Service							
		Exhibits the ability to:							
		• assist tax customers with basic state laws and procedures which pertain to divisional applications							
		• provide inspection and permit results to inspectors and stake holders	✓						Observation

A – Applies to this position
C – Certified for this employee

Sample Skill Hierarchy Certification Training Methods
Classification: *Customer Service Representative*

A	C	Requirements for Skill Block 2	Type of Training					What method will be used to certify the skill/competency?
			On-the-Job	In-House Training	Coach	Job Rotation	Vendor School	College/University	
		• assist customers by utilization of computer system for information retrieval	✓						Observation

A – Applies to this position
C – Certified for this employee

Sample Skill Hierarchy Certification Training Methods
Classification: *Customer Service Representative*

A	C	Requirements for Skill Block 3	On-the-Job	In-House Training	Coach	Job Rotation	Vendor School	College/ University	What methods will be used to certify the skill/competency?
		Administrative Support							
		Exhibits the ability to:							
		• distribute paychecks	✓						Observation
		• assist with preparing W-2's for distribution	✓						
		• assist with the Kronos Time-clock System	✓	✓					Certificate-PR Kronos Training Observation
		Documentation							
		Demonstrates the ability to:							
		• prepare and update plans review checklists	✓		✓				Observation
		• deposit funds into correct accounting line and document for records			✓				Observation
		• code suits and bankruptcies into the system							

A – Applies to this position
C – Certified for this employee

Sample Skill Hierarchy Certification Training Methods
Classification: *Customer Service Representative*

A	C	Requirements for Skill Block 3	Type of Training						What methods will be used to certify the skill/competency?
			On-the-Job	In-House Training	Coach	Job Rotation	Vendor School	College/ University	
		Processing							
		Demonstrates the ability to:							
		• receive and issue applications for permits using the Building Permit Program	✓						Observation
		• match invoices to DPO's, checking addresses, and enter at the proper time	✓	✓	✓				Certificate-Accounts Payable Training Observation
		• prepare liens for filing							
		• review and approve all check requests for payment							
		• contact insurance companies regarding non-payment							
		• provide utility releases	✓						Observation
		• send adjusted tax statements to property owners for payment							
		• prepare requests for any tax refunds to be submitted to accounts payable							
		• process cash receipts, including returned expense funds, refunds and credits	✓	✓					Observation
A	C	Requirements for Skill Block 3	Type of Training						

A – Applies to this position
C – Certified for this employee

Sample Skill Hierarchy Certification Training Methods
Classification: *Customer Service Representative*

		On-the-Job	In-House Training	Coach	Job Rotation	Vendor School	College/University	What methods will be used to certify the skill/competency?
	• audit check requests for accuracy							
	• assist with end-of-year processing and distribution of longevity, take-home vehicles and mileage							
Database/System Utilization								
	Demonstrates the ability to:							
	• cancel invoice, purchase order, or employee payment requests on computer system	✓						
	• establish new vendor files on computer	✓				✓		Certificate-TRIMS Training
	• enter accurate payments into system	✓		✓				Observation
	• enter insurance information on patients' accounts							
	• process deed transfer tape		✓					
	• enter data from invoices and purchase orders, check requests for capital projects, void checks; and schedule for payment							Observation

A – Applies to this position
C – Certified for this employee

Sample Skill Hierarchy Certification Training Methods
Classification: *Customer Service Representative*

A	C	Requirements for Skill Block 3	Type of Training						What methods will be used to certify the skill/competency?
			On-the-Job	In-House Training	Coach	Job Rotation	Vendor School	College/University	
		• upload and download into insurance company's data banks							
		Analysis							
		Demonstrates the ability to:							
		• review vendor inquiries and statements	✓						
		• review computer reports or other financial documents	✓		✓				Observation
		• audit time sheets for accuracy and input time sheet data bi-weekly	✓	✓					Certificate-Payroll Training Observation
		• check all accounts for payment status and send current statement or delinquent statement accordingly							
		• review credit card usage and charges for all departments fuel usage	✓						Observation
		• review monthly departmental billings for all warehouse as well as automotive parts used by departments	✓						Observation

A – Applies to this position
C – Certified for this employee

Sample Skill Hierarchy Certification Training Methods

Classification: *Customer Service Representative*

A	C	Requirements for Skill Block 3	On-the-Job	In-House Training	Coach	Job Rotation	Vendor School	College/ University	What methods will be used to certify the skill/competency?
		• match documents showing monies owed to documents for method of payment			✓				Observation
		• research all statements or permits with past due amounts	✓						Observation
		• research payroll problems and make adjustments as necessary	✓	✓					Observation
		• review payment and DPO inquiries							
		Inventory/Supplies							
		Demonstrates the ability to:							
		• identify if correct part is still in production and can be substituted	✓						Observation
		• use technical manuals to research parts requests	✓						Observation
		Customer Service							
		Exhibits the ability to:							
		• answer general questions from vendors regarding status of payments toward accounts	✓						Observation

A – Applies to this position
C – Certified for this employee

Sample Skill Hierarchy Certification Training Methods
Classification: *Customer Service Representative*

A	C	Requirements for Skill Block 3	Type of Training						What methods will be used to certify the skill/competency?
			On-the-Job	In-House Training	Coach	Job Rotation	Vendor School	College/ University	
		• provide equipment services for shop	✓						Observation
		• assist customers with inquiries concerning billing or permit procedures and information	✓		✓				Observation
		• make phone calls to collect delinquent accounts	✓						
		Training							
		Exhibits the ability to:							
		• training individuals to perform entry level work	✓		✓				Observation
		• present training at new employee orientation on payroll and timesheets							

A – Applies to this position
C – Certified for this employee

Appendix F – Page 14

©Copyright 2003, 2004 - All rights reserved - The Waters Consulting Group, Inc

Sample Skill Hierarchy Certification Training Methods

Classification: *Customer Service Representative*

A	C	Requirements for Skill Block 4	On-the-Job	In-House Training	Coach	Job Rotation	Vendor School	College/ University	What method will be used to certify the skill/competency?
		Support							
		Exhibits the ability to:							
		• maintain automated tank gauging system required by law	✓						Observation
		Documentation							
		Demonstrates the ability to:							
		• update and maintain current and accurate records of property ownership							Standard Defined by HR Policies
		• update payroll information training manual with new laws and/or policies		✓					
		• obtain data for workers compensation		✓					Standard Defined by Risk Policies
		• update and maintain individual accounts or contractor files	✓	✓	✓				Observation
		• maintain information in spreadsheet programs	✓	✓	✓				Observation
		• transfer information from one document to another	✓				✓		Observation

A – Applies to this position
C – Certified for this employee

Sample Skill Hierarchy Certification Training Methods
Classification: *Customer Service Representative*

A	C	Requirements for Skill Block 4	On-the-Job	In-House Training	Coach	Job Rotation	Vendor School	College/ University	What method will be used to certify the skill/competency?
		• utilize legal guidelines to process documents							
		• assign procedure codes to EMS billing utilizing an intermediate knowledge of the ICD9 codes							
		Processing							
		Demonstrates the ability to:							
		• process requests from departments to move expenses from one to another, or different accounts	✓						Observation
		• bill or collect revenue for other departments	✓						Observation
		• prepare/obtain authorization/notarization for release of lien			✓				
		• process over the counter permits							Observation
		Database System/Utilization							
		Demonstrates the ability to:							

A – Applies to this position
C – Certified for this employee

Sample Skill Hierarchy Certification Training Methods
Classification: *Customer Service Representative*

A	C	Requirements for Skill Block 4	On-the-Job	In-House Training	Coach	Job Rotation	Vendor School	College/ University	What method will be used to certify the skill/competency?
		• generate claims from computer system for paper and electronic claims	✓						Observation
		• void payment on a computer and transfer money to correct account or refund	✓		✓				Observation
		• enter adjustments for third party sick pay, car allowance credits and housing for W-2's	✓						Observation
		• perform daily/monthly reconciliation reports	✓		✓				Observation
		Analysis							
		Demonstrates the ability to:							
		• visually review time sheets and computer reports for errors	✓						Observation
		• identify and analyze delinquent accounts for further legal action	✓						Observation
		• balance deposits and adjustments	✓	✓	✓				Observation
		• assist with budget request for payroll related issues			✓				
		• review permit applications			✓				Observation

A – Applies to this position
C – Certified for this employee

Appendix F – Page 17

©Copyright 2003, 2004 - All rights reserved - The Waters Consulting Group, Inc

Sample Skill Hierarchy Certification Training Methods
Classification: *Customer Service Representative*

A	C	Requirements for Skill Block 4	On-the-Job	In-House Training	Coach	Job Rotation	Vendor School	College/University	What method will be used to certify the skill/competency?
		• maintain recaps by pay period, monthly, quarterly, and annually (fiscal and calendar)	✓						Observation
		• recognize inaccurate information and research the issue							
		Inventory/Supplies							
		Demonstrates the ability to:							
		• order and maintain standard fuel monitoring devices to be installed and repaired on vehicles	✓						Observation
		Customer Service							
		Exhibits the ability to:							
		• send statements to attorney office for suits							
		• collect fines from citizens	✓						Observation
		Teamwork							
		Demonstrates the ability to:							

A – Applies to this position
C – Certified for this employee

Sample Skill Hierarchy Certification Training Methods
Classification: *Customer Service Representative*

A	C	Requirements for Skill Block 4	On-the-Job	In-House Training	Coach	Job Rotation	Vendor School	College/ University	What method will be used to certify the skill/competency?
		• coordinate with department and division managers responsible for the projects	✓		✓				Observation
		Training							
		Exhibits the ability to:							
		• teach/instruct classes	✓	✓					Observation
		Directing Others							
		Displays the ability to:							
		• oversee input of vendor invoices and check requests		✓					Observation
		• monitor work for accuracy, proof work and make corrections	✓		✓				Observation
		• oversee temporary personnel assignments and results	✓			✓			Observation

A – Applies to this position
C – Certified for this employee

Sample Skill Hierarchy Certification Training Methods
Classification: *Customer Service Representative*

A	C	Requirements for Skill Block 5	On-the-Job	In-House Training	Coach	Job Rotation	Vendor School	College/ University	What method will be used to certify the skill/competency?
		Support							
		Exhibits the ability to:							
		• provide hazardous waste removal for shop	✓						Observation
		Documentation							
		Demonstrates the ability to:							
		• fill out Texas workers compensation commission forms for injured employees		✓					Observation
		• fill out subpoenas and other court documents							
		• maintain documentation, registrations and testing for all fuel tanks	✓						Observation
		• use the appropriate medical ICD-9 codes for insurance purposes							
		Processing							
		Demonstrates the ability to:							

A – Applies to this position
C – Certified for this employee

Sample Skill Hierarchy Certification Training Methods
Classification: *Customer Service Representative*

A	C	Requirements for Skill Block 5	On-the-Job	In-House Training	Coach	Job Rotation	Vendor School	College/University	What method will be used to certify the skill/competency?
		• file liens with the appropriate governmental agency							
		• calculate and prepare federal tax deposits for approval and transmit information timely							
		• prepare 1099-miscellaneous for IRS							
		• review simple permits		✓	✓				Observation
		• review plans for compliance with accessibility requirements							Certificate - ICBO
		Database System/Utilization							
		Demonstrates the ability to:							
		• use an accounts payable system	✓						
		• process supplemental tax adjustments tape							
		• produce bill print file and coordinate on printing	✓						
		• run complex reports							
		• retrieve data elements for preparing advanced documents							
A	C	Requirements for Skill Block 5			Type of Training				

A – Applies to this position
C – Certified for this employee

Sample Skill Hierarchy Certification Training Methods
Classification: *Customer Service Representative*

		On-the-Job	In-House Training	Coach	Job Rotation	Vendor School	College/ University	What method will be used to certify the skill/competency?
Analysis								
Demonstrates the ability to:								
	• assist with annual audit-special reports and request for information for audit and budget	✓						
	• balance quarterly payroll earnings/deductions and work with accountant to balance liability accounts							
	• reconcile and recover overpayments of injury leave monies and correct underpayments							
	• research, calculate and process back-pays, repays and leave adjustments	✓						Observation
	• research, analyze, correct and maintain files on erroneous payments	✓						Observation
	• review financial processes and procedures and make recommendations for changes within prescribed policies	✓		✓				Observation

A – Applies to this position
C – Certified for this employee

Sample Skill Hierarchy Certification Training Methods

Classification: *Customer Service Representative*

A	C	Requirements for Skill Block 5	On-the-Job	In-House Training	Coach	Job Rotation	Vendor School	College/ University	What method will be used to certify the skill/competency?
		• interpret/audit information and enter data	✓		✓				Observation
		• develop/create spreadsheets	✓						Observation
		• verify accuracy of information from tape or download files							
		• analyze differences between final account and source documents	✓						
		• recognize and resolve program and/or software problems							
		Customer Service							
		Exhibits the ability to:							
		• inform customers of advanced state tax laws							
		• answer employee and citizen questions	✓	✓	✓				Observation
		• assess and resolve billing disputes	✓						
		• assist customers in accessing the plats and computer records	✓						Observation

A – Applies to this position
C – Certified for this employee

Appendix F – Page 23

©Copyright 2003, 2004 - All rights reserved - The Waters Consulting Group, Inc

Sample Skill Hierarchy Certification Training Methods
Classification: *Customer Service Representative*

A	C	Requirements for Skill Block 5	Type of Training						What method will be used to certify the skill/competency?
			On-the-Job	In-House Training	Coach	Job Rotation	Vendor School	College/ University	
		Training							
		Exhibits the ability to:							
		• provide organization-wide training on new systems and procedures	✓						Observation
		• organize nationwide training on new systems or procedures							
		Directing Others							
		Displays the ability to:							
		• apply knowledge of administrative policies	✓	✓	✓				Observation
		• communicate department policies	✓	✓	✓				Observation
		• coordinate work schedules and work flow within the department and with other departments	✓		✓				Observation
		Promotional Gate							

A – Applies to this position
C – Certified for this employee

Sample Skill Hierarchy Certification Training Methods
Classification: *Customer Service Representative*

A	C	Requirements for Skill Block 6	Type of Training						What method will be used to certify the skill/competency?
			On-the-Job	In-House Training	Coach	Job Rotation	Vendor School	College/ University	
		Directing Others							
		Displays the ability to:							
		• recommend staffing needs and make hiring decisions	✓		✓				Observation
		• authorize overtime and leave for employees	✓		✓				Observation
		• counsel employees regarding disciplinary and other various problems	✓	✓	✓				Observation
		• receive and resolve employee complaints	✓		✓				Observation
		• conduct annual reviews and determine salary increases for employees	✓		✓				Observation

A – Applies to this position
C – Certified for this employee

Sample Skill Hierarchy Certification Training Methods

Classification: *Inspector*

A	C	Requirements for Skill Block 1	On-the-Job	In-House Training	Coach	Job Rotation	Vendor School	College/ University	What method will be used to certify the skill/competency?
		Administrative Support							
		Exhibits the ability to:							
		• review construction plans for compliance with specific codes, general design standards, ordinances and other local and state laws	✓						Observation
		• route calls and visitors to appropriate sources	✓						Observation
		• make copies of documents and send faxes	✓						Observation
		Support							
		Demonstrates the ability to:							
		• present case to applicable boards for rehabilitation or other action							
		Documentation							
		• Demonstrates the ability to:							
		• maintain own individual files on correspondence, records, reports, and cards	✓						Observation

A – Applies to this position
C – Certified for this employee

Sample Skill Hierarchy Certification Training Methods

Classification: *Inspector*

A	C	Requirements for Skill Block 1	On-the-Job	In-House Training	Coach	Job Rotation	Vendor School	College/ University	What method will be used to certify the skill/competency?
		• maintain log entries of construction and enforcement of codes	✓	✓					Observation
		• maintain photographic case records	✓						Observation
		• maintain telephone log	✓	✓					Observation
		• maintain records of court orders, results of citations, State and Federal requirements	✓		✓				Observation
		• document the status of sites inspected, actions taken at sites, and corrections required, or construction quantities	✓	✓					Observation
		Analysis							
		Demonstrates the ability to:							
		• interpret occupancy applications and certifications and other dept's data (such as H.T.E.)	✓						Observation
		• investigate alleged violations of local and state laws, ordinances, or codes	✓						Observation
		• interpret construction specifications	✓	✓					Observation
		Customer Service							
		Exhibits the ability to:							

A – Applies to this position
C – Certified for this employee

Sample Skill Hierarchy Certification Training Methods
Classification: *Inspector*

A	C	Requirements for Skill Block 1	On-the-Job	In-House Training	Coach	Job Rotation	Vendor School	College/ University	What method will be used to certify the skill/competency?
		• assess fees from citizens and stakeholders	✓						Observation
		• refer customer to and coordinate contact with various organizations	✓						Observation
		• conduct on-site inspections to verify compliance or resolve conformity issues	✓		✓				Observation
		• schedule own inspections, re-inspections and complaint inspections ensuring timely completion	✓						Observation
		• independently oversee cleanup and repairs while on-call	✓						Observation
		• respond to complaints and requests for information by phone, by letter, or in person	✓	✓	✓				Observation
		Training/Certification							
		Exhibits the ability to:							
		• complete department cross-training Phase I	✓	✓					Observation
		• complete an applicable State license or certification or 20-hours outside technical exhibiting proficiency					✓		License

A – Applies to this position
C – Certified for this employee

Sample Skill Hierarchy Certification Training Methods
Classification: *Inspector*

A	C	Requirements for Skill Block 2	Type of Training						What method will be used to certify the skill/competency?
			On-the-Job	In-House Training	Coach	Job Rotation	Vendor School	College/ University	
		Administrative Support							
		Exhibits the ability to:							
		• produce reports summarizing reconciliations	✓						Observation
		• proficiently utilize software such as mainframe database, word-processing, e-mail, scheduling	✓	✓					Certificate Observation
		• prepare and update checklists or development worksheets	✓		✓				Observation
		Support							
		Demonstrates the ability to:							
		• write/issue notices or citations for violations of applicable codes, regulations or laws, and follow through with appropriate actions	✓	✓					Observation
		Documentation							
		Demonstrates the ability to:							
		• maintain division files on correspondence, records, reports and cards	✓						Observation
		Processing							

A – Applies to this position
C – Certified for this employee

Sample Skill Hierarchy Certification Training Methods
Classification: *Inspector*

A	C	Requirements for Skill Block 2	On-the-Job	In-House Training	Coach	Job Rotation	Vendor School	College/ University	What method will be used to certify the skill/competency?
		Demonstrates the ability to:							
		• update all inspection check lists to current codes	✓						Review – Work
		• set up pre-construction meetings for all commercial projects	✓	✓					Review – Work
		• conduct research and issue occupancy applications							
		Analysis							
		Demonstrates the ability to:							
		• interpret codes and ordinances	✓						Observation
		• conduct surveys with other regional cities on their methods and approval procedures	✓	✓					Review - Work
		• conduct research to determine correct information regarding assigned inspection activities	✓						Observation
		• examine floodplain determinations	✓						Observation
		Customer Service							
		Exhibits the ability to:							

A – Applies to this position
C – Certified for this employee

Sample Skill Hierarchy Certification Training Methods
Classification: *Inspector*

A	C	Requirements for Skill Block 2	Type of Training						What method will be used to certify the skill/competency?
			On-the-Job	In-House Training	Coach	Job Rotation	Vendor School	College/ University	
		• provide meetings to guide contractors and property owners through "code-interpretation" procedures	✓						Observation
		• pre-walk through inspection with all parties concerned for a temporary certificate of occupancy	✓						Observation
		• facilitate construction and enforcement through mediation							
		Training/Certification							
		Exhibits the ability to:					✓		
		• successfully complete certification for area of specialty or pass State examination	✓	✓					Certificate

A – Applies to this position
C – Certified for this employee

Sample Skill Hierarchy Certification Training Methods

Classification: *Inspector*

A	C	Requirements for Skill Block 3	On-the-Job	In-House Training	Coach	Job Rotation	Vendor School	College/ University	What method will be used to certify the skill/competency?
		Administrative Support							
		Exhibits the ability to:							
		• appear in court as a witness for the State in a trail by Judge and jury	✓	✓					Observation Certificate
		• proficiently use spreadsheet and presentation software	✓	✓					Observation Certificate
		Documentation							
		Demonstrates the ability to:							
		• collect, update and organize files and ordinances for the division	✓						Observation
		Processing							
		Demonstrates the ability to:							

A – Applies to this position
C – Certified for this employee

Sample Skill Hierarchy Certification Training Methods
Classification: *Inspector*

A	C	Requirements for Skill Block 3	On-the-Job	In-House Training	Coach	Job Rotation	Vendor School	College/ University	What method will be used to certify the skill/competency?
		• assist with periodic reports to management	✓						Observation
		Analysis							
		Demonstrates the ability to:							
		• monitor incoming revisions for building projects and other construction projects	✓	✓					Observation
		• examine engineering plans for private development and capital improvement projects	✓						Observation
		• analyze various computer reports and ledger sheets to report to management	✓	✓					Observation
		• complete audits of all projects overseen	✓	✓					Review - Projects Finalized with Full Compliance
		• determine or recommend material and/or equipment needs	✓						Observation

A – Applies to this position
C – Certified for this employee

Sample Skill Hierarchy Certification Training Methods

Classification: *Inspector*

A	C	Requirements for Skill Block 3	On-the-Job	In-House Training	Coach	Job Rotation	Vendor School	College/ University	What method will be used to certify the skill/competency?
		• offer suggestions regarding compliance issues within the limits of applicable laws and regulations	✓	✓	✓				Observation
		• review documents which record entries and deletions from accounts and computer files	✓	✓					Observation
		• contact other states and municipalities for information and interpretations of new and existing code references	✓						Observation
		Training/Certification							
		Exhibits the ability to:							
		• complete department cross-training Phase II	✓						Observation
		• exhibit proficiency and/or obtain certification in additional inspection or enforcement area	✓	✓			✓		Certificate Observation
		Teamwork							
		Demonstrate the ability to:							

A – Applies to this position
C – Certified for this employee

Sample Skill Hierarchy Certification Training Methods
Classification: *Inspector*

A	C	Requirements for Skill Block 3	On-the-Job	In-House Training	Coach	Job Rotation	Vendor School	College/ University	What method will be used to certify the skill/competency?
		• consult with departments on issues and questions regarding plan, code or policy interpretation	✓	✓	✓				Feedback

Type of Training spans: On-the-Job | In-House Training | Coach | Job Rotation | Vendor School | College/University

A – Applies to this position
C – Certified for this employee

Appendix F – Page 35

©Copyright 2003, 2004 - All rights reserved - The Waters Consulting Group, Inc

Sample Skill Hierarchy Certification Training Methods

Classification: *Inspector*

A	C	Requirements for Skill Block 4	On-the-Job	In-House Training	Coach	Job Rotation	Vendor School	College/ University	What method will be used to certify the skill/competency?
		Documentation							
		Demonstrates the ability to:							
		• record data in a mainframe or personal computer spreadsheet program	✓						Observation
		• make entries in journals, mainframe computer data entry screens, and various spreadsheet programs		✓					Observation
		• maintain and update departmental records, job status records, vehicle, radio, computer records and code enforcement records	✓						Observation
		• prepare progress reports for projects	✓						Observation
		• maintain records of court order results of citation, State and Federal requirements	✓		✓				Observation
		Processing							
		Demonstrates the ability to:							
		• analyze and post information to records, reports, cards and files	✓						Observation
		Analysis							
		Demonstrates the ability to:							

A – Applies to this position
C – Certified for this employee

Sample Skill Hierarchy Certification Training Methods
Classification: *Inspector*

A	C	Requirements for Skill Block 4	On-the-Job	In-House Training	Coach	Job Rotation	Vendor School	College/ University	What method will be used to certify the skill/competency?
		• research records and compile information for use in testimony	✓						Observation
		• review and evaluate work products, methods, and procedures	✓		✓				Observation
		• write new policies pertaining to newly adopted codes or new methods of construction	✓		✓				Observation
		• examine designs of street, alley, drainage, water and sanitary sewer projects	✓						Observation
		• examine specifications for design projects	✓						Observation
		• review and rewrite policies pertaining to the applicable construction codes and ordinances	✓		✓				Observation
		Customer Service							
		Exhibits the ability to:							
		• make topical presentations to homeowners associations, classrooms and other departments	✓						Observation
		• answer employee and citizen questions regarding areas of responsibility	✓						Observation
		• consult with citizens and/or contractors, developers and designers about permits and regulations verbally and in writing	✓						Observation

A – Applies to this position
C – Certified for this employee

Sample Skill Hierarchy Certification Training Methods

Classification: *Inspector*

A	C	Requirements for Skill Block 4	On-the-Job	In-House Training	Coach	Job Rotation	Vendor School	College/ University	What method will be used to certify the skill/competency?
		Teamwork							
		Demonstrates the ability to:							
		• prepare and conduct safety meetings	✓	✓					Observation
		• coordinate duties and projects with other departments and outside agencies involved in Enforcement or Inspection activities	✓	✓					Observation
		• organize and attend plan review meetings and meetings with various the Boards or Commissions	✓	✓					Observation
		• meet with other departments regarding health and safety issues	✓	✓					Observation
		Directing Others							
		Displays the ability to:							
		• control and account for expenditures		✓		✓		✓	Observation
		• monitor work for accuracy, proof work and make corrections	✓						Observation
		• monitor inspectors activity on field inspections for consistency	✓		✓				Review – Consistency of Inspections
		• establish, manage and coordinate schedules	✓		✓		✓		Observation

A – Applies to this position
C – Certified for this employee

Sample Skill Hierarchy Certification Training Methods
Classification: *Inspector*

A	C	Requirements for Skill Block 4	Type of Training					What method will be used to certify the skill/competency?
			On-the-Job	In-House Training	Coach	Job Rotation	Vendor School	College/ University	
		Training/Certification							
		Exhibits the ability to:							
		• obtain additional certifications for inspection, enforcement and leadership areas, or obtain 20 hours of training applicable exhibiting proficiency.	✓	✓	✓	✓	✓		Certificate
		Promotional Gate							

A	C	Requirements for Skill Block 5	Type of Training					What method will be used to certify the skill/competency?
			On-the-Job	In-House Training	Coach	Job Rotation	Vendor School	College/ University	
		Documentation							
		Demonstrates the ability to:							
		• maintain systematic, complete, and accurate records of division activities and services	✓			✓			Observation
		Analysis							
		Demonstrates the ability to:							

A – Applies to this position
C – Certified for this employee

Sample Skill Hierarchy Certification Training Methods

Classification: *Inspector*

A	C	Requirements for Skill Block 5	On-the-Job	In-House Training	Coach	Job Rotation	Vendor School	College/ University	What method will be used to certify the skill/competency?
		• audit time sheets for accuracy and input time sheet data weekly	✓						Observation
		• develop, maintain, and review reports and/or division performance assessments	✓						Observation
		• review computer reports and other financial documents such as the budget	✓						Observation
		• prepare and recommend the adoption of long-range and immediate plans	✓		✓		✓		Observation
		• review new codes and ordinances, and make suggestions	✓				✓		Observation
		Customer Service							
		Exhibits the ability to:							
		• make presentations to community education programs, homeowners associations and others upon request	✓		✓				Observation
		Directing Others							
		Displays the ability to:							
		• assign activities and projects, and monitor work flow	✓						Observation

A – Applies to this position
C – Certified for this employee

Sample Skill Hierarchy Certification Training Methods

Classification: *Inspector*

A	C	Requirements for Skill Block 5	On-the-Job	In-House Training	Coach	Job Rotation	Vendor School	College/ University	What method will be used to certify the skill/competency?
		• provide counseling and/or training to employees in need of skill development	✓	✓					Observation
		• give infield training to field inspectors on all subjects	✓	✓	✓	✓	✓		Review – Staff Skill Application
		• oversee the maintenance of accurate and complete financial records for the division	✓				✓		
		• measure the division's performance	✓	✓			✓		Review – Performance Measures
		• direct the budget preparation based on reasonable budget estimates, work programs and supporting data for the division	✓	✓			✓		Review – Budget Proposals
		• recruit and select employees		✓			✓		Observation
		• motivate employees to help meet department and organization goals	✓	✓			✓		Observation
		• review employee performance on a regular basis	✓	✓	✓				Observation

A – Applies to this position
C – Certified for this employee

APPENDIX G

SKILL HIERARCHY TABLE

The Public Sector's Guide to Skill-based Pay

SKILL HIERARCHY TABLE

Skill Hierarchy Table - Template

Skill Zone	Skills Attained	Skill Sub-Zone
1		Sub-Zone 1.0
		Sub-Zone 1.1
		Sub-Zone 1.2
		Sub-Zone 2.0
2		Sub-Zone 2.1
		Sub-Zone 2.2
		Sub-Zone 2.3
		Sub-Zone 2.4
		Sub-Zone 2.5
		Sub-Zone 3.0
3		Sub-Zone 3.1
		Sub-Zone 3.2
		Sub-Zone 3.3
		Sub-Zone 3.4
4		Sub-Zone 4.1
		Sub-Zone 4.2
		Sub-Zone 4.3
		Sub-Zone 4.4
		Sub-Zone 4.5

Appendix G – Page 1
©Copyright 2003, 2004 - All rights reserved - The Waters Consulting Group, Inc

APPENDIX H

SKILL OBJECTIVES TABLE

The Public Sector's Guide to Skill-based Pay

SKILL OBJECTIVES TABLE

Skill Objectives Table - Template

Position or Skill Group:
Skill ID:
Action: What should the employee be able to do?

Proof/Measurement: How well must it be done?

Speed/Time	Accuracy	According To…	Proof {Sign-Off? Certificate? Other?}

Standards: Under what conditions do you want the employee to be able to do it?

Items Given	Items Excluded	Setting/Conditions	Other

Safety Criteria
Equipment Needed

Location of Skill Mastery Demonstration: (check all that apply)	Field (on-the-job) ☐	Lab Set-up/Training ☐	Classroom instruction ☐
Estimated Time requirement to complete demonstration:			

APPENDIX I

SKILL INVENTORY SCALE AND FORM TEMPLATE

The Public Sector's Guide to Skill-based Pay

EMPLOYEE SKILL INVENTORY ANALYSIS SCALE AND RATING SHEET

Skill Inventory Analysis Scale

	Employee Skill Inventory Analysis Scale
1	**Cannot** perform the Skill in question. Can only perform skill with detailed and thorough supervision.
2	Can perform **some** aspects of the skill. May require general supervision and feedback.
3	**Can** perform the Skill in question, completely and without supervision (unless specifically required by the Skill Objective).
0	**N/A** – This skill is not applicable to this position at this time. A score of zero down not have a negative impact on the overall score

Skill Inventory Rating Sheet – Sample Template

Skill Zone _____

Skill Sub Zone _____

1.   Rating _____
2.   Rating _____
3.   Rating _____
4.   Rating _____

Average Score for Sub-Zone _____

Skill Sub Zone _____

1. Rating _____
2. Rating _____
3. Rating _____
4. Rating _____

Average Score for Sub-Zone _____

Skill Sub Zone _____

1. Rating _____
2. Rating _____
3. Rating _____

Average Score for Sub-Zone _____

Skill Zone _____

Skill Sub Zone _____

1. Rating _____
2. Rating _____
3. Rating _____

Average Score for Sub-Zone _____

APPENDIX J

SAMPLE SKILL-BASED PAY POSITION QUESTIONNAIRE

SKILL-BASED PAY POSITION QUESTIONNAIRE

CITY OF SAMPLE

PLACE
EMPLOYEE INFORMATION STICKER
HERE

(PLACE STICKERS FOR MULTIPLE EMPLOYEES ON BACK OF LAST PAGE)

THE WATERS
CONSULTING
GROUP, INC.

2695 Villa Creek Drive, Suite 104   Dallas, Texas 75234   www.watersconsulting.com

Skill-based Pay Position Questionnaire Instructions
City of Sample

Brief Explanation of Book

The purpose of this Skill-based Pay Position Questionnaire book is to collect information from employees regarding their jobs in a standardized format. Instructions are provided for each section and are found on the even numbered pages. Sections to be completed by employees are found on the odd numbered pages.

Following completion of this questionnaire, please forward to your supervisor. The supervisors and/or manager will review the information you provide for content and accuracy. You may be asked to complete the questionnaire in a group session format with several employees who perform similar duties. If at any time you have questions or require assistance to complete the questionnaire please refer to your supervisor or manager.

General Instructions

The following guidelines should be helpful in completing this questionnaire:

1. Please PRINT as neatly as possible.
2. Use only blue or black ink.
3. Read each item carefully and answer completely.
4. Be brief but specific in accurately describing the job. Make sure you are <u>not</u> describing your personal qualifications or how you would like this job to be. Describe only the actual job duties and qualifications, as they currently exist.

Skill-based Pay Position Questionnaire
City of Sample

Introduction

The Waters Consulting Group, Inc. (WCG) has been selected to design a Skill-Based Pay System for your organization. The first phase of the project involves the completion of the **Skill-based Pay Position Questionnaires**. Refer all initial questions regarding the completion of this questionnaire to your supervisor. Further questions concerning the job analysis process may be addressed via email to The Waters Consulting Group, Inc. at **information@watersconsulting.com** or by calling toll free at **1-800-899-1669**.

The examination of the **Skill-based Pay Position Questionnaire**s is one of the critical first steps in developing and maintaining an effective compensation program.

- They provide the basis for assessing and determining the relative scope.

- They serve as a communication tool to be used in surveys comparing the salaries of jobs with comparable jobs in similar organizations.

Thank you for your input and cooperation!

Deadline:
Please return your questionnaire to your supervisor by

Skill-based Pay Position Questionnaire Instructions
City of Sample

A. Instructions - Identification / General Information

This section is your general information including your name, job title and department. Please answer all questions as completely and accurately as possible.

Employee Name:	Joe Sample
If more than one Employee participated in completing this questionnaire, put "Multiple Employees" and attach a list of all participants to this form.	
Current Job Title:	Utility Technician II
Department Name:	Water Resources
Immediate Supervisor's Name:	John Director
Immediate Supervisor's Title:	Water Resources Director

Length of Service with Organization: 10 Years   9 Months

Length of Service in Current Job: 2 Years   1 Months

Describe your normal work schedule

Monday - Friday 7:00 a.m. to 4:00 p.m.

B. Instructions - Brief Analysis of the Job

This section is intended to capture a brief description of your job. Explain your job as if you were speaking to someone, unfamiliar with what you do, over coffee. The purpose of your job should differ from the duties by changing the focus from what you do to stating why the work is performed. The duties will explain how the "purpose of this job" is accomplished.

The purpose of this job is to: Use this space to summarize the general purpose of the job.

This is accomplished by: Briefly describe how your job's purpose is accomplished.

Other duties include: Then list any important duties outside of your job's general purpose.

The purpose of this job is to: provide multi-skilled services in operation and maintenance of the associated assets of the Edmond Water System.
This is accomplished by: installing, monitoring, repairing and maintaining water treatment plant systems equipment and facilities. Additionally responsible for monitoring and recording water usage.
Other duties include: providing emergency services on an -as-needed basis and administrative duties as necessary

Skill-based Pay Position Questionnaire
City of Sample

A. Identification / General Information

Employee Name:	
If more than one Employee participated in completing this questionnaire, put "Multiple Employees" and attach a list of all participants to this form.	
Current Job Title:	
Department Name:	
Immediate Supervisor's Name:	
Immediate Supervisor's Title:	

Length of Service with Organization: ___ Years ___ Months

Length of Service in Current Job: ___ Years ___ Months

Describe your normal work schedule

B. Brief Description of the Job

The purpose of this job is to:
This is accomplished by:
Other duties include:

Skill-based Pay Position Questionnaire Instructions
City of Sample

C. Instructions - Essential Functions

In this section we would like to obtain more detailed information into the functions you perform. Take a moment to review the description you provided in Section B. Now complete Section C using essential functions and tasks to explain how you accomplish your duties.

Function: List the primary or the most important functions that you perform. List only functions that require more than 5% of your time on a yearly basis.

Percentage of Time: Estimate the percentage of total working time per year that is taken up with that duty. These estimates should be made after all essential functions have been listed. The total percentages must equal 100%.

Physical Strength Code: Write ONE letter that best describes the strength demands of the essential function during a typical 8-hour workday. Use the codes listed below.

Physical Strength Codes

S = Sedentary	L = Light	M = Medium	H = Heavy	VH = Very Heavy
Exerting up to 10 lbs. occasionally or negligible weights frequently; sitting most of the time.	Exerting up to 20 lbs. occasionally, 10 lbs. frequently, or negligible amounts constantly **OR** requires walking or standing to a significant degree.	Exerting 20-50 lbs. occasionally, 10-25 lbs. frequently, or up to 10 lbs. two-thirds or more of the time.	Exerting 50-100 lbs. occasionally, 25-50 lbs. frequently, or up to 10-20 lbs. two-thirds or more of the time.	Exerting over 100 lbs. occasionally, 50-100 lbs. frequently, or up to 20-50 lbs. two-thirds or more of the time.

Tasks performed to accomplish this function: Use the space provided to list the tasks used to accomplish the function.

(Additional examples can be found on page 8)

Function: Provide multi-skilled services for the operation of the Edmond Water System.	**Percentage of Time:**	35%	**Physical Strength Code:**	M
Tasks performed to accomplish this function:					
1. Conducting routine installation, monitoring, maintenance and emergency					
2. Monitors and services water systems by investigating/locating repair sites					
3. Manages work requirements & inventory by determining equipment/supply needs					

What skills do you use to accomplish this function: Use the space provided to list the skills used to accomplish the function.

(Additional examples can be found on page 8)

Function: Provide multi-skilled services for the operation of the Edmond Water System.	**Percentage of Time:**	35%	**Physical Strength Code:**	M
Skills used to accomplish this function:					
1. Knowledge of all water systems and water treatment plant facilities systems					
2. Collect appropriate data and test water quality					
3. Ability to conduct inventory of parts and order replacements or purchases					

Skill-based Pay Position Questionnaire
City of Sample

C. Essential Functions

1. Function:	Percentage of Time:	Physical Strength Code:
	%	

Tasks performed to accomplish this function:

What skills do you use to accomplish this function:

2. Function:	Percentage of Time:	Physical Strength Code:
	%	

Tasks performed to accomplish this function:

What skills do you use to accomplish this function:

Skill-based Pay Position Questionnaire Instructions
City of Sample

C. Essential Functions (continued)

3. Function:	Percentage of Time:	Physical Strength Code:
	%	

Tasks performed to accomplish this function:

What skills do you use to accomplish this function:

4. Function:	Percentage of Time:	Physical Strength Code:
	%	

Tasks performed to accomplish this function:

What skills do you use to accomplish this function:

Skill-based Pay Position Questionnaire
City of Sample

D. Essential Functions (continued)

5. Function:	Percentage of Time:	Physical Strength Code:
	%	

Tasks performed to accomplish this function:

What skills do you use to accomplish this function:

6. Function:	Percentage of Time:	Physical Strength Code:
	%	

Tasks performed to accomplish this function:

What skills do you use to accomplish this function:

Skill-based Pay Position Questionnaire Instructions
City of Sample

D. Equipment, Certifications and Other Requirements

Machines, Tools, Equipment and Work Aids: List machines, tools and/or equipment that are required for this job (Not including Computer Equipment and Software).

Backhoe, bulldozer, shovel, rake, truck
Light and Heavy Equipment; Hand and Power Tools; Various Meters, Testing & Measuring Equipment; Laboratory Equipment; Computers; Printers and Related

Computer Equipment and Software: List all computer equipment and software that is required for this job.

Personal computer, printer, scanner, related software

Primary Work Location: Please check the type of location where the primary job duties are performed.
- ☐ Office Environment
- ☐ Warehouse
- ☒ Shop
- ☐ Vehicle
- ☐ Recreation Centers/Neighborhood Centers
- ☐ Outdoors (Specify) _____
- ☐ Other (Specify) _____

Protective Equipment Required: List protective equipment, if any, which is required for this job.

Safety glasses, gloves, hard hat, steel toe boots
OR
Rubber gloves, face mask

Certification and Other Requirements: (List any licenses, certifications, statutory requirements, or registrations required for this job. This does not necessarily mean the license you have, but what is required to hire or promote someone into this position, either internally or from the outside. Use exact name of license, certification, etc.)

1. Certified Hydrostatic Technician
2.
3.
4.
5.
Yes or No, Is a valid drivers license required? Yes
If Yes, what type? Commercial Driver's License

Skill-based Pay Position Questionnaire
City of Sample

D. Equipment, Certifications and Other Requirements

Machines, Tools, Equipment and Work Aids:

Computer Equipment and Software:

Primary Work Location:
- ☐ Office Environment
- ☐ Warehouse
- ☐ Shop
- ☐ Vehicle
- ☐ Recreation Centers/Neighborhood Centers
- ☐ Outdoors (Specify) _____
- ☐ Other (Specify) _____

Protective Equipment Required:

Certification and Other Requirements: (List any licenses, certifications, statutory requirements, or registrations required for this job. This does not necessarily mean the license you have, but what is required to hire or promote someone into this position, either internally or from the outside. Use exact name of license, certification, etc.)

1.	
2.	
3.	
4.	
Yes or No, is a valid drivers license required?	
If Yes, what type?	

E. Career Path Definition

Please indicate other city jobs that are related to this position as part of a career family.

Other jobs in the City to which I or others that hold my same position might be promoted.	1. *Supervisor or Manager*
	2.
	3.
My Current Job	
Other jobs in the City that would prepare applicants for my current position.	1. *Assistant or Seasonal Employee*
	2.
	3.

F. Supervisory and Management Responsibilities

Supervisory Responsibility: (Yes) or No, does this position involve directing the work of others?

If Yes, please list the job titles (not working titles) and number of employees you supervise.

Job Title(s)	Number of Employees
1. *Assistant*	One
2. *Seasonal Employee*	Three
3.	
4.	
5.	
6.	
7.	
8.	

Nature of Work Direction: If you answered "Yes" to the question above, please indicate the nature of work direction provided by the job by placing an "X" next to it.

	Work requires the occasional direction of helpers, assistants, seasonal employees, interns, volunteers or temporary employees.
X	Work requires functioning as a lead worker performing essentially the same work as those directed and includes overseeing work quality, training, instructing, and scheduling work.
	Work requires supervising and monitoring performance for a regular group of employees or a work unit including providing input on hiring/disciplinary actions and work objectives/effectiveness and realigning work as needed.
	Work requires managing and monitoring work performance by directing subordinate supervisors or administrators including making final decisions on hiring and disciplinary actions, evaluating program/work objectives and effectiveness, and realigning work and staffing assignments, as needed.
	Work requires managing and monitoring work performance of senior department managers including evaluating program/work objectives and effectiveness, establishing broad organizational goals and realigning work and staffing for the department.

Skill-based Pay Position Questionnaire
City of Sample

E. Career Path Definition

Please indicate other City jobs that are related to this position as part of a career family.

Other jobs in the City to which I or others that hold my same position might be promoted.	1.
	2.
	3.
My Current Job	
Other jobs in the City that would prepare applicants for my current position.	1.
	2.
	3.

F. Supervisory and Management Responsibilities

Supervisory Responsibility: Yes or No, does this position involve directing the work of others?

If Yes, please list the job titles (not working titles) and number of employees you supervise.

Job Title(s)	Number of Employees
1.	
2.	
3.	
4.	
5.	
6.	
7.	
8.	

Nature of Work Direction: If you answered "Yes" to the question above, please indicate the nature of work direction provided by the job by placing an "X" next to it.

	Work requires the occasional direction of helpers, assistants, seasonal employees, interns, volunteers or temporary employees.
	Work requires functioning as a lead worker performing essentially the same work as those directed and includes overseeing work quality, training, instructing, and scheduling work.
	Work requires supervising and monitoring performance for a regular group of employees or a work unit including providing input on hiring/disciplinary actions and work objectives/effectiveness and realigning work as needed.
	Work requires managing and monitoring work performance by directing subordinate supervisors or administrators including making final decisions on hiring and disciplinary actions, evaluating program/work objectives and effectiveness, and realigning work and staffing assignments, as needed.
	Work requires managing and monitoring work performance of senior department managers including evaluating program/work objectives and effectiveness, establishing broad organizational goals and realigning work and staffing for the department.

G. Signature/Approval - Instructions

After completing the Skill-based Pay Position Questionnaire, please sign the form and return the form to your supervisor.

Skill-based Pay Position Questionnaire
City of Sample

G. Signature/Approval

To the best of my ability, I have filled out this questionnaire, and believe it to be an accurate analysis of my job.

x	
Employee Signature	Date

x	
Supervisor Signature	Date
Comments:	

x	
Department Head Signature (if applicable)	Date
Comments:	

x	
Human Resources Director Signature	Date
Comments:	

©Copyright 2003, 2004 - All rights reserved - The Waters Consulting Group, Inc

> **Check to be sure:**
> All sections are completed.
> You have signed and dated Section G.
> **Return your questionnaire to your supervisor by the deadline:**

Thank you for your input and cooperation!

THE WATERS CONSULTING GROUP, INC.

2695 Villa Creek Drive, Suite 104   Dallas, Texas 75234   www.watersconsulting.com

APPENDIX K

SAMPLE BROADBANDED JOB DESCRIPTIONS

Career Path: Accounting

Brief Description of the Path:
The duties performed in this career path support accounting functions for the department. Administrative duties include sorting and distributing mail, filing papers, entering data in the computer and maintaining office supplies. Other duties include preparing financial reports, processing claims, analyzing accounts, maintaining petty cash funds, issuing checks, preparing billings and other accounting related duties. Incumbent may also assist with budget preparation, prepare various schedules, analyses and reports, manage accounts and process various contracts.

Typical Position Titles That Fall Under This Path:
Division Director Secretary-Accounting
Accounts Payable Specialist
Accounting Clerk
Senior Accounts Payable Specialist

Financial Coordinator
Accounts Payable Manager
Budget Coordinator

Path Requirements

Formal Education:
The minimum level of education required for this career path is a high school diploma or equivalent. A two-year Associate's degree is preferred.

Experience:
Over five years experience performing administrative and accounting duties is required.

Certifications, Licenses and Other Requirements:
Valid Texas Class C Driver's License

Supervisory:
Progression through this career path may include the development of leadership competencies.

Career Path: Accounting

Physical Demands

Overall Strength Demands:

_____ Sedentary   __X__ Light   _____ Medium   _____ Heavy   _____ Very Heavy

Codes: for each physical demand code listed:
C = Continuously   F = Frequently   O = Occasionally   R = Rarely   N = Never

Physical Action	Frequency Code	Description
Standing	O	Making copies, faxing
Sitting	C	To perform desk work
Walking	O	To other offices and office equipment
Lifting	R	Files, checks, boxes
Carrying	R	Supplies, files
Pulling	R	File drawers
Pushing	R	File drawers
Fine Dexterity	C	To use computer keyboard, calculator
Reaching	R	For supplies and files
Kneeling	R	To retrieve files
Crawling	N	
Twisting	R	From computer to telephone
Climbing	O	Step stool, stairs
Balancing	R	On step stool
Seeing	C	To read, perform computer work
Hearing	C	To communicate with co-workers and on telephone
Talking	F	To communicate with co-workers and on telephone
Using Foot Controls	N	

Career Path: Accounting

Machines, Tools, Equipment and Work Aids:
Computer and related software, calculator, fax machine, telephone, copier, printer, hole punch, typewriter

Environmental Factors:
Exposure to and frequency:

N = Never   Y = Yearly   M = Monthly   W = Weekly   D = Daily

ENVIRONMENTAL FACTORS					
Dirt and Dust	N	Extreme Temperatures	Y	Noise and Vibration	N
Fumes and Odors	N	Wetness/Humidity	N	Darkness or Poor Lighting	N

HEALTH AND SAFETY					
Mechanical Hazards	N	Chemical Hazards	N	Electrical Hazards	N
Fire Hazards	N	Explosives	N	Communicable Diseases	N
Physical Danger or Abuse	N	Other (specify)			

WORK LOCATION(S)					
Office Environment	X	Warehouse		Shop	
Vehicle		Outdoors		Other:	

Protective Equipment Required:
N/A

Non-physical Demands:

N = Never   R = Rarely   O = Occasionally   F = Frequently   C = Continuously

Time Pressures	C	Emergency Situations	R
Frequent Change of Tasks	F	Irregular Work Schedule/Overtime	F
Performing Multiple Tasks Simultaneously	C	Working Closely with Others As Part of a Team	F
Tedious or Exacting Work	C	Noisy/Distracting Environment	R

Contacts

Internal and External

The incumbents in this career path contact others within the organization. These contacts may involve similar work units or departments within the agency, which may be involved in decision making or providing approval or decision making authority for purchases, products or projects. Incumbents may work within the community to identify service needs and implement programs designed to fill service gaps. Work may also include contact with individuals outside the agency belonging to professional or peer organizations. Working with various regulatory agencies may also be required of the employee.

Career Path: Accounting

Signatures - Review and Comment

I have reviewed this career path analysis and its attachments and find it to be an accurate description of the demands of this career path.

_____ _____ _____
                                 Signature of Employee   Date

_____ _____ _____
Job Title of Supervisor   Signature of Supervisor   Date

_____ _____ _____
Job Title of Director   Signature of Director   Date

Comments: _____

_____

_____

The above statements are intended to describe the general nature and level of work being performed by individuals assigned to this career path. They are not intended to be an exhaustive list of all responsibilities, duties, and skills required of personnel so classified in this path. This career path description is subject to change as the needs and requirements of the positions in the career path change.

Career Path: Support Services Provider- Customer Service Representative

Brief Description of the Path:
The duties performed in this career path provide various support duties to the department. Duties may include providing information, services or supplies to customers or other departments, monitoring activities, maintaining inventory, answering telephones, providing clerical support, or performing other duties as assigned. Administrative duties include completing various reports, processing documents relative to the department, handling various fund accounts including payroll and completing other duties as assigned. Supervisory duties include overseeing staff and establishing production standards and priorities.

Typical Position Titles That Fall Under This Path:

Permit Specialist	Clerk 1
Payroll Clerk	Clerk 2
General Ledger Clerk	Clerk 3
General Services Clerk	Recreation Attendant
Payroll Coordinator	Warehouse Supervisor
Accounts Payable Supervisor	Parts Worker
Ambulance Billing Clerk	Accounts Payable Clerk
Permit Specialist Supervisor	

Path Requirements

Formal Education:
The minimum education required for this career path is a high school diploma or the equivalent.

Experience:
At least six months experience is required.

Certifications, Licenses and Other Requirements:
Valid Texas Class C Driver's License

Various other certificates, licenses and other requirements may be required as the incumbent progresses through the career path.

Direct Reports/Leadership:
Progression through this career path may include the development of leadership competencies.

Career Path: Support Services Provider-Customer Service Representative

Physical Demands

Overall Strength Demands:
_____ Sedentary   **X** Light   _____ Medium   _____ Heavy   _____ Very Heavy

Codes: for each physical demand code listed:
C = Continuously   F = Frequently   O = Occasionally   R = Rarely   N = Never

Physical Action	Frequency Code	Description
Standing	F	At copier, to assist citizens
Sitting	F	To perform work at desk
Walking	F	To other departments or office equipment
Lifting	F	Supplies, boxes, equipment
Carrying	F	Supplies, boxes, equipment
Pulling	F	File drawers, equipment
Pushing	F	File, drawers, equipment
Reaching	F	For supplies, books
Kneeling	O	To retrieve equipment
Crawling	O	To retrieve equipment
Twisting	O	From computer to telephone, to retrieve equipment
Climbing	O	Step stool, ladder
Balancing	O	On step stool, ladder
Seeing	C	To read, perform work on the computer, take inventory
Hearing	C	To communicate with co-workers and customers and on telephone
Talking	C	With co-workers and on telephone
Using Foot Controls	F	To drive
Fine Dexterity	F	For computer keyboard

Career Path: Support Services Provider-Customer Service Representative

Machines, Tools, Equipment and Work Aids:
Mail processing machines, copier, GBC binder, computer and related software, calculator, printer, microfilm machine, fax machine, typewriter, architectural scale, telephone, paper shredder, postage machine, paper cutter, folding machine, hole punch, laminator, bursting machine, check signer, two-way radio, cash register, hand tools, power tools, forklift, manuals, hand truck, pick up truck, plat books and maps

Environmental Factors:
Exposure to and frequency:
N = Never   Y = Yearly   M = Monthly   W = Weekly   D = Daily

ENVIRONMENTAL FACTORS					
Dirt and Dust	W	Extreme Temperatures	W	Noise and Vibration	W
Fumes and Odors	W	Wetness/Humidity	W	Darkness or Poor Lighting	W

HEALTH AND SAFETY					
Mechanical Hazards	W	Chemical Hazards	M	Electrical Hazards	M
Fire Hazards	Y	Explosives	N	Communicable Diseases	W
Physical Danger or Abuse	M	Other (specify)			

WORK LOCATION(S)					
Office Environment	X	Warehouse	X	Shop	X
Vehicle	X	Outdoors	X	Other:	

Protective Equipment Required:
Steel toe boots, seat belt, hard hat, gloves, eye protection, dust mask, hearing protection, skin protection

Non-physical Demands:

N = Never   R = Rarely   O = Occasionally   F = Frequently   C = Continuously

Time Pressures	F	Emergency Situations	O
Frequent Change of Tasks	F	Irregular Work Schedule/Overtime	F
Performing Multiple Tasks Simultaneously	F	Working Closely with Others As Part of a Team	F
Tedious or Exacting Work	F	Noisy/Distracting Environment	F

Career Path: Support Services Provider-Customer Service Representative

Contacts
(Contacts vary depending on department and position)

Contacts within the City

DEPARTMENT	CONTACT/TITLE	FREQUENCY	PURPOSE OF CONTACT
Finance	Accountant	Weekly	Assist with DPO discrepancies
General Services	Director	Weekly	Printing, paper
Purchasing	Buyer	Weekly	DPO's, price agreements
Fleet Services	Director	Weekly	Supplies and vendors
Environmental Health	Division Manager	Monthly	Fuel tank management
Police and Fire	Officer, EMS Coordinator	Daily	Vehicle maintenance, EMS information/verification, coordination of FA information
Human Resources	Systems Administrator	Daily	Verifying employee items
ACS	Help desk	Daily	Computer related items
Utility Billing	Cashiers	Daily	Cash receipt packets

Contacts outside City

ORGANIZATION	CONTACT/TITLE	FREQUENCY	PURPOSE OF CONTACT
Other cities	Parts	Monthly	Locating vendors or parts
American Payroll	President	Monthly	Informational meetings
Comptroller	Various	Monthly	Reports
Vendors	Various	Weekly	Vending repairs
SFGA	Adjuster	Daily	Workers Compensation
Utility companies	Various	Daily	Utility releases for C/O's
Attorneys offices	Lawyers	Daily	Coordinating information on delinquent accounts and law suits

Contacts with Vendors/Suppliers & General Public

ORGANIZATION	CONTACT/TITLE	FREQUENCY	PURPOSE OF CONTACT
Automotive vendors	Sales	Daily	parts
General public		Daily	Filling in for office staff, answering questions, providing information
Fuel vendors	Sales	Monthly	Fuel delivery
Auto repair shops	Representative	Weekly	Repair service
Office supply stores	Sales	Weekly	Supplies

Career Path: Support Services Provider-Customer Service Representative

Signatures - Review and Comment

I have reviewed this career path analysis and its attachments and find it to be an accurate description of the demands of this job.

_____   _____   _____
                                         Signature of Employee   Date

_____   _____   _____
Job Title of Supervisor   Signature of Supervisor   Date

_____   _____   _____
Job Title of Department Head   Signature of Department Head   Date

Comments:_____

_____

_____

The above statements are intended to describe the general nature and level of work being performed by individuals assigned to this job. They are not intended to be an exhaustive list of all responsibilities, duties, and skills required of personnel so classified in this position. This job description is subject to change by the City as the needs and requirements of the job change.

Career Path: Technical Support Provider-Facility

Brief Description of the Path:
The duties performed in this career path provide cleaning, maintenance and repair services to facilities in the City. Administrative duties include contacting various vendors for supplies, writing reports, keeping logs and inventory and managing special projects. Supervisory duties include assigning work duties, completing performance evaluations and resolving employee complaints. Other duties include assisting other departments and assisting with special projects.

Typical Position Titles That Fall Under This Path:
Craft Technician
Pool Maintenance Technician
Custodian
Facility Maintenance Worker
Craft Technician Supervisor

Path Requirements

Formal Education:
The minimum education required for this career path is a high school diploma or the equivalent. As incumbent progresses through this career path, additional training beyond high school in the area of plumbing, electrical or mechanical work is preferred.

Experience:
Over one year custodial experience is required.

Certifications, Licenses and Other Requirements:
Valid Texas Class C Driver's License

Various other certificates, licenses and other requirements may be required as the incumbent progresses through the career path.

Direct Reports/Leadership:
Progression through this career path may include the development of leadership competencies.

Career Path: Technical Support Provider-Facility

Physical Demands

Overall Strength Demands:

____ Sedentary   ____ Light   _X_ Medium   ____ Heavy   ____ Very Heavy

Codes: for each physical demand code listed:
C = Continuously   F = Frequently   O = Occasionally   R = Rarely   N = Never

Physical Action	Frequency Code	Description
Standing	C	Performing maintenance and cleaning duties
Sitting	O	Desk work, driving
Walking	F	To and from facilities, reviewing work
Lifting	F	Equipment and supplies
Carrying	F	Equipment and supplies
Pulling	O	Broom, dolly, mop, vacuum, carts
Pushing	O	Broom, dolly, mop, vacuum, carts
Reaching	F	For supplies, changing light bulbs. Painting
Kneeling	O	Gaining access into compartments, general maintenance and cleaning
Crawling	O	Under buildings, in attics, cleaning carpets
Twisting	O	In small compartments, sweeping, mopping, general maintenance
Climbing	O	Ladders, stairs, scaffolding
Balancing	O	On ladders, stairs and scaffolding
Seeing	C	Observing work area, reading
Hearing	C	Communicating with others on radio and telephone, troubleshooting
Talking	C	Communicating with others on radio and telephone
Using Foot Controls	F	Driving, operating vacuums
Fine Dexterity	F	Computer keyboard

Career Path: Technical Support Provider-Facility

Machines, Tools, Equipment and Work Aids:
Computer and related software, telephone, calculator, table saw, drill press, pressure jet, roto-rooter, electric welder, grinder, sander, hand tools, Ohm meter, various electric meters, drill, vacuum pump, refrigerant gauge, recovery machine, thermometer, scale, staple gun, grease gun, electric blower, carpet shampoo equipment, broom, vacuum cleaner, dust mop, mop and bucket, buffer, truck, ladder

Environmental Factors:
Exposure to and frequency:

N = Never   Y = Yearly   M = Monthly   W = Weekly   D = Daily

ENVIRONMENTAL FACTORS					
Dirt and Dust	D	Extreme Temperatures	W	Noise and Vibration	D
Fumes and Odors	D	Wetness/Humidity	W	Darkness or Poor Lighting	D

HEALTH AND SAFETY					
Mechanical Hazards	W	Chemical Hazards	W	Electrical Hazards	W
Fire Hazards	W	Explosives	Y	Communicable Diseases	D
Physical Danger or Abuse	W	Other (specify)			

WORK LOCATION(S)					
Office Environment	X	Warehouse	X	Shop	X
Vehicle	X	Outdoors	X	Other:	

Protective Equipment Required:
Eye protection, dust mask, rubber gloves, back support, steel toe boots, face shield, SCBA, welding gloves, wet suit

Non-physical Demands:

N = Never   R = Rarely   O = Occasionally   F = Frequently   C = Continuously

Time Pressures	F	Emergency Situations	O
Frequent Change of Tasks	F	Irregular Work Schedule/Overtime	O
Performing Multiple Tasks Simultaneously	F	Working Closely with Others As Part of a Team	C
Tedious or Exacting Work	O	Noisy/Distracting Environment	F

Career Path: Technical Support Provider-Facility

Contacts

Contacts within the City

DEPARTMENT	CONTACT/TITLE	FREQUENCY	PURPOSE OF CONTACT
All Departments	Various	Daily	Service requests
Parks Department	Assistant Park Manager	Weekly	Assisting with special projects
Facility Maintenance	Supervising Technician	Monthly	Assisting with special projects
Fleet Services	Various	Monthly	Requisitioning supplies
Building Maintenance	Various	Weekly	Reporting serious repairs
Administration & Planning	Staff members	Weekly	Setting up meetings

Contacts outside City

ORGANIZATION	CONTACT/TITLE	FREQUENCY	PURPOSE OF CONTACT
Metrocrest Center	Director	Monthly	Replacing light bulbs
Adult Senior Services	Director	Monthly	Service requests

Contacts with Vendors/Suppliers & General Public

ORGANIZATION	CONTACT/TITLE	FREQUENCY	PURPOSE OF CONTACT
Walmart		Monthly	Supplies
Turner Hardware Store		Weekly	Supplies
Bank		Weekly	Getting change
Southwest Supply		Monthly	Supplies
Apollo Paper		Monthly	Supplies
Detco Industries		Monthly	Supplies
National Sanitary	Sales	Monthly	Supplies
Voss Electric	Sales	Monthly	Supplies
Plumbing suppliers	Sales	Monthly	Supplies
Electric suppliers	Sales	Monthly	Supplies
Pool suppliers	Sales	Weekly	Supplies

Career Path: Technical Support Provider-Facility

Signatures - Review and Comment

I have reviewed this career path analysis and its attachments and find it to be an accurate description of the demands of this job.

_____ _____
Signature of Employee   Date

_____   _____ _____
Job Title of Supervisor   Signature of Supervisor   Date

_____   _____ _____
Job Title of Department Head   Signature of Department Head   Date

Comments:_____
_____
_____

The above statements are intended to describe the general nature and level of work being performed by individuals assigned to this job. They are not intended to be an exhaustive list of all responsibilities, duties, and skills required of personnel so classified in this position. This job description is subject to change by the City as the needs and requirements of the job change.

APPENDIX L

SAMPLE PAY STRUCTURES

Sample Proposed System

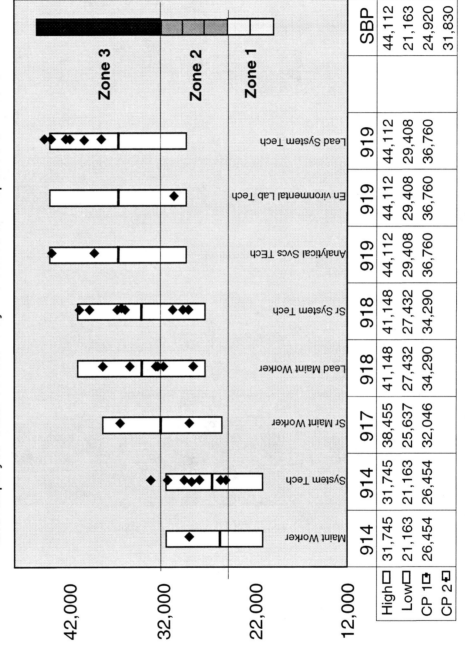

Sample Proposed System
SBP Group 1

Proposed Skill Zones

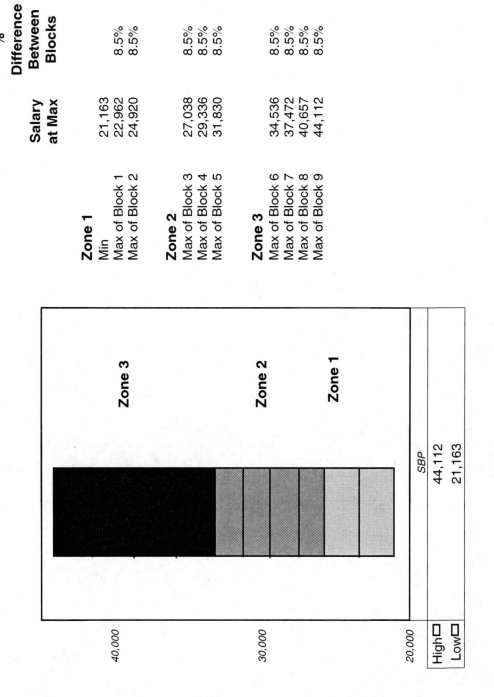

	Salary at Max	% Difference Between Blocks
Zone 1		
Min	21,163	
Max of Block 1	22,962	8.5%
Max of Block 2	24,920	8.5%
Zone 2		
Max of Block 3	27,038	8.5%
Max of Block 4	29,336	8.5%
Max of Block 5	31,830	8.5%
Zone 3		
Max of Block 6	34,536	8.5%
Max of Block 7	37,472	8.5%
Max of Block 8	40,657	8.5%
Max of Block 9	44,112	8.5%

Appendix L ©Copyright 2003, 2004 - All rights reserved - The Waters Consulting Group, Inc

APPENDIX M

SAMPLE POLICY AND ADMINISTRATION STRUCTURES

Skill-based Pay Policy And Procedures

PHILOSOPHY

The general pay philosophy of the Organization is to provide an equitable compensation system for all employees. Skill development and solid job performance are the primary factors supporting this philosophy.

The goals of the pay structure are:

1. To directly support the City's and/or department's goals by focusing on skill acquisition and development based upon actual needs identified by the Committee; and

2. To lead to a more flexible utilization of the work force as employees acquire a breadth and depth of skills across a range of operations.

This policy establishes the procedures and rules for the implementation and administration of the Learning & Results-Based Pay Pilot. Employee pay will be based on the level of training, skills, and certifications possessed and how they demonstrate/translate those skills to their performance.

ROLES AND RESPONSIBILITIES OF SYSTEM ADMINISTRATORS

The administration of the Learning and Results-Based Pay Pilot is shared under the direction of the Director of Human Resources and the Director of each Pilot Department. The supervisors and employees have important roles in making the Organization's Learning and Results-Based Pay Pilot successful.

1. The Director of HR (or designee) is responsible for the following:

    1.1. Communicating Skill-based pay issues with the Department Program Manager (Department HR Coordinator, if applicable) and/or Department Supervisor and the Department Director.

    1.2. Conducting annual salary surveys to adjust the salary structure as a percent of the cost of labor movement. Updating the salary schedule, as necessary.

    1.3. Monitoring measurement of employees' skill development submitted by the Department Director.

    1.4. Having final approval for all slotting of current employees and new hires into pay system.

    1.5. Provide ongoing oversight to ensure process is equitable and administered effectively.

    1.6. Inputting and tracking employees' pay increases based on performance and skill acquisition.

This is a sample of a working document. Each organization's Policy/Administration guidelines will vary.

Skill-based Pay Policy And Procedures

    1.7. Supporting the department with training coordination and funding.

    1.8. Maintaining responsibility for related issues connected to the Learning and Results-Based Pay Pilot.

2. The Department Director, through the Department Program Manager or Supervisor, is responsible for:

   2.1. Reviewing and finalizing changes and updates of Learning and Results-Based Pay related documents. Final copies of all documents will be presented to HR for their approval.

   2.2. Monitoring and funding their department's training.

   2.3. Monitoring movement through skill zones.

   2.4. Approving assessments of employees' skills as needed.

   2.5. Developing annual salary projections based on estimated employee skill acquisition.

   2.6. Certifying employee performance and skill acquisition pay increases.

   2.7. Ensuring process is equitable and administered effectively.

3. The Department Supervisor(s) and/or Department Program Manager are responsible for the constant improvement of their employees and overseeing employees' participation in the Learning and Results-Based Pay Program. These activities include:

   3.1. Managing the employee evaluation process and the Performance Evaluation Instrument.

   3.2. Conducting assessments of employees' skills as needed.

   3.3. Reviewing employee skills completion documentation for accuracy, validity, and completeness.

   3.4. Selecting, developing and coordinating training.

   3.5. Developing a projected training plan and budget.

   3.6. Conducting a mid-year and year-end review of employees' performance and skill zone requirements; determining appropriate pay increase. Completing the appropriate documentation, sending it to the Director for approval and, finally, to Human Resources for tracking and compensation.

   3.7. Meeting with their employees a minimum of every six months to review the employees' performance, skill development and progression, coaching the employee, and resolving any other issues their employees may have pertaining to the program.

This is a sample of a working document. Each organization's Policy/Administration guidelines will vary.

Skill-based Pay Policy And Procedures

- 3.8. Scheduling training and development time for employees to fulfill skill acquisition requirements, and scheduling other employees to fill in for the employees who are scheduled for training or assessments.
- 3.9. Regularly communicating to employees the importance of the program and updating them on any overall program changes.
- 3.10. Acting as an assessor when required.
- 3.11. Motivating all employees in their individual participation in the program.

4. The employee is ultimately responsible for their career development and the timely movement through skill zones. This includes:
   - 4.1. Reviewing and verifying the accuracy of their completed skills.
   - 4.2. Discussing their progress and performance every six months with their supervisor.
   - 4.3. Submitting all required original certifications/verification forms to the Department Program Manager and/or Supervisor when they are received.
   - 4.4. Signing up for training, properly scheduling with supervisor, and attending all regularly scheduled required classes.
   - 4.5. Participating in all scheduled skill assessments.

COMPENSATION AND PAY INCREASES

Pay increases are earned by the employee and requested, recommended and justified by the Department Director. The amount of the pay increase for each skill zone can be found in the City's Skill Zone Table for each job.

PAY INCREASE COMPONENTS:
All pilot employees will no longer be evaluated at their anniversary date, but will be evaluated every six months (includes a mid-year and year-end review). The mid-year review will be in December; the year-end review will be in June.

An employee's pay increase is based on three components: performance evaluation, skill progression, and skill attainment. (described in detail below).

The reviews must be completed by the supervisor, reviewed by the Department Director, and approved by Human Resources by June 15th and December 15th for inclusion in the employee's official personnel file with the *Personnel Status Report (PSR)*. Pay increases will not be given until Human Resources has approved the reviews.

Pay Increase Components:

This is a sample of a working document. Each organization's Policy/Administration guidelines will vary.

Skill-based Pay Policy And Procedures

1. Performance Evaluation – evaluates the core competencies and performance behaviors necessary for effective job performance. An employee may receive an associated annual pay increase for receiving a "meets expectations" or higher on the this component.
2. Skill Progression Evaluation – evaluates whether the employee has progressed in obtaining skills. An employee may receive an associated annual pay increase for receiving a "meets expectations" or higher on the this component.
3. Skill Zone Attainment – evaluates whether the employee has successfully completed a skill zone within the six month period. Once an employee "completes" a new skill zone, their pay will move to the minimum of the next higher skill zone (see the City's Skill Zone Table for the associated pay increase).

An employee must receive a "meets expectations" or higher on their performance evaluation to be eligible for the skill progression pay increase and the pay increase associated with completing a skill zone. An employee who does not "meet expectations" on the their performance evaluation must be reevaluated in six months and receive a "meets expectations" or higher on the next performance evaluation prior to obtaining the skill progression and skill zone attainment pay increase.

Each Pay Increase Component has an associated rating scale and pay increase percentage as follows:
1. <u>Performance Evaluation</u>
   - Exceeds expectations = 2%
   - Meets expectations = 1%
   - Does not meet expectations = 0%

2. <u>Skill Progression Evaluation</u>
   - Meets expectations = 2%
   - Does not meet expectations = 0%

3. <u>Skill Zone Attainment</u>
   - Completes a new skill zone = see the City's Skill Zone Table for associated pay increase
   - Does not complete a new skill zone = 0%

Human Resources reserves the right to determine what General Wage Increase, if any, will be obtained by the pilot jobs based on market analysis.

PAY INCREASE PROCESS:

Still need to define what would be the most effective process b/ dept. and HR, what documentation needs to be completed, who needs to sign-off on what, etc. How we translate skill certifications into semi/annual pay increases.

This is a sample of a working document. Each organization's Policy/Administration guidelines will vary.

Skill-based Pay Policy And Procedures

MONITORING MOVEMENT THROUGH SKILL ZONES

The Department Program Manager and/or Department Supervisor will monitor an employee's progress through the skill zones. The City's Skill Zone Table and the Certification Manual determines the requirements for all job classifications. All documentation for the completion of the skills will be the certification forms and training certificates that are kept in the Department Program Manager/Supervisor's Office. Copies will be submitted to Human Resources for verification.

All salary increases are effective at the beginning of the nearest pay period.

Employees are not eligible to move out of their current skill-based pay zone until all requirements for that zone have been met. Once they are met, the employee will receive a "skill zone attainment" pay increase at their next six month evaluation period provided they have "met expectations" on their most recent Performance Evaluation.

CRITERIA FOR MOVEMENT TO THE NEXT SKILL ZONE:

An employee is eligible to move to the next higher skill zone when she or he meets the following criteria:

1. **"Meets Expectations" Rating or higher on their most recent Performance Evaluation.** The completed and approved Performance Evaluation with a "meets expectations" or higher serves as sufficient documentation that an employee has fulfilled this requirement.

2. **Completion of the time requirement** by December 15th or June 15th. The time requirement for each skill zone is stated in the Skill Zone Table.

3. **Completion of skills within the Skill Zone.** Corroboration from the Department Director that the employee is certified for all the skills as defined in the respective skill zone.

VERIFICATION FOR MOVEMENT TO THE NEXT SKILL ZONE:

Employee progression through the skill zones and training requirements are documented in the following manner:

1. *Internal Training Verification:* The *Class Data Sheet* with the required signature(s) will fulfill the certification and documentation requirement.

2. *External Training Verification:* Certificates or other appropriate documentation issued by the classes that have been approved by Program Manager and/or Supervisor, or official transcripts received will fulfill the certification and documentation requirement.

3. *Technical Skill Verification:*

   Every skill must be assessed to the criteria as written in the certification manual for that skill. Once an employee has become competent in a skill, he or she must verify competency through an assessment process (demonstration). Successful

This is a sample of a working document. Each organization's Policy/Administration guidelines will vary.

Skill-based Pay Policy And Procedures

assessment (mastery) of the skill, in accordance with defined standards, gives the employee credit for that skill. The employee verification process will be as follows:

3.1. Employee requests an assessment from the supervisor and/or designee.

3.2. The Supervisor or another assessor arranges an assessment in accordance with the standards defined in the Certification Manual.

- The assessment must include at least one supervisor as an assessor.

3.3. The employee demonstrates the skill for the assessors and is evaluated.

- The demonstration may be either on-the-job or in a designated training area; however, at least one of the two demonstrations for an assessment must be on-the-job.

3.4. On the *Skill Verification Form,* the assessor marks "mastery" or "non-mastery". The decision by the assessors must be unanimous as to the employee having mastered the skill, or the employee is marked as "non-mastery" for that skill.

3.5. All assessors and the employee are required to sign the form.

- If the employee is marked "non-mastery" for that skill, the reason why must be noted in the comments section of the form.

- If not verified for the skill, the employee may reschedule an assessment after 30 calendar days. See "Recertification" section for action if the employee is unable to demonstrate the skills in the allotted time frame.

- If the employee is verified for the skill, the original *Skill Verification Form* is kept in the Department Program Manager or Supervisor's Office; a copy of the form is given to the employee.

- If at any point during the demonstration the skill is not performed by the employee to the required safety standards, the demonstration is to be stopped immediately and the employee's skill verification form is marked as "non-mastery".

3.6. An assessor's duty is to not only verify that the employee can perform the skill safely, accurately, consistently, and effectively, but also coach an employee who is does not demonstrate the skill to the required criteria. <u>After the demonstration and the verification form is completed</u>, it is the duty of the assessors to provide constructive feedback (i.e. coaching) to the employee receiving the "non-mastery".

3.7. An employee will receive a 2% increase for completing a skill zone if their current pay is above the minimum pay level of next highest skill zone.

TRAINING

TRAINING FUNDS:

This is a sample of a working document. Each organization's Policy/Administration guidelines will vary.

Skill-based Pay Policy And Procedures

Training funds for the pilot projects will be determined and approved through the budget process. The Department Supervisor will be responsible for developing a training plan and projected training costs for the upcoming year. This plan will be submitted along with the department's budget submission. Once funds are approved, Human Resources will work with the Department to finalize allocated training funds and training plan.

TRACKING TRAINING NEEDS:

It will be the responsibility of the Department Supervisor and/or Program Manager to track the training needs for each employee involved in the pilot. This includes ongoing dialogue regarding training needed, scheduling necessary training for the employee (on-the-job or classroom), and the certification demonstration.

Human Resources will provide necessary technical support with the tracking software.

CERTIFICATION EXAMS

An employee is required to pay for a certification exam and upon receiving the certification will be reimbursed for the cost of obtaining that certification. The employee will not be reimbursed for unsuccessful attempts to obtain required certifications. The Department will pay for renewals but not for re-certification of suspended or revoked licenses.

OTHER REIMBURSEMENTS

Mileage will not be reimbursed when a City vehicle is available, and mileage will only be reimbursed with prior approval of the employee's supervisor. Meals will not be reimbursed unless there is an approved overnight stay.

UTILITIES: STIPEND PAY

As the operation necessitates and as the employee demonstrates the necessary skills, the Utilities Director may temporarily assign a limited number of employees in the "Chief Waterworks Operator" function who have achieved 1-5 skill zones. Employees designated as a "Chief Waterworks Operator" will receive an annual stipend equivalent to $2400 for as long as they are performing in that capacity. The Department Director has the discretion to rotate employees in this function as the operation necessitates or based on the employee's performance.

MINIMUM SKILL ZONE REQUIREMENT

The employee is ultimately responsible for their own career development and timely movement through the mandatory skill zones.

An employee is required to reach a minimum skill zone within a designated period of time (as stated in the City's Skill Zone Table). Any employee who does not meet this

Skill-based Pay Policy And Procedures

requirement or has indicated in writing that they are not willing to achieve the minimum skill zone will be subject to administrative action, up to and including termination.

Factors that may be considered in determining the appropriate administrative response include the employee's work history, length of employment (permanent employee versus non-permanent employee), current job performance, past performance evaluations and the existence of past disciplinary action.

RECERTIFICATION

An employee's pay will be lowered to the maximum pay level of the skill zone they are able to demonstrate if the employee loses a certification, a license, is unable to certify for in skill in the allotted timeframe, or does not recertify in a required skill as identified in the Certification Manual. An employee is responsible for maintaining all licenses, certifications and skills required by the Learning and Results-Based Pay Program. An employee must also follow all rules, regulations, and safety procedures required for any verified skill, whether federal, state, or local government. In addition, a supervisor may deem it necessary to recommend an employee for reassessment for a Skill-based requirement upon repeated or gross sub-par performance, or a serious safety violation.

TRANSITION EMPLOYEES

Transition employees are all current employees in the Learning and Results-Based Pay Program who have been placed into the Program from the regular step compensation system that was in effect before the pilot.

1. An initial assessment of current employees' skills will be completed by an internal department committee (consisting of a combination of the employee's supervisor, department supervisors/manager, and department director, or designee). The committee will rate each employee's skills, and the employee will be assigned to the skill zone and pay level commensurate to the skill assessment. Human Resources will review placements to ensure consistent application, thoroughness of documentation and identification of trends.

2. All current employees must fill in any "gaps" in prior zones before advancing in the Plan by verifying for all skills where they were assessed to not have "mastered", beginning with Skill Zone 1 and continuing through their present Skill Zone. Once the gaps are filled in, the employee will move through the Program as required by the Plan.

3. All current employees whose pay is above the pay rate in their designated skill zone must demonstrate all skills up to their present skill zone prior to advancing to the next skill zone. Their pay will be frozen until they demonstrate all the skills up to their present skill zone (i.e., they will receive no additional merit increase).

4. Employees initially placed in the program will not be limited by time restrictions outlined in the Certification Manual. This will allow them to fulfill prior skill requirements as quickly as possible and move out of transition status. Once an

Skill-based Pay Policy And Procedures

employee has moved out of transition status, the employee will move through the Program as required by the Plan.

5. The time allotted for obtaining missing skills (gaps) will be double the time outlined for the skill zones in the Skill Zone Table. An employee who does not obtain the required missing skills in the allotted time will have their pay lowered and frozen to the maximum pay level of the skill zone they demonstrate.

NEW EMPLOYEES

New employees are new hires to the Organization or current employees who transfer to the pilot classification. A new employee who is either a new hire or a transfer to the pilot job classification is required to meet the terms of his or her *Skill-based Pay/Skill Zone Placement and Conditions document*, that was decided at the beginning of the six months probationary period. Any employee who does not meet the terms of this notice will have his or her pay adjusted to the level where their skills are determined to be at that point in time. The employee will then move through the Program as required by the Certification Manual, fulfilling all skill, time, and evaluation requirements.

Human Resources, in partnership with the Department, will determine what skill zone and associated pay level the new employee is to be hired.

- There is a need upon bringing a new employee into the Skill-based Pay Program that he or she be assessed and placed as fairly and accurately as possible into a skill zone before hiring.
- Before an offer of employment is made, the candidate(s) will complete a pre-employment review (based on the certification requirements) to determine the most appropriate skill zone to initially place them. The review will include participation of the Department Program Manager, the Supervisor, and a committee of hiring decision-makers. The employee will be placed at the appropriate skill zone for a six month period.
- After being hired and before the six-month probationary period is complete, the new employee will fill in any gaps in The organization specific requirements that would bring the new employee in-line with the designated skill zone requirements he or she was initially hired with.
- At the end of the six-month probationary period, the new employee will then be given a final placement into the Program. His/her placement will be based on the level of skills they demonstrate. He or she, from then on, will move through the Program as required by the Plan.
- If the employee's skills are below the original assessment, the employee will be placed at the maximum pay level of skill zone they demonstrate. If the employee's skills are above the original assessment, the employee will be placed at the minimum pay level of the skill zone they demonstrate (once they complete the timegate for their current skill zone).
- The second six-month time requirement is waived so that the wait for the second evaluation is not longer than six months (to integrate into the December and June evaluation cycle). To be eligible for this one time event, the employee must fulfill all required skill and evaluation requirements.

This is a sample of a working document. Each organization's Policy/Administration guidelines will vary.

Skill-based Pay Policy And Procedures

TRANSITION OUT OF THE PILOT

Should the decision be made in the future to eliminate the Learning & Results Based Pay Pilot Program and return to the City's current classification and pay system, an employee's compensation shall revert to that which would have been paid if the employee had not been included in the pilot program. The employee will be placed into the appropriate class specification. Employees would revert to their former anniversary dates.

This is a sample of a working document. Each organization's Policy/Administration guidelines will vary.

FORMS FOR THE ADMINISTRATION OF THE PAY SYSTEM

LEARNING & RESULTS-BASED PAY JOBS

The Learning and Results-Based Pay jobs have been defined by a career path oriented class specification. A manual describing the skill requirements and certification procedures has been prepared for each job. A Skill Zone Table has been established for each career path that outlines the training requirements and skills for each skill zone.

Skill zones are separated by time requirements, which provide the employee time to use newly acquired skills and allow the City to benefit from the time and effort spent on the employee's skill development. The time requirements are established as years of work experience in the specific position (or related position) required for movement into the next skill zone.

DEVELOPMENT OF PAY RANGES FOR EACH SKILL ZONE:
The challenge in the design process is to appropriately link the market data to the skill zones identified by the Committee. The following information provides a first step in making the link between the market and the Skill-based pay plan.

- A skill zone is the measurement unit of value-added contribution by an employee to the work process.

- Skill zones were identified by the Committee.

- The pay attached to a skill zone represents a blend between the market data and the value of the skills to the City. As an employee completes more skill zones, the potential contribution by the employee increases, and is reflected through corresponding increases in pay. The individual pay attached to each skill zone have been designed to capture the market data for the entry level and the senior level positions.

- The minimum time required for an individual to remain in each skill zone is presented.

Below is specific information relating to each Learning and Results-Based Pay job, including:

1. Market analysis of the job
2. Class Specification
3. Skill Zone Table (includes skill zones, skills, and time requirements)
4. Certification Manual

* need to add information

This is a sample of a working document. Each organization's Policy/Administration guidelines will vary.

Skill-based Pay Policy And Procedures

MARKET ANALYSIS

Market data has been obtained from IPAC for the entry level and the senior levels of the pilot jobs. The data has been aged to July 1, 2002, using 3% to define market movement. Job descriptions were obtained from the participating cities to aid in job matching. To facilitate the review process, the minimum education and experience requirements and the certification requirements have been extracted from the job descriptions and added to the market data for each job.

The following summarizes the market data for each job:

04-37 Water Treatment Operator I
Entry Level Position

Minimum Education:	In general, most positions require a high school diploma.
Minimum Education:	Requirements vary from no experience to 3 to 5 years.
Certification Requirements:	Most positions identify either a Class IV or a Class III requirement.
Average Pay Range	$22,163 to $34,295
Average Salary	$26,792

04-38 Sr. Water Treatment Operator
Senior Level Position

Minimum Education:	In general, most positions require a high school diploma and some level of additional training.
Minimum Education:	Requirements vary from 6 months experience to 3 to 5 years.
Certification Requirements:	Most positions identify either a Class II or a Class I requirement.
Average Pay Range	$27,922 to $42,725
Average Salary	$35,067

This is a sample of a working document. Each organization's Policy/Administration guidelines will vary.

FORMS FOR THE ADMINISTRATION OF THE PAY SYSTEM

- Will need to add other pilot group's market data, class specs, skill zone tables and certification manuals

Skill-Based Pay Governing Policy

INTRODUCTION

The general pay philosophy of the organization is to provide an equitable compensation system for all employees. Skill development and solid job performance are the primary factors supporting this philosophy.

The purpose of the Skill-Based Pay plans is to attract, retain and motivate employees through the payment of financial compensation commensurate with the individual's ability, responsibility and contribution to attainment of the organization goals. From an individual standpoint, the program is designed to inspire the development of skill attainment for each employee and to recognize and reward outstanding performance and value to the organization. From an organizational perspective, the Skill-based Pay plan is designed to achieve both internal and external pay equity.

I. POLICY SUMMARY

Skill-based pay varies from traditional compensation methodologies in that it is person-based rather than job based. In a job-based compensation system, the nature of the work and the value of the job is the focus of determining pay decisions for individual employees. In a Skill-based Pay plan, employees are encouraged and rewarded for increasing their knowledge, skills and competency, and their ability to contribute to the attainment of organizational or department goals.

The organization's Water and Wastewater Utilities Department has a commitment to increased productivity and reduced staffing by developing a more flexible, team-oriented approach to operations. When applying their philosophy, employee versatility and skill level becomes an important factor in the achievement of the department's mission. Skill-based Pay provides a method of defining the department's skill needs and establishes a method of encouraging employees to meet those needs by acquiring additional skills and competencies. The system gives employees the ability to grow and develop without the limitations of traditional job descriptions and the hierarchy they tend to create.

II. STRUCTURE OF THE SKILL-BASED PAY PLAN

A. This policy establishes the procedures and rules for the Skill-based Pay plan for the organization's Water and Wastewater Utility employees who complete specific training and demonstrate a variety of skills that apply to the Municipal Water Utility Industry. Employee pay will be based on the level of training, skills, and certifications possessed.

B. Instead of a traditional, hierarchical job structure based upon narrowly defined jobs, this plan utilizes a broadbanding approach that combines several former job titles into two broader career paths. Employee teams, selected to represent six key groups of positions, developed an inventory of skills associated with each career path, ranging from basic to highly advanced. In addition, opportunities for

Skill-Based Pay Governing Policy

cross training in skills associated with related areas of expertise were developed. Each skill was defined and ranked to assure that as an employee meets the requirement for certification in the skill, significant value will be added to the operation of the Water and Wastewater Utility Department. This is accomplished by establishing a much broader skill pool from which to perform the various tasks of the Department. The premise for this
approach is that employees will be encouraged to acquire a wider range of skills and accept broader responsibilities in order to advance through the career path.

C. Each new job has been defined by a new broader career path oriented job description. A manual describing the skill requirements and certification procedures has been prepared establishing eight skill pay zones or groups for each job. Skills have also been grouped vertically according to technical or career subjects into "tracks" in the Skill-based Pay Manual of Certification Standards. A Skill Based Table has been established for each career path that outlines the training requirements and skill zones for each zone and track. The Skill Based Tables have a Foundation and Development Track and at least one Technical Certification Track for Water or Wastewater. These skill zones and training requirements are presented in more detail in the Manual of Certification Standards.

D. The Department of Human Resources will maintain the Water and Wastewater Departments' Skill-based Pay plan. The Skill-Based Pay plan includes a schedule listing the monthly salary at the minimum and maximum of Pay Zones 1-8 for each pay grade (i.e., each pay grade is divided into eight pay zones). The *minimum* represents the minimum salary level for a new employee meeting the minimum qualifications of the jobs career definitions. The maximum of Zone 8 represents the maximum salary level for the position.

   1) Pay Zones are separated by "gates" which provide the employee time to use newly acquired skills and allow the Organization to benefit from the time and effort spent on the employee's skill development. The gates are established as years of work experience in the specific position (or related position) required for movement into the next zone. A twelve year career ladder "minimum time frame" is allocated as follows:

      | Zone 1 to Zone 2 | -- | Six (6) month gate |
      | Zone 2 to Zone 3 | -- | One (1) year gate |
      | Zone 3 to Zone 4 | -- | One (1) year gate |
      | Zone 4 to Zone 5 | -- | One (1) year gate |
      | Zone 5 to Zone 6 | -- | Two (2) year gate |
      | Zone 6 to Zone 7 | -- | Two (2) year gate |
      | Zone 7 to Zone 8 | -- | Two (2) year gate |
      | Zone 8 | -- | Three (3) year gate |

Suggestion: Part-time employees use the same Skill Zone Plans as full-time employees of the same job title. Employees who fail to meet the skill zone requirements are ineligible for raises tied to individual movement within the range.

This is a sample of a working document. Each organization's Policy/Administration guidelines will vary.

Skill-Based Pay Governing Policy

III. COMPENSATION PLICY RECOMMENDATIONS

A. Advancement through the pay plan will be based on the employee's performance review and completion of the requirements outlined in the Manual of Certification Standards. Employees must complete all certification requirements in the technical skills to get credit for the skill for compensation purposes. The employee is required to fully complete the skills listed at each level, as well as the time requirement for the level, before attempting to certify the skills in a higher level. Employees in some positions may be required to complete multiple technical tracks to advance past a pre-established point in a pay grade. These requirements are clearly laid out in the Skill Zone Table.

B. Each position falls into a specific classification and pay range, and the pay ranges are divided into eight pay zones associated with the eight skill zones. Employees must meet the requirements set forth in the Manual of Certification Standards for each zone of the position prior to entering the next pay zone. The pay zones are also separated by the time "gates" described above. Within each zone, requirements are grouped into two basic categories: Foundation/Developmental Training and Technical Skill Development. The department is required to monitor movement of employees through the skill zones.

C. Employee performance reviews are conducted twice a year, following an October 1st and April 1st cycle. Employees may be eligible for performance pay increases based upon their performance evaluation and completion of additional skill certification requirements. It is important to note that performance pay increases are not automatic. The amount of the skill-based increase is allocated evenly at the appropriate review date.

D. The Water and Wastewater Department Directors may temporarily assign employees to higher level positions in order to insure continuance of work projects, supervision, etc. Persons temporarily assigned to a higher paying position are placed in a "differential pay" category effective the first full day of the change. An employee placed in a differential pay category may receive the greater of the "minimum" salary for the position or a ten-percent salary increase.

E. An employee demoted to a classification with a lower pay grade or lower maximum salary, either voluntarily or involuntarily, shall be compensated at a rate which is determined by the Water and Wastewater Department Director and the Director of Human Resources.

This is a sample of a working document. Each organization's Policy/Administration guidelines will vary.

Skill-Based Pay Governing Policy

F. An employee who moves to a new classification in the same pay grade may receive an increase in compensation with the approval of the Water and Wastewater Department Head and the Director of Human Resources if the salary falls within a higher skill zone.

G. The rate of pay of an employee reclassified to another classification in a higher pay grade may be increased by ten percent, or adjusted to the "minimum" of the new range, whichever is greater.

H. New employees meeting the minimum job requirements are hired at the "minimum" salary. There may be circumstances where a new employee offers an unusual skill level, the number of qualified applicants is lacking, or there may be market conditions or specific job duties requiring higher compensation levels, in which the employee may be offered compensation above the "minimum," contingent upon available funding as directed below:

1) Starting salaries above the minimum within the first two zones require the approval of the Water and Wastewater Department Director.

2) Starting salaries within the third Zone up to the maximum of Zone four require the approval of the Director of Water and Wastewater Utilities and the Director of Human Resources.

3) Starting salaries at or above Zone four require the approval of the Director of Water and Wastewater Utilities, Director of Human Resources and an Assistant Organization Manager.

4) A position may be temporarily filled at a pay rate below the "minimum" when qualified applicants are not available or when the applicant does not meet the minimum requirements of the job. This represents the *training rate* for employees who lack the skills for a particular position, but who are able and willing to develop these skills on the job. Employees hired at the training rate are increased to the "minimum" pay rate once they gain the minimum skills and qualifications required for the position.

IV. CLASSIFICATION SYSTEM

Several beginning and advanced level job classes were combined into single job classes (i.e., former Service Provider and Sr. Service Provider were combined with other position titles into a single Water Utility Operator job class). Pay zones 1 – 6 will be considered the entry to intermediate level, while pay zones seven and eight will be advanced level positions. Advancement past certain designated pay zones may require an advanced level vacancy and therefore an interview and promotion process for those employees moving past the designated pay zone.

Skill-Based Pay Governing Policy

SYSTEM ADMINISTRATION

A. The administration of the Skill-based Pay plan for the Water and Wastewater Utility is shared under the direction of the Director of Human Resources and the Water and Wastewater Department Director. The HR Director is responsible for the following:
   1) Communication of skill-based pay issues with the workforce (may include training others, communicating with employee groups, etc.).
   2) Conducting salary surveys annually to adjust the salary structure as a percent of the cost of labor movement.
   3) Updating the system annually.
   4) Working with the Water and Wastewater Utility Department to change and update skill zones as the system develops
   5) Monitoring measurement of employees' skill development submitted by the Water and Wastewater Utility Department.
   6) Having final approval for all slotting of new hires into pay zones
   7) Being responsible for related issues connected to the Skill-based Pay plan.

B. The Water and Wastewater Utility Department shares in the responsibility for administration of the Skill-based Pay plan. The department's responsibilities include:
   1) Submitting in writing changes and updates of skill zones to Human Resources.
   2) Selecting, developing, monitoring and funding their department's training.
   3) Managing their department's employee evaluation process (Progress Reviews) including entering Progress Review data into the PAMS System.
   4) Monitoring movement through skill zones.
   5) Conducting certification and re-certification of employees' skills as needed.

VI. CERTIFICATION AND REVIEW PROCESS

A. Within each zone, skills are grouped into two basic categories. Employee progression through the skill zones and training requirements is evaluated in the following manner:

   1) 1.*Foundation and Development Training:* When employees receive training through the organization's Supervisory Development Program or training from an outside source, they will receive a "certificate" from the instructor or institution indicating the training has been completed. This serves as documentation for completing the formal training course, and should include the employee's name, date of training, instructor's name and signature, how many training hours completed and topic of the training. Training hours must be pre-approved by the department director (Form A attached). The documentation will be maintained within the department's files and are subject to audit by the Human Resources staff.

   2) *Technical Skills:* When an employee has become competent in a skill zone, they may "certify" in that skill. This gives the employee credit for the skill zone. This certification is used to establish the employees pay. To certify,

Skill-Based Pay Governing Policy

an employee must inform their supervisor they are ready to test for the skill zone. Two supervisors or one supervisor and one lead person in the same position are required to evaluate the employee as they demonstrate the skills necessary to certify for the skill zone. The supervisor and the Department Head are required to document the certification or failure to certify. If the employee satisfies the certification requirement, the supervisor fills out the certification form and furnishes a copy to the employee, the department and maintains a copy for the employee's file. This form includes the employee's name, position, date of testing, the supervisors' names and signatures, and the skill zone tested (see attached form A). Again, this document will be maintained within the departments' files and is subject to audit by the Human Resources staff. Failure to successfully complete the certification requirements requires the employee to wait a minimum of 30 days before testing again.

3) *On-The-Job-Performance (Progress Review):* The completed and approved Progress Review form (with a "good" rating, or higher) serves as sufficient documentation an employee has fulfilled this requirement. This document must be submitted to Human Resources for inclusion in the employee's official personnel file. The standard status change forms must also be submitted to Human Resources for processing and inclusion in the employee's personnel file if a skill-based merit increase is involved.

B. Monitoring Skill Based Pay Plan Movement
The department will monitor an employee's progress through skill zones by using the Skill Zone Table. Using the Skill Zone Table as a spreadsheet, the supervisor will put the employee's name at the top of the first page and highlight those skill zones completed. The documentation of the completion of the skills will be the certification forms and training certificates that are kept in the employees training file.

A hard copy of an updated spreadsheet or worksheet must be maintained in each department and made available for review by Human Resources staff members during on-site audits. The hard copy must be signed and dated by the employee's supervisor.

1) Eligibility for Skill-Based Pay - When a pay increase involves movement into the next higher pay zone, the employee must meet the following criteria:
   - No disciplinary actions pending
   - An overall "good" rating on the employee's performance appraisal (a score of 5 and above)
   - Certification from the Water and Wastewater Utility Department Director that the employee has satisfied the criteria as defined in the respective pay zone

   The rate of an employee's movement through a pay range is dependent upon individual performance, skill development, and the time requirements established for the respective zone.

Skill-Based Pay Governing Policy

A total of two Progress Reviews per employee are administered annually. The amount of the skill-based increase is allocated evenly at the appropriate review date. All departments utilize an October 1st/April 1st review cycle.

Employees receiving a Progress Review rating of less than 5.0 will not be eligible for a pay increase during the respective review period, regardless of skill zones and training that have been completed.

Employees are not eligible to move out of their current pay zone until all requirements have been met. The requirements include both skill zones and years of experience.

Performance pay increases are NOT automatic. Increases must be earned by the employee and requested, recommended and justified by the Water and Wastewater Utility Department Director. Awarding or withholding performance pay is a management prerogative and responsibility.

All salary increases are effective at the beginning of the nearest pay period.

2) Demotions - An employee who is either voluntarily or involuntarily demoted to a classification with a lower pay range or lower maximum salary shall be compensated at a rate determined by the Director of Water and Wastewater Utilities and the Director of Human Resources. The salary for employees receiving voluntary or involuntary demotions must be placed below the maximum pay level of the assigned pay range.

Skill-Based Pay Policy and Administration Guidelines

POLICY SUMMARY

There are three categories of employees: full-time regular, part-time and temporary. The plan utilizes a BroadBanding approach, which requires an extensive change in responsibilities/duties for an employee to move into a new job class or pay range.

PAY RANGES

Each position falls into a specific classification and pay range, and the pay ranges are divided into four zones. Employees are required to meet specific criteria documented in the zoning plan PRIOR to entering the next pay zone for their classification's pay range. The pay zones are separated by "gates" which provide the employee time to use newly acquired skills and allows the Organization to benefit from the time and effort spent on the employee's skill development. The gates are based on years of work experience. A twelve year career ladder "minimum time frame" exists. Within each zone, skills are grouped into four basic categories: formal training, cross training, on-the-job performance (Progress Reviews) and certification/education. Each category has an assigned weight based upon its departmental impact. Departments are required to monitor movement of employees through the zoning plans.

Personnel Services maintains the Organization's pay plan which lists salaries by pay grade. New employees are hired at the "calculated minimum" of the approved salary grade. There may be circumstances where a new employee may be offered compensation above the minimum, contingent upon available funding. Examples include an exceptional skill level offered by the employee, tight market conditions, or the existence of a limited number of qualified applicants. In these cases, the appropriate zone associated with the salary request dictates the level of management approval required.

Employees may be eligible for performance pay increases based upon their performance evaluation. Performance pay increases are not automatic. A total of two Progress Reviews will be administered annually for each employee. The amount of the skill-based increase is allocated evenly at the appropriate review date. All departments shall utilize an October 1st/April 1st review cycle.

Department Directors may temporarily assign employees to higher level positions in order to insure continuance of work projects, supervision, etc. Persons temporarily assigned to a higher paying position are placed in a "differential pay" category effective the first full day of the change. Employees placed in a differential pay category receive the greater of the "calculated minimum" salary for the position or a ten-percent salary increase, unless otherwise authorized by the Organization Manager. An employee either voluntarily or involuntarily demoted to a classification with a lower pay grade or lower maximum salary shall be compensated at a rate which is determined by the affected employee's Department Director and the Director of Personnel Services.

CLASSIFICATION SYSTEM

EMPLOYEE STATUS

There are three categories of employee status:

1. Full time regular employees are scheduled to work forty hours per week in regular positions (NOTE: Full-time Fire civil service personnel work a total of 56 hours per a seven consecutive day work cycle and 112 hours per a fourteen consecutive day work cycle).

2. Part time employees work less than thirty-five hours per week. The number of hours a part-time employee works should be limited to thirty-five per week. Part-time employees working twenty or more hours per week will be eligible for the same benefits as full-time employees except for health and life insurance. Health and life insurance are not available to part-time employees regardless of the number of hours they work.

3. Part-time employees accrue benefits in proportion to the number of annual budgeted hours for that position at the following rate: at least 20 hours but not greater than 25 hours per week accrue at 62% of full-time; at least 25 but not greater than 30 hours accrue at 75% and at least 30 but not greater than 35 accrue at 87%). Accrual rates will not fluctuate between pay periods but may be adjusted on an annual basis.

4. Temporary employees work less than 1,000 hours per year and are hired for a specific job. Temporary employees are not eligible to receive holiday pay and are not eligible for benefits available to full-time and part-time employees. At a total of 999 hours, temporary employees must be terminated unless they have written authorization from the Organization Manager to continue as temporary.

JOB CLASSIFICATIONS

Personnel Services maintains the Position Classification Plan.

Exempt positions (System A) are grouped according to pay classifications which are determined by the following factors: knowledge required, experience, organizational control, human relations, planning, budget responsibility, authority exercised, complexity and working conditions.

Skill-Based Pay Policy and Administration Guidelines

Non-exempt (System B) position factors include knowledge required, experience, organizational control, human relations, responsibility, authority exercised, complexity and working conditions.

With BroadBanding, a job will require an extensive change in responsibilities/duties to move into a new job class or pay range. When extensive changes occur, Department Directors may submit written requests through the Organization Manager, Deputy Organization Manager or Assistant Organization Manager to Personnel Services to reclassify the current position(s). This could involve reclassifying the position to an existing job class or creating a new job class (with BroadBanding, most reclassification requests will involve reclassifying to an existing job class).
Again, it should be noted an extensive change in a position is required to move it into a higher or lower classification under BroadBanding. Position Classification Request packets are available in Personnel Services.

Personnel Services evaluates the request and makes a recommendation to the Organization Manager. The Organization Manager is the final authority for determining job classifications.

Several journey and advanced journey level job classes were combined into single job classes (i.e., former Accounting Technician and Sr. Accounting Technician were combined into a single Accounting Technician job class). Job classes with a Series 300 or Series 400 designation on the position listing are indicative of these journey/advanced journey level combinations. Both Series 300 and Series 400 job classes with the same title share the same pay grade; however, employees in Series 300 job classes may only progress to the top of Zone 3, while those in Series 400 job classes may progress to the maximum pay level of Zone 4.

SYSTEM ADMINISTRATION

The administration of the Skill-based Pay system is under the direction of the Director of Personnel Services, who is responsible for the following:

- Communication of Skill-based Pay issues with the workforce (may include training others, communicating with employee groups, etc.).
- Conducting salary surveys annually to adjust the salary structure as a percent of the cost of labor movement.
- Updating the system annually by working with individual departments to change and update skill zones as the system develops (see Section III, E, 2, a, 1-4). -Monitoring measurement of employees' skill development submitted by departments (see Section III, E, 3, a, 1-2).
- Having final approval for all slotting of new hires into zones through Zone 2 (see Section III, C).
- Being responsible for related issues connected to the skill-based system.

This is a sample of a working document. Each organization's Policy/Administration guidelines will vary.

Skill-Based Pay Policy and Administration Guidelines

Consistent with the goals of the Organization's quality initiative, departments share in the responsibility for administration of the Skill-based Pay system. The department's responsibilities include:
- Submitting in writing changes and updates of skill zones to Personnel Services.
- Selecting, developing, monitoring and funding their department's training.
- Managing their department's employee evaluation process (Progress Reviews) including entering Progress Review data into the PAMS System.
- Monitoring movement through career ladders.
- Conducting re-certification of employees' skills as needed. (i.e. specific certificates).

EMPLOYEE COMPENSATION

The general pay philosophy of the Organization of Sample is to provide an equitable compensation program for all employees. Skill development and solid job performance are the primary factors supporting this philosophy.

The purpose of the pay system is to attract, retain and motivate employees through the payment of financial compensation commensurate with the individual's ability, responsibility and contribution to the Organization's goal. From an individual standpoint, the program is designed to inspire the development and progress of each employee and to recognize and reward outstanding performance. From an organizational perspective, the pay plan is designed to achieve both internal and external pay equity.

PAY PLAN ZONES

Personnel Services maintains the pay plan. The plan includes a schedule listing the monthly salary at the minimum, the calculated minimum and maximum of Pay Zones 1-4 for each pay grade (i.e., each pay grade is divided into four zones along with the minimum salary). The calculated minimum represents the minimum salary level for a new employee meeting the minimum qualifications of the job. The maximum of Zone 4 represents the maximum salary level of the pay grade. The salary range from the minimum to the calculated minimum represents a training rate for employees not meeting the minimum qualifications for the job (see Section III, C).

Pay zones are separated by "gates" which provide the employee time to use newly acquired skills and allows the Organization to benefit from the time and effort spent on the employee's skill development. The gates are established, as years of work experience in the specific position (or related position) required for movement into the next zone. A twelve year career ladder "minimum time frame" is allocated as follows:
- Zone 1 to Zone 2 – Two (2) year gate

This is a sample of a working document. Each organization's Policy/Administration guidelines will vary.

Skill-Based Pay Policy and Administration Guidelines

- Zone 2 to Zone 3 – Three (3) year gate
- Zone 3 to Zone 4 –Three (3) year gate
- Zone 4 –Intended to last a minimum of four years; four (4) year gate.

Salaries are listed on a monthly basis for exempt and non-exempt classifications. Executive, administrative and professional employees are generally classified as exempt (System A). All others are classified as non-exempt (System B)

PART TIME EMPLOYEES

Part-time employees are paid in accordance with the same pay plan as full- time employees. (i.e. use of same zoning plans, salary schedules, etc.)

STARTING SALARY

New employees meeting the minimum job requirements are hired at the "calculated minimum" salary. There may be circumstances where a new employee offers an unusual skill level, the number of qualified applicants is lacking, or there may be market conditions or specific job duties requiring higher compensation levels, in which the employee may be offered compensation above the "calculated minimum," contingent upon available funding. Starting salaries at the training rate ("actual minimum salary") require the approval of the department director and the Director of Personnel Services.

Starting salaries above the calculated minimum within the first zone require the approval of the department director. Starting salaries within the second zone up to the maximum of Zone 2 require the approval of the department director and the Director of Personnel Services. Starting salaries at or above Zone 3 require the approval of the department director, Director of Personnel Services and the appropriate Assistant Organization Manager or Deputy Organization Manager.

A position may be temporarily filled at a pay rate below the "calculated minimum" when qualified applicants are not available or when the applicant does not meet the minimum requirements of the job. This represents the training rate for employees who lack the skills for a particular position, but who are able and willing to develop these skills on the job. Employees hired at the training rate are increased to the "calculated minimum" pay rate once they gain the skills and qualifications required for the position.

PAY ZONE GUIDELINES

Pay zones distinguish:

- Positions within the same or comparable classifications which have inherently higher levels of responsibility

Skill-Based Pay Policy and Administration Guidelines

- Positions which require certification or proficiency above comparable positions or other positions within the same classification
- Positions which routinely serve as lead worker for other comparably classified employees
- Positions which, due to market conditions or internal job equity, require starting salaries above those established for the range or for which do not support paying employees above a certain point within the ranges, or
- Positions for which market data or internal job equity do not support paying salaries as high as the established maximum of the range.

NOTE: Meeting the development criteria does not entitle an employee to enter the next pay zone, but only makes the employee eligible.

Part-time employees use the same Zoning Plans as full-time employees of the same job title. Employees who fail to meet the zoning requirements are ineligible for raises tied to individual movement within the range.

CERTIFICATION AND REIVEW PROCESS

Within each zone, skills are grouped into four basic categories. Employee progression through the four skill zones is evaluated in the following manner:

Formal Training: When employees receive WIN! Training or receive training from an outside source, they will receive a "certificate" from the instructor indicating the training has been completed. This serves as documentation for completing the formal training course, and should include the employee's name, date of training, instructor's name and signature, how many training hours completed and topic of the training. Training hours must be pre-approved by the employee's department director. The documentation will be maintained within the departments' files and are subject to audit by Personnel Services' staff.

Cross Training: When an employee cross-trains in another position, the department is required to document the training. This form includes the employee's name, date of training, supervisor's name and signature, how many training hours completed, and position and duties trained upon. Again, this document will be maintained within the departments' files and is subject to audit by Personnel Services' staff.

On-The-Job-Performance: The completed and approved Progress Review form (with a "good" rating or higher) serves as sufficient documentation an employee has fulfilled this requirement. This document must be submitted to Personnel Services for inclusion in the employee's official personnel file. The standard status change forms must also be submitted to Personnel Services for processing and inclusion in the employee's personnel file if a skill-based merit increase is involved.

This is a sample of a working document. Each organization's Policy/Administration guidelines will vary.

Skill-Based Pay Policy and Administration Guidelines

Certification/Education: A copy of the certificate, license, or transcript indicating completion of certification or education is furnished to the employee's department head as documentation of accomplishments of skills in the zone. Once again, this documentation will be maintained within the department's files and is subject to audit by Personnel Services' staff.

Each category has an assigned weight based on its departmental impact. Original weights were determined by each department's management and staff. Any changes to the weights must be approved by Personnel Services. It should be noted the On-The-Job-Performance (Progress Review) category is mandated at a minimum weight of 50%. Personnel Services maintains the zoning plans for each job class. The zoning plans are aligned to promote equity across departmental lines [i.e., alignment of training and cross-training hours, minimum 50% weight for the On-The-Job-Performance (Progress Review) category]. The zoning plans are recorded in Personnel Services on standardized forms (see Exhibit II) based upon input received from the Organization department.

MONITORING CAREER LADDER MOVEMENT

Departments will monitor movement of employees through the zoning plans:

Spreadsheet: A computerized spreadsheet for monitoring movement is available for departments who have the capability to utilize Excel. Specifically, the supervisor may enter into the spreadsheet the date of the Progress Review and the percent of each skill zone completed at the time of the review. The spreadsheet maintains a record of the percent completed. When all skill zones in a zone are completed, the spreadsheet indicates this by showing the word "completed" next to the zone.

Worksheet: A handwritten worksheet is available for those departments without access to Excel. The supervisor may enter the data of the Progress Review, and the percent of each skill zone completed at the time of the review, and calculate by hand how much of each skill zone has been completed. A hard copy of the completed spreadsheet or worksheet must be maintained in each department and made available for review by Personnel Services' staff members during on-site audits. The hard copy must be signed and dated by the employee's supervisor.

CALCULATING SKILL-BASED PAY

When a merit increase involves movement into the next higher pay zone, the employee must meet the following criteria:
- No disciplinary actions pending.
- An overall "Good" rating on the employee's performance appraisal (a score of 5 and above).

This is a sample of a working document. Each organization's Policy/Administration guidelines will vary.

Skill-Based Pay Policy and Administration Guidelines

- Certification from the Department Director the employee has satisfied the criteria as defined in the respective zoning plan.

Classified employees participate in the Skill-based Pay system. Part-time employees use the same Zoning Plans as full-time employees with the same job title.

The rate of an employee's movement through a pay range is dependent upon individual performance, skill development, and the time requirements established for the respective zone. A fixed amount is set by the Organization Council each year during the budget process. A 3% annual increase for Skill-based Pay increases has been established as a reasonable goal, unless it creates a hardship for the overall Organization budget. This figure does not include adjustments to the salary structure (i.e., market adjustments to salary ranges).

A total of two Progress Reviews per employee are administered annually. The amount of the skill-based increase is allocated evenly at the appropriate review date. All departments utilize an October 1st/April 1st review cycle.

Additional merit pay increases of one percent (1%) based on performance are provided to employees receiving a rating of at least 7.5 to 8.9 on the Progress Review; however employees receiving an overall Progress Review Score of 9.0 or higher may receive an equivalent salary increase of 2% annually.
- For example, if an employee receives an 8.1 Progress Review rating in April, a 7.7 rating in October, is on schedule for completing the requirements of the zoning plan (Exhibit I), and the Organization Council had previously approved a 3% annual increase for SBP, the employee would be eligible for a 4% annualized merit increase (1.5% + 0.5% = 2% increase in April and 1.5% +0.5% = 2% increase in October; 4% combined increase for year). Using the same example, if the Progress Review ratings are 9.3 and 9.1 respectively, the employee would be eligible for a 5% annualized merit increase (1.5% + 1% = 2.5% increase in April and 1.5% + 1% = 2.5% increase in Oct.; 5% combined increase). Finally, using the same example, if the April and October Progress Review ratings are 7.2 and 9.3 respectively, the employee would be eligible for a 4.5% increase (1.5% + 0.5% = 2% increase in April and 1.5% + 1.0% = 2.5% increase in October; 4.5% combined increase).
- Employees receiving a Progress Review rating of less than 5.0 will not be eligible for a pay increase during the respective review period, regardless of formal training, cross training and/or certification/education that might have been completed.

Employees who are on schedule for completing the requirements of their zoning plan, but who have not met the time requirements established for the zone, will receive skill-based merit increases up to, but not exceeding, the maximum pay of the zone. For example, an employee with a salary deep into Zone 1 has just

Skill-Based Pay Policy and Administration Guidelines

been reviewed (9.3 rating) and is eligible for a 2.5% increase (1.5% + 1.0%). However, the employee started above the "calculated minimum," has only been in Zone 1 for one year, and a 1.8% salary increase would place the employee at the maximum of Zone 1. In this case, the employee would receive a 1.8% increase instead of a 2.5% increase. Employees may receive special merit pay increases within their pay zone. Employees are not eligible to move out of their current pay zone until all requirements have been met. The requirements include both skill zones and years of experience.

Employees are eligible for Skill-based Pay increases if they are on schedule for completing the requirements of the Zoning Plans. To make this determination, it is necessary for employees to have completed a sufficient amount of the Zone's requirements to receive the increase (Exhibit I details the percentage to be completed at each Progress Review cycle). Please note these increases are in relation to performance increases.

To determine the percentage, the supervisor figures the percentage of each skill zone completed, and multiplies this amount by the weight assigned to the skill zone. An example for calculating Skill-based Pay is provided in Exhibit III and forms for use in figuring Skill-based Pay are provided in Form D (manual) and/or Form E (computerized); forms attached.

Performance pay increases are not automatic. Increases must be earned by the employee and requested, recommended and justified by the Department Director. Awarding or withholding performance pay is a management prerogative and responsibility. All salary increases are effective at the beginning of the nearest pay period.

DEMOTIONS

An employee who is either voluntarily or involuntarily demoted to a classification with a lower pay range or lower maximum salary shall be compensated at a rate determined by the affected employee's Department Director and the Director of Personnel Services. The salary for employees receiving voluntary or involuntary demotions must be placed below the maximum pay level of the assigned pay range.

TRANSFERS

An employee who applies and is selected for a position in the same job classification in another Organization department, or who applies and is selected for a position in a new classification in another Organization department within the same pay range, may receive an increase in compensation with the approval of the Director of Personnel Services within Zone 2, or the Director of Personnel Services and the appropriate Assistant Organization Manager or Deputy

Skill-Based Pay Policy and Administration Guidelines

Organization Manager if the salary falls within Zone 3 or 4. The salary increase should follow the same criteria outlined for new hires [see "Starting Salary"].

RECLASSIFIED EMPLOYEES

If an employee's position is reclassified to another classification in a higher pay range, the rate of pay may be increased by ten percent (10%), or adjusted to the "calculated minimum" of the new range, whichever is greater. If an employee's position is reclassified to another classification in a lower pay range, or to another position in the same pay grade, the rate of pay will typically not be adjusted, provided the employee is below the maximum salary level of the pay range of the newly classified position.

All salary adjustments should follow the same criteria outlined for new hires [see "Starting Salary"].

APPENDIX N

SAMPLE CERTIFICATION MANUAL

Skill Zone 1

Track 1
Foundation and Development Skill Blocks

In order to complete the requirements for Skill Zone 1, Track 1, the following skills must be demonstrated:

1.1.1	City Policy/Departmental Directives Review
1.1.2	Defensive Driving
1.1.3	First Aid / CPR
1.1.4	Basic Haz-Mat.
1.1.5	Confined Space Entry
1.1.6	Two- way Radio Protocol

The complete instructions, requirements and procedures used to complete the skills listed above are outlined in the remaining section to follow.

1.1.1 City Policy and Departmental Directives Review

To Do: Review "City Policy and "Departmental Directives"

Proof: Get sign-off of supervisor on checklist

How To:

The "City Directives" and "Departmental Policies" will help you to become familiar with the organization. Get a copy from your supervisor.

You should review this information during the first week of your employment.

You should ask questions to your supervisor if you do not understand something in either one of the books.

You supervisor will review the policies with you and will help you to complete the checklist on the following page.

The checklist will be placed in your file to show proof of completion of this item.

1.1.2 Defensive Driving

To Do: City Sponsored Training Course(s)

Proof: Written Test with a Passing Score and a City Class Certificate

How To:

- You must contact the Field Training Coordinator to make arrangements to complete a defensive driving class.

- The Field Training Coordinator will enroll employees in the City's course or other arrangements will be made if classes are unavailable.

- You may be enrolled in a local defensive driving course or may be enrolled in a home study course.

- You must provide documentation of the defensive driving course completion. A copy of the documentation will be maintained in your personnel file.

1.1.3 First Aid / CPR

To Do: City Sponsored Training Course

Proof: Give a copy of passing certificate to your supervisor

- Complete classroom training on first aid procedures and cardiopulmonary resuscitation (CPR) as provided by the contract Service Company. (Classroom training may be completed on treatment facility site when the class size is large enough to permit it, however single or small groups of employees will be sent to the contract service company office for training.)

- Provide proof of successful class completion to your supervisor upon returning to work.

1.1.4 Basic Haz-Mat

To Do: Attend class for Basic Haz-Mat

Proof: Give proof of attendance to your supervisor

How To:

- Go to the Field Training Coordinator within 45 days of employment to sign up to attend the one-day training class.

- After you attend the class, give your supevisor a copy of your certificate. The documentation will be kept in your personnel file.

1.1.5 Confined Space Entry

To Do: On-the-Job Training and City-Sponsored Training Course(s)

Proof: Demonstrated Skill with Supervisor's Sign-Off Certificate and a City Class Certificate

How To:

- You must complete confined space entry and practice.

- The training will be provided through the Field Training Coordinator.

- Documentation of the training will be signed by the employee and by the field training coordinator and maintained in the employee's personnel file.

1.1.6 Two way Radio Protical

To Do: Receive On-the-Job Training and Demonstrate Skill

Proof: Demonstrated Skill Certificate

How To:

- In order to demonstrate knowledge of effective two-way radio communications, study the equipment users manual(s) for the two-way radio communications system(s).

- Have your supervisor locate this information for you if you do not have it in your possession. You will be required to pass a city-sponsored class on the proper operation of this equipment. Have your supervisor sign you up for this class. The pass/fail class will focus primarily on these items:

    1. Identification of radio equipment components
    2. Proper radio terminology (what to say)

3. Procedures for emergency radio usage
4. Demonstration of learned techniques and procedures

- Once you have completed the class, make sure to provide your supervisor with a class certificate as proof of successful completion. Your supervisor may also ask that you demonstrate your skills and further proof. If so, have your supervisor complete a "Demonstrated Skill Certificate" as well.

Track 2
Water Utility Operator Technical Skill Block

In order to complete the requirements for Skill Zone 1, Track 2, the following skills must be demonstrated:

> 1.2.1 Water Mainlines
>
> 1.2.2 Valves
>
> 1.2.3 Fire Hydrants
>
> 1.2.4 Service Connections
>
> 1.2.5 Disinfection/Sanitation
>
> 1.2.6 Basic Equipment Operation

The complete instructions, requirements and procedures used to complete the skills listed above are outlined in the remaining section to follow.

1.2.1 Water Mainlines

To Do: On-the-Job Training and City-Sponsored Training Course(s)

Proof: Get a "Demonstrated Skill Certificate" from your Field Training Coordinator on each item listed below.

How To:
- In order to demonstrate and identify the understanding of Water Mainlines, the following skills must be demonstrated.

    1. Identify Components
    2. Identify three types of mainline water pipe.
    3. Install, repair clamp and compression coupling.

4. Use water system maps to identify at least three appurtenances.

- Once you have completed the demonstration, make sure to provide your supervisor with proof of successful completion. Your supervisor may also ask that you demonstrate your skills and further proof. If so, have your supervisor complete a "Demonstrated Skill Certificate" as well.

1.2.2 Valves

To Do: On-the-Job Training and City-Sponsored Training Course(s)

Proof: Get a "Demonstrated Skill Certificate" from your Field Training Coordinator on each item listed above. Give a copy of passing certificates to your supervisor.

How To:

- In order to demonstrate the understanding of Valves, the following skills must be demonstrated

    1. Locate and mark valves.
    2. Basic operations of valves.
    3. Adjust top section to grade.
    4. Clean out valve.

- Once you have completed the demonstration, make sure to provide your supervisor with proof of successful completion. Your supervisor may also ask that you demonstrate your skills and further proof. If so, have your supervisor complete a "Demonstrated Skill Certificate" as well.

1.2.3 Fire Hydrants

To Do: On-the-Job Training and City-Sponsored Training Course(s)

Proof: Get a "Demonstrated Skill Certificate" from your Field Training Coordinator on each item listed above. Give a copy of passing certificates to your supervisor.

How To:

- In order to demonstrate the knowledge and understanding of Fire Hydrants, the following skills must be demonstrated.

    1. Identify three brands by manufacturer and determine mainline size
    2. Demonstrate proper operation
    3. Clean and paint

- Once you have completed the demonstration, make sure to provide your supervisor with proof of successful completion. Your supervisor may also ask that you demonstrate your skills and further proof. If so, have your supervisor complete a "Demonstrated Skill Certificate" as well.

1.2.4 Service Connections

To Do: On-the-Job Training and City-Sponsored Training Course(s)

Proof: Get a "Demonstrated Skill Certificate" from your Field Training Coordinator on each item listed above. Give a copy of certificates to your supervisor.

How To:

- In order to demonstrate the knowledge and understanding of Service Connections, the following skills must be demonstrated.

    1. Identify components from mainline to private service line

    2. Identify the equipment needed to install a service connection

    3. Identify the hand tools needed to install or repair service connection

    4. Identify the parts used to repair a service connection

- Once you have completed the demonstration, make sure to provide your supervisor with proof of successful completion. Your supervisor may also ask that you demonstrate your skills and further proof. If so, have your supervisor complete a "Demonstrated Skill Certificate" as well.

1.2.5 Disinfection/Sanitation

To Do: On-the-Job Training and City-Sponsored Training Course(s)

Proof: Get a "Demonstrated Skill Certificate" from your Field Training Coordinator on each item listed above. Give a copy of certificates to your supervisor.

How To:

- In order to demonstrate the knowledge and understanding of, the following must be demonstrated.

    1. Personal hygiene at work

    2. Excavation standard to assure sanitation

    3. List water line disinfection standards

- Once you have completed the demonstration, make sure to provide your supervisor with proof of successful completion. Your supervisor may also ask that you demonstrate your skills and further proof. If so, have your supervisor complete a "Demonstrated Skill Certificate" as well.

1.2.5 Basic Equipment Operation

To Do: On the Job Training

Proof: Demonstrated Skill Certificate

How To:

- Employee shall contact supervisor or Field Training Coordinator and make arrangements for on the job training.

- During this hands on training you will be instructed how to demonstrate the basic equipment operations.

- Once you have completed the demonstration, make sure to provide your supervisor with proof of successful completion. Your supervisor may also ask that you demonstrate your skills and further proof. If so, have your supervisor complete a "Demonstrated Skill Certificate" as well.

Track 3
Wastewater Collection Mechanical/Technical Skill Blocks

In order to complete the requirements for Skill Zone 1, Track 3, the following skills must be demonstrated:

> 1.3.1 Wastewater Mainlines
>
> 1.3.2 Manholes
>
> 1.3.3 Inflow/infiltration
>
> 1.3.4 Service Connections
>
> 1.3.5 Disinfection/Sanitation
>
> 1.3.6 Basic Equipment Operation

The complete instructions, requirements and procedures used to complete the skills listed above are outlined in the remaining section to follow.

1.3.1 Wastewater Mainlines

To Do: On-the-Job Training and City-Sponsored Training Course(s)

Proof: Get a "Demonstrated Skill Certificate" from your Field Training Coordinator on each item listed below.

How To:
- In order to demonstrate and identify the understanding of Wastewater Mainlines, the following skills must be demonstrated.

    1. Identify three types of sewer pipe

2. Restrict flow for repairs or maintenance

3. Install a rubber adapter

- Once you have completed the demonstration, make sure to provide your supervisor with proof of successful completion. Your supervisor may also ask that you demonstrate your skills and further proof. If so, have your supervisor complete a "Demonstrated Skill Certificate" as well.

1.3.2 Manholes

To Do: On-the-Job Training and City-Sponsored Training Course(s)

Proof: Get a "Demonstrated Skill Certificate" from your Field Training Coordinator on each item listed below.

How To:
- In order to demonstrate and identify the understanding of Wastewater Manholes, the following skills must be demonstrated.

    1. Identify the components

    2. Identify the hazards that can be found in a manhole

- Once you have completed the demonstration, make sure to provide your supervisor with proof of successful completion. Your supervisor may also ask that you demonstrate your skills and further proof. If so, have your supervisor complete a "Demonstrated Skill Certificate" as well.

1.3.3 Inflow/Infiltration

To Do: On-the-Job Training and City-Sponsored Training Course(s)

Proof: Get a "Demonstrated Skill Certificate" from your Field Training Coordinator on each item listed below.

How To:
- In order to demonstrate and identify the understanding of Inflow/Infiltration, the following skills must be demonstrated.

    1. Define I & I

2. Name three sources of I & I

3. Describe three I & I investigation techniques

- Once you have completed the demonstration, make sure to provide your supervisor with proof of successful completion. Your supervisor may also ask that you demonstrate your skills and further proof. If so, have your supervisor complete a "Demonstrated Skill Certificate" as well.

1.3.4 Service Connections

To Do: On-the-Job Training and City-Sponsored Training Course(s)

Proof: Get a "Demonstrated Skill Certificate" from your Field Training Coordinator on each item listed below.

How To:
- In order to demonstrate and identify the understanding of Wastewater Service Connections, the following skills must be demonstrated.

    1. Explain what a service connection is

    2. Identify the components from main line to property line

    3. Identify the tools needed to install a sewer service

    4. Identify the materials needed to install a sewer service

- Once you have completed the demonstration, make sure to provide your supervisor with proof of successful completion. Your supervisor may also ask that you demonstrate your skills and further proof. If so, have your supervisor complete a "Demonstrated Skill Certificate" as well.

1.3.5 Disinfection/Sanitation

To Do: On-the-Job Training and City-Sponsored Training Course(s)

Proof: Get a "Demonstrated Skill Certificate" from your Field Training Coordinator on each item listed below.

How To:
- In order to demonstrate and identify the understanding of Wastewater Disinfection / Sanitation, the following skills must be demonstrated.

1. Personal hygiene at work

2. Demonstrate proper disinfection of SSO

- Once you have completed the demonstration, make sure to provide your supervisor with proof of successful completion. Your supervisor may also ask that you demonstrate your skills and further proof. If so, have your supervisor complete a "Demonstrated Skill Certificate" as well.

1.3.6 Basic Equipment Operations

To Do: On the Job Training

Proof: Demonstrated Skill Certificate

How To:

- Employee shall contact supervisor or Field Training Coordinator and make arrangements for on the job training.

- During this hands on training you will be instructed how to demonstrate the basic equipment operations.

- Once you have completed the demonstration, make sure to provide your supervisor with proof of successful completion. Your supervisor may also ask that you demonstrate your skills and further proof. If so, have your supervisor complete a "Demonstrated Skill Certificate" as well.

APPENDIX O

SAMPLE SKILL LISTS AND RATINGS

Skill List and Ratings for Support Services Provider-Accountant

Task	Rater 1	Rater 2	Rater 3	Rater 4	Avg	St. Dev
preparing and analyzing cashflow projections and available investment vehicles to make investment decisions	11	10	11	11	**10.75**	0.5
ensuring financial mainframe system is operating correctly	9	9	11	12	**10.25**	1.5
contacting vendor to resolve serious system problems	8	12	10	10	**10**	1.633
coordinating city budget process	9	10	10	10	**9.75**	0.5
preparing for bond referendums, debt impact analysis, and formulating financing strategies	10	9	10	10	**9.75**	0.5
assisting city treasurer to market debt for city	11	7	9	11	**9.5**	1.915
making hiring decisions	7	9	9	12	**9.25**	2.062
ensuring debt service payments are released on time and for the correct amounts	10	8	9	9	**9**	0.816
maintaining debt service schedules	10	7	9	10	**9**	1.414
preparing budget document for GFOA distinguished budget presentation award	7	9	10	10	**9**	1.414
assisting with the annual audit and preparation of annual financial statements for GFOA distinguished award	8	9	7	11	**8.75**	1.708
tracking all expected cash flow	8	10	7	9	**8.5**	1.291
maintaining accounting processes	7	10	8	9	**8.5**	1.291
generating monthly backups of financial software	9	7	10	7	**8.25**	1.5
preparing and compiling financial data necessary for arbitrage rebate calculation and legal compliance	9	6	9	9	**8.25**	1.5
researching and troubleshooting system related problems	6	8	9	10	**8.25**	1.708
reviewing and approving all check requests for payment	8	8	8	8	**8**	0
acts as city liaison to the community services funding committee	8	8	8	8	**8**	0
ensuring timeclock system is operating correctly	7	8	8	9	**8**	0.816
monitoring and reporting on fixed assets	7	8	9	8	**8**	0.816
providing on the job guidance to employees	6	10	8	8	**8**	1.633
ensuring system control tables are functioning properly	7	9	8	8	**8**	0.816

Appendix O – Page 1

©Copyright 2003, 2004 - All rights reserved - The Waters Consulting Group, Inc

Skill List and Ratings for Support Services Provider-Accountant

Skill						
determining investable balances and funds disbursement	7	8	8	8	**7.75**	0.5
assisting in preparing financial statements for specific funds	7	7	7	9	**7.5**	1
compiling and developing audit work papers, budget activity and financial statements	7	6	8	9	**7.5**	1.291
meeting with city, department and division managers to coordinate decision making on accounting issues	6	7	7	10	**7.5**	1.732
resolving employee complaints	7	7	7	9	**7.5**	1
assisting controller in preparing and monitoring Accounting Division Budget	7	7	7	8	**7.25**	0.5
conducting external research and providing assistance to committees	6	8	7	8	**7.25**	0.957
processing debt service invoices	8	7	7	7	**7.25**	0.5
providing training on financial system and timeclock system	6	9	7	7	**7.25**	1.258
conducting annual performance reviews	5	8	7	8	**7**	1.414
instructing the securities clearance department of the bank to settle trades purchased and sold	7	7	7	7	**7**	0
monitoring cash in the bank and CDs to ensure legal compliance	7	7	7	7	**7**	0
coordinating federal, state and legal agency surveys	7	6	7	8	**7**	0.816
performing special projects	8	7	6	7	**7**	0.816
supervising and performing testing of new system releases	8	8	5	7	**7**	1.414
reviewing payroll registers and disbursements for any discrepancies	5	8	6	8	**6.75**	1.5
maintaining grant revenue	7	7	7	6	**6.75**	0.5
providing analysis required to support city treasurer on projects or assignments	6	8	5	8	**6.75**	1.5
verifying broker/dealer trade confirmations and bank confirmations	7	6	7	7	**6.75**	0.5
preparing annual budgets for employee health and disability fund and debt service fund	6	7	7	7	**6.75**	0.5
safe keeping software-update user data as well as bank's data	8	6	7	6	**6.75**	0.957
analyzing and comparing	6	7	6	8	**6.75**	0.957

Skill List and Ratings for Support Services Provider-Accountant

current period general ledger activity to bank activity						
monitoring accounting for arbitrage restricted funds	7	7	6	6	**6.5**	0.577
utilizing computer software to produce schedules and reports	8	6	5	7	**6.5**	1.291
coordinating with department and division managers responsible for projects	6	5	6	8	**6.25**	1.258
reviewing financial processes and procedures	6	6	5	8	**6.25**	1.258
scheduling work	5	5	7	8	**6.25**	1.5
using an on-line accounts payable system	5	6	5	9	**6.25**	1.893
researching inquiries and communicating finding in verbal and written format	5	6	6	8	**6.25**	1.258
reviewing and reconciling data	6	6	5	8	**6.25**	1.258
update training manuals as needed	7	6	6	6	**6.25**	0.5
reviewing income and expense activity	6	7	4	7	**6**	1.414
initiating wire transfers, intra-bank transfers and stop payments	8	4	5	7	**6**	1.826
preparing detailed worksheet of financial information	5	6	5	8	**6**	1.414
preparing regular reports containing financial information	6	6	5	7	**6**	0.816
researching and resolving any discrepancies	6	6	6	6	**6**	0
reviewing and interpreting information obtained from sub-ledger reports and/or spreadsheets	6	5	5	8	**6**	1.414
assessing and resolving billing disputes	6	6	7	4	**5.75**	1.258
retrieving market information daily through on-line financial software	6	6	4	7	**5.75**	1.258
approve all journal entries posted in system	5	5	5	8	**5.75**	1.5
determining salary increases for employees	6	6	5	6	**5.75**	0.5
communicating with city departments on accounting issues	5	6	4	7	**5.5**	1.291
entering investment trade information into software	6	7	4	5	**5.5**	1.291
making necessary journal entries to reverse the charges at the start of a new fiscal year	4	6	7	5	**5.5**	1.291
preparing investment tickets to complete journal entries and provide a description of the	6	5	4	7	**5.5**	1.291

Skill List and Ratings for Support Services Provider-Accountant

security transactions						
recommending and providing training to employees	4	6	4	8	**5.5**	1.915
performing records management	6	4	6	6	**5.5**	1
reviewing and approving accounting reconciliation	5	4	5	7	**5.25**	1.258
printing bank balance reports and financial market information reports	4	6	5	6	**5.25**	0.957
ensuring daily financial reports are reviewed in a timely manner	6	5	5	5	**5.25**	0.5
preparing monthly journal entries for accounting and reviewing monthly portfolio reports prepared by the treasury analyst	6	6	4	5	**5.25**	0.957
processing cash receipts	5	5	4	6	**5**	0.816
Recommending staffing needs	4	6	4	6	**5**	1.155
reviewing vendor inquiries and statements	.	5	8	7	**5**	1.528
safekeeping receipts daily	6	3	4	7	**5**	1.826
communicating with payroll coordinator as needed	4	6	5	5	**5**	0.816
ensuring computer software current	5	7	3	5	**5**	1.633
funding our health claims every two weeks and ensuring the city is up to date	5	6	5	4	**5**	0.816
obtaining statistical information from outside sources	5	5	5	5	**5**	0
representing the finance department in committees	5	5	5	5	**5**	0
coordinating bi-weekly meeting with information technology, purchasing and accounts payable in dealing with system issues	5	3	5	6	**4.75**	1.258
handling investor and citizen inquiries	.	6	5	8	**4.75**	1.528
approving all capital project invoices and check requests	4	5	4	5	**4.5**	0.577
downloading information from mainframe	4	4	4	6	**4.5**	1
preparing investment calendar to reflect maturities and purchases	4	5	4	5	**4.5**	0.577
acquiring monthly market pricing on each security the city owns through a communication software	4	4	4	5	**4.25**	0.5
calculating interest on retainers for repayment to contractors	4	4	4	5	**4.25**	0.5
organizing the investment	4	5	4	4	**4.25**	0.5

Skill List and Ratings for Support Services Provider-Accountant

ticket for each security purchased and file by portfolio						
removing fixed assets	4	4	4	4	**4**	0

APPENDIX P

SAMPLE SKILL OBJECTIVES

Example Skill Objective

Skill ID: 1.1.1	Skill: Basic Safety			
	# Demos: **N/A**	Demo Interval: **N/A**	# Assessors: **1**	Proctor? **Y**

ACTION - Performance: What should the employee be able to do?

Complete Training on the following topics:
1. Asbestos Awareness
2. Back Safety
3. Confined Space to include Blower Safety (video)
4. Defensive Driving
5. Electrical Safety work practices
6. Hazard Communication
7. Hearing Protection
8. PPE
9. Excavation and Fall Protection Safety
10. Machine Guarding
11. Compressed Air Safety/Use (viewing of the CBT)
12. Welding and Cutting Torch Safety
13. Basic Traffic Control (Flagger)
14. Competent Person
15. Threat Recognition (Snakes to Security)
16. Good housekeeping
17. Additional Resources: City OSHM Manual, and Central Safety Services Web. Site.
18. Auto Crane and Rigging Safety

STANDARDS - Conditions: Under what conditions do you want the employee to be able to do it? (Think about actual job conditions)

All weather conditions

PROOF - Criteria/Measurement: How well must it be done?

Attendance and active participation and successful completion of Training.

Safety and Certification Criteria

Location of assessment demonstration: (check all that apply)	Computer Based ☒	Field (on-the-job) ☒	Lab Set-up/Training ☐	Classroom instruction ☒

Equipment Needed

RECERTIFICATION:: YES____   NO __X*__   IF YES, FREQUENCY_____

*Attendance of annual OSHA training is required.

Example Skill Objective

Skill ID: 1.1.2	Skill: Housekeeping		
# Demos: N/A	Demo Interval: N/A	# Assessors: 1	Proctor? Y

ACTION - Performance: What should the employee be able to do?

1. Completion of 5 – Star Training
2. Perform the following housekeeping duties:
   a. Mopping and Sweeping
   b. Spill Response for common workplace chemicals and materials including cleaning solvents, gasoline, oil or spent materials and debris
   c. Cleaning Computers (incl. vacuuming keyboards)
   d. Job Site Clean-up
   e. Disposal for common workplace chemicals and materials including cleaning solvents, gasoline, oil or spent materials and debris
   f. Recycling
   g. Cleaning Vehicles (Exterior and Interior)

STANDARDS - Conditions: Under what conditions do you want the employee to be able to do it? (Think about actual job conditions)

PROOF - Criteria/Measurement: How well must it be done?

According to criteria set by/within the 5 – Star System
Attendance and active participation and successful completion of Training.

Safety and Certification Criteria

Location of assessment demonstration: (check all that apply)	Computer ☐ Based	Field ☒ (on-the-job)	Lab ☐ Set-up/Training	Classroom ☒ instruction

Equipment Needed

Basic housekeeping equipment and tools

RECERTIFICATION:: YES____ NO__X__ IF YES, FREQUENCY_____

Example Skill Objective

Skill ID: 1.1.3	Skill: Basic Customer Service			
	# Demos: N/A	Demo Interval: N/A	# Assessors: N/A	Proctor? Y

ACTION - Performance: What should the employee be able to do?

Completion of KASSETT Training (City's Customer Service Training program)

STANDARDS - Conditions: Under what conditions do you want the employee to be able to do it? (Think about actual job conditions)

Under any condition or situation

PROOF - Criteria/Measurement: How well must it be done?

Attendance and active participation and successful completion of Training.

Safety and Certification Criteria

Location of assessment demonstration: (check all that apply)	Computer ☐ Based	Field ☐ (on-the-job)	Lab ☐ Set-up/Training	Classroom ☒ instruction

Equipment Needed

RECERTIFICATION:: YES____ NO _X_ IF YES, FREQUENCY_____

Example Skill Objective

Skill ID: 1.2.1	Skill: Power Tool Operation		
# Demos: 2	Demo Interval: N/A	# Assessors: 1	Proctor? N/A

ACTION - Performance: What should the employee be able to do?

3. Operate (manual, gas, hydraulic, and electric)
    a. Power saws
    b. Drills
    c. Grinders
    d. Hammers
    e. Tapping machines
    f. Pipe Threaders
    g. Drill Presses
    h. Concrete saws
    i. Cement mixers
    j. Pneumatic tools and impact wrenches
    k. Jackhammers
    l. Tampers
    m. Vacuuming equipment
    n. Dewatering equipment

STANDARDS - Conditions: Under what conditions do you want the employee to be able to do it? (Think about actual job conditions)

Confined space
Limited movement
All weather conditions
Within traffic right of way limitations

PROOF - Criteria/Measurement: How well must it be done?

According to criteria set by/within the 5 – Star System
Attendance and active participation and successful completion of Training

Safety and Certification Criteria

As recommended by Manufacturer
Appropriate PPE
Follow Housekeeping standards

Location of assessment demonstration: (check all that apply)	Computer ☐ Based	Field ☒ (on-the-job)	Lab ☐ Set-up/Training	Classroom ☒ instruction

Equipment Needed

Basic housekeeping equipment

Example Skill Objective

Skill ID: 1.2.2	Skill:	Concrete Construction		
# Demos: 1		Demo Interval: N/A	# Assessors: 1	Proctor? N/A

ACTION - Performance: What should the employee be able to do?

Plan to construct
Form
Bend rebar to specifications
Calculate volume of materials
Mix, Pour and Finish

STANDARDS - Conditions: Under what conditions do you want the employee to be able to do it? (Think about actual job conditions)

In the field
All weather conditions

PROOF - Criteria/Measurement: How well must it be done?

According to Tucson Water standard specifications and details

Safety and Certification Criteria

Appropriate PPE
Follow Housekeeping standards

Location of assessment demonstration: (check all that apply)	Computer ☐ Based	Field ☒ (on-the-job)	Lab ☐ Set-up/Training	Classroom ☒ instruction

Equipment Needed

Levels
Hammer
Wheel barrel
Electric saw
Concrete vibrator
Mixers
Assorted hand tools
Trowels
Hand tamper
Builders level

RECERTIFICATION:: YES____ NO _X_ IF YES, FREQUENCY_____

Appendix P – Page 5
©Copyright 2003, 2004 - All rights reserved - The Waters Consulting Group, Inc

Example Skill Objective

Skill ID: 1.2.3	Skill: Basic Locating			
	# Demos: 6	Demo Interval: N/A	# Assessors: 1	Proctor? N/A

ACTION - Performance: What should the employee be able to do?
Locate Tucson Water assets and generate a bluestake request Reference Valve maps and As-Builts Set-up traffic control Notify customers of scheduled outages Excavate (pothole to locate assets and other utilities)
STANDARDS - Conditions: Under what conditions do you want the employee to be able to do it? (Think about actual job conditions)
Any time there is a need to dig In traffic Any weather condition
PROOF - Criteria/Measurement: How well must it be done?
100% Based on accuracy of valve map In accordance with Bluestake law and limits
Safety and Certification Criteria
PPE Traffic Hazards

Location of assessment demonstration: (check all that apply)	Video ☐	Computer Based ☐	Field ☒ (on-the-job)	Lab ☒ Set-up/Training	Classroom ☒ instruction

Equipment Needed
Shovel Valve wrench Laptop Valve map system Paint sprayer Pin Locators Assorted valve wrenches
RECERTIFICATION: YES____   NO__X__   IF YES, FREQUENCY_____

Example Skill Objective

Skill ID: 1.3.1	Skill:	Distribution: Basic Piping		
# Demos: 10		Demo Interval: N/A	# Assessors: 1	Proctor? N/A

ACTION - Performance: What should the employee be able to do?

Install or repair a metering service
Repair or replace water pipes
Identify pipe type and size
Identify pipefitting parts
Identify coupling method (primer and glue, threaded, mechanical)
Thread pipe
Measure and fabricate plumbing 2"-4" with associated valves, materials and equipment

Completion of the following training courses:
Piping Practices Tools
Using Pipe and Fittings
Large diameter pipe cleaning
Plumbing and Pipefitting
Shut-off valve design and application considerations
Selecting shut-off valves and accessories
Installing shut-off valves
Maintaining shut-off valves
2" – 48" 2500 Resilient wedge gate valve

STANDARDS - Conditions: Under what conditions do you want the employee to be able to do it?
(Think about actual job conditions)

PROOF - Criteria/Measurement: How well must it be done?

In accordance to Tucson Water standard, specifications and details
No leaks
No failure
Successful completion and participation of courses listed above

Safety and Certification Criteria

PPE
Shoring

Location of assessment demonstration: (check all that apply)	Video ☐	Computer Based ☒	Field ☒ (on-the-job)	Lab ☒ Set-up/Training	Classroom ☒ instruction

Equipment Needed

Primer, Glue, Fittings, Cutters, Basic tools, Tapping machine

RECERTIFICATION: YES____   NO__X__   IF YES, FREQUENCY_____

Example Skill Objective

Skill ID: 1.3.2	Skill:	Distribution: Repair and Replacement of 16" pipe or smaller		
	# Demos: ( )	Demo Interval: N/A	# Assessors: 1	Proctor? N/A

ACTION - Performance: What should the employee be able to do?

Replace sections of water pipe ( )
Repair sections of water pipe ( )
Identify size of mains, and types of pipes and materials needed for repair ( )
Prep job site for excavation to include obtaining permits and bluestake clearance, and traffic control ()
Backfill and compact trench and install temporary pavement to standards
Repair water pipe leaks
Exercise system valves
Open and close valves
Purge wells or distribution system to waste
Flush and disinfect pipe
Sanitize and disinfect pipeline
De-water
Locate and excavate valve boxes, meter boxes and vaults
Repair and replace valves
Replace fire hydrants, valves and assorted water work fittings

Completion of the following training courses:
Meter replacement
New Service Installation
How to repair and replace a meter box
How to install, complete and service a residential meter
How to back-fill and compact dirt

STANDARDS - Conditions: Under what conditions do you want the employee to be able to do it?
(Think about actual job conditions)

In the field
Work in confined spaces for long periods of time
Within traffic right of way limitations
All weather and traffic conditions

PROOF - Criteria/Measurement: How well must it be done?

No damage
Tucson Water standard specification and details
Accurately distinguishes appropriate material and equipment for the job
Maintain water system pressure and work passes leak test (no leaks)

Safety and Certification Criteria PPE Traffic Control Lock Out/Tag Out Confined Space Respirator Excavation permitting Permitting					
Location of assessment demonstration: (check all that apply)	Video ☐	Computer ☒ Based	Field ☒ (on-the-job)	Lab ☐ Set-up/Training	Classroom ☒ instruction
Equipment Needed Various power hand tools Shoring De-watering pumps Pressure Sprayer					
RECERTIFICATION: YES____ NO _X_ IF YES, FREQUENCY_____					

Example Skill Objective

Skill ID: 1.3.3	Skill: ADEQ Water Distribution Grade 1 Note: Progression to Craft level and successful completion of probation will require Distribution Grade 1 certification. Water Treatment Grade 1 certification (exam) is similar to the Distribution Grade 1. You may opt to take both certifications consecutively to progress to Craft level.			
	# Demos:	Demo Interval: N/A	# Assessors: 1	Proctor? N/A
ACTION - Performance: What should the employee be able to do?				
STANDARDS - Conditions: Under what conditions do you want the employee to be able to do it? (Think about actual job conditions)				
PROOF - Criteria/Measurement: How well must it be done?				
Safety and Certification Criteria				
Location of assessment demonstration: (check all that apply)	Video ☐	Computer Based ☐	Field ☒ (on-the-job)	Lab ☒ Set-up/Training	Classroom ☒ instruction
Equipment Needed				
RECERTIFICATION: YES____ NO__X__ IF YES, FREQUENCY_____				

Example Skill Objective

Skill ID: 1.3.4	Skill: Maintenance of Equipment			
	# Demos: 4	Demo Interval: N/A	# Assessors: 1	Proctor? N/A

DETERMINE AVAILABLE CBT'S AND ACTIONS

ACTION - Performance: What should the employee be able to do?

Completion of the following training courses:
Lubricating greases: Types, applications and equipment
Lubricating oil: Types, properties and handling
Centrifugal pumps: Operation and Maintenance
Vertical Turbine and Horizontal pump Operations
Industrial Seals: Types, materials and properties
Industrial Seals: Mechanical Face-Troubleshooting and Installation

STANDARDS - Conditions: Under what conditions do you want the employee to be able to do it?
(Think about actual job conditions)

In the Plant
In the field

PROOF - Criteria/Measurement: How well must it be done?

Attendance, participation and successful completion of the training courses
No future failure

Safety and Certification Criteria

PPE
Lockout Tagout

Location of assessment demonstration: (check all that apply)	Video ☐	Computer Based ☒	Field ☒ (on-the-job)	Lab ☐ Set-up/Training	Classroom ☐ instruction

Equipment Needed

Grease gun
Basic hand tools

RECERTIFICATION: YES____   NO__X__   IF YES, FREQUENCY_____

Example Skill Objective

Skill ID: 1.4.1	Skill: Basic Water System functions and equipment		
# Demos:	Demo Interval: N/A	# Assessors: N/A	Proctor? Y

ACTION - Performance: What should the employee be able to do?

Read and interpret valve maps
Physically locate wells, booster stations, reservoirs and pressure regulating stations
Inspect vehicles
Utilize radios and cellular phones
Obtain construction plans and As-Builts
Performs inspections of equipment and tools
Performs calculations (volumes, flows, gallons per minute, etc) for disinfection dosages for sanitation
Takes readings and records of water pressures and flow and chlorine residual
Mechanically disconnects above or below grade piping and assemblies

Completion of the following training courses:
Tucson Water Systems
Reading Engineering Plans

STANDARDS - Conditions: Under what conditions do you want the employee to be able to do it? (Think about actual job conditions)

All weather conditions
Confined spaces

PROOF - Criteria/Measurement: How well must it be done?

Attendance and active participation and successful completion of Training.

Safety and Certification Criteria

PPE
Lockout/tagout double block and bleed
Competent Person
ADEQ Distribution Grade 1

Location of assessment demonstration: (check all that apply)	Computer ☐ Based	Field ☐ (on-the-job)	Lab ☐ Set-up/Training	Classroom ☒ instruction

Equipment Needed
Assorted hand and power tools

RECERTIFICATION:: YES____ NO__X__ IF YES, FREQUENCY_____

Example Skill Objective

Skill ID: 1.4.2	Skill:	Tank Maintenance		
	# Demos: 1	Demo Interval: N/A	# Assessors: 1	Proctor? N/A

ACTION - Performance: What should the employee be able to do?

Scrub, mop and squigey liners or coatings
Remediate and dispose of media (sand, oil contaminated soil, dirt, debris)
Conduct basic inspection of storage tanks and hydro-pneumatic vessels
Maintain and repair of fittings, gauges, ladders and hatches

Completion of the following training course:
Hydro-Pneumatic Pressure Vessels-Purpose, Functions, and Maintenance

---

STANDARDS - Conditions: Under what conditions do you want the employee to be able to do it?
(Think about actual job conditions)

Ability to work in high humidity
Ability to work in a confined space

PROOF - Criteria/Measurement: How well must it be done?

Attend, participate and successfully complete training courses
Meet Tucson Water quality standards

Safety and Certification Criteria

PPE
Lockout Tagout
Confined Space
Double Block and Bleed

Location of assessment demonstration: (check all that apply)	Video ☐	Computer Based ☐	Field ☒ (on-the-job)	Lab ☐ Set-up/Training	Classroom ☐ instruction

Equipment Needed

High Pressure Blower
Basic hand tools
Air Monitor

RECERTIFICATION: YES____ NO _X_ IF YES, FREQUENCY_____

Example Skill Objective

Skill ID: 1.5.1	Skill: Inventory			
	# Demos:	Demo Interval: N/A	# Assessors: 1	Proctor? N/A

ACTION - Performance: What should the employee be able to do?

Conduct physical inventory
Determine onsite material requirements
Pick-up materials and equipment
Ensure trucks are properly supplied
Haul and dispose of debris
Purchase materials
Determine dimension and serial numbers of items
Utilize and references catalog for ordering
Utilize scales
Utilize forklift
Use discretion and verify information provided by sales associates for field fit situations
Utilize manufacturer website.

STANDARDS - Conditions: Under what conditions do you want the employee to be able to do it? (Think about actual job conditions)

All weather conditions

PROOF - Criteria/Measurement: How well must it be done?

Within driver's license limits
Physical inventory must be 95% accurate
Orders must be 100% accurate
No re-stocking charges

Safety and Certification Criteria

Back safety
Forklift
Use of material safety data sheets

Location of assessment demonstration: (check all that apply)	Video ☐	Computer Based ☐	Field ☒ (on-the-job)	Lab ☒ Set-up/Training	Classroom ☒ instruction

Equipment Needed

Computer, Paper and Pen, Forklift, Pallet jacks, Hand trucks, Scales

RECERTIFICATION: YES_X*__   NO___   IF YES, FREQUENCY_____

*Forklift recertification

Example Skill Objective

Skill ID: 1.6.1	Skill: ADEQ Water Treatment Grade 1 Note: Progression to Craft level and successful completion of probation will require Distribution Grade 1 certification. Water Treatment Grade 1 certification (exam) is similar to the Distribution Grade 1. You may opt to take both certifications consecutively to progress to Craft level.				
# Demos:		Demo Interval: N/A	# Assessors: 1		Proctor? N/A
ACTION - Performance: What should the employee be able to do?						
STANDARDS - Conditions: Under what conditions do you want the employee to be able to do it? (Think about actual job conditions)						
PROOF - Criteria/Measurement: How well must it be done?						
Safety and Certification Criteria						
Location of assessment demonstration: (check all that apply)	Video ☐	Computer Based ☐	Field ☒ (on-the-job)	Lab ☒ Set-up/Training	Classroom ☒ instruction
Equipment Needed						
RECERTIFICATION: YES____ NO__X_ IF YES, FREQUENCY_____						

APPENDIX Q

SAMPLE VISUALS AND PRESENTATIONS

Introducing Skill-based Pay

Sample Employee Presentation

Presented by: THE WATERS CONSULTING GROUP, INC.
2695 Villa Creek Drive • Suite 104 • Dallas • Texas • 75234 • www.watersconsulting.com

Overview

1. Introduction to Skill-Based Pay
2. Skill-Based Pay Policy Issues
3. Skill-Based Pay at at your organization

Skill-based vs. Traditional

Skill-based Pay Systems

- **Person-Based** – Focuses on an individual's ability to contribute to the organization
- **Emphasizes Learning** – By promoting the acquisition of new skills
- Employees are paid for the range of job-related skills and competencies they demonstrate

Traditional Pay Systems

- **Job-Based** – Nature of the work performed and value of that work drives compensation
- Pay is based on the value of the tasks required for the job

Appendix Q ©Copyright 2003, 2004 - All rights reserved - The Waters Consulting Group, Inc

Principles of SBP

Q: *How does Skill-based Pay work?*
A: Pay progression is determined and based on competencies (skills, behaviors, knowledge) associated with superior performance

Q: *What situations lead organizations to consider this technique?*
A:
1) Large skilled, technical or professional workforce and/or presence of career ladders
2) Focus on work teams and need for workforce flexibility
3) Slower growth rates/fewer opportunities

Standard Characteristics of SBP

1. Provides a means by which employees can increase their pay without climbing the hierarchical ladder
2. Supports the organization's and/or department's goals by focusing skill acquisition and development on actual needs
3. More flexible utilization of workforce as employees acquire a breadth and depth of skills across a range of operations – multiple tasks performed with a leaner staff

Potential Benefits of SBP

- Promotes greater flexibility for organization and person
- Improves problem solving by moving it to the person
- Improves communication both upward and downward
- Supports employment security (more valuable)
- Helps to attract and retain talented employees
- Shifts the supervisory role from "task master" to "teacher"

Differences in Skill-based Pay

While Skill-based pay systems share common characteristics, the design and implementation of the pay system will differ as each Skill-based plan is customized to meet the unique needs of each organization.

Implement: Yes or No?

Skill-based pay plans <u>should not be</u> implemented because the organization feels it needs to be doing what other organizations are doing.

👍

Skill-based pay plans <u>should be</u> implemented based on sound reasoning, such as for increases in employee motivation, increases in productivity and increases in workforce flexibility.

Skill-based Pay Results Model

The focus is on enhancing an individual's ability to contribute to the overall good of the organization

- Organizational Readiness
- Acceptable Environment?
  - Yes → Set up skill-based pay committees with SMEs → Develop Skill Hierarchies → Develop and price skill blocks → Design Training & Certification Programs → Prepare skill inventory for each employee
  - No → Do not use Skill-based Pay

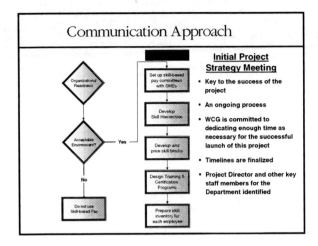

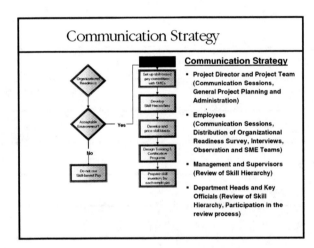

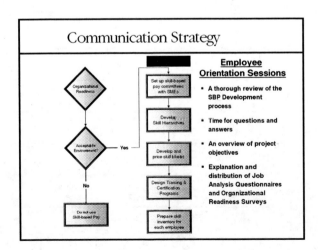

Appendix Q ©Copyright 2003, 2004 - All rights reserved - The Waters Consulting Group, Inc

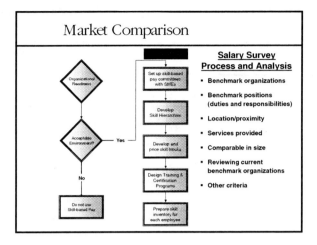

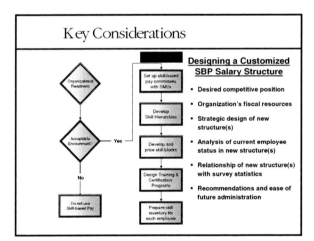

Broadbanding Defined

Broadbanding – commonly refers to the collapsing of many salary grades into bands for numerous purposes such as for improving organizational effectiveness by managing career development and overseeing pay.

Broadbanding – reduces much of the hierarchy associated with a traditional pay structure to support a flatter, leaner, more customer-focused organization.

(Abosch & Hand, 1994)

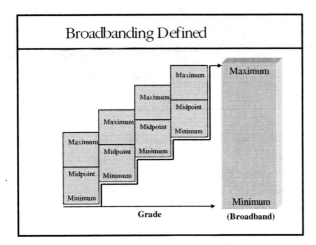

Benefits of Broadbanding

- Supports a flexible and fluid organization by making it easier to restructure work and reorganize teams

- Encourages lateral employee movement and development by flattening or eliminating the pyramid driven job family career ladders

- Supports teamwork by de-emphasizing differences in level and status

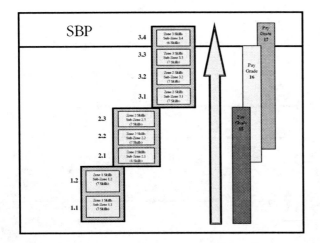

Skill Certification

How are employee skills and competencies certified and re-certified?

- Certification might involve one or more of several methods including:

  1. Paper/Pencil Testing
  2. Completion of Approved Course Work
  3. Completion of Training Sessions
  4. Actual Demonstration of Competence in Skill

Skill Objectives

- What is the skill an employee must be able to perform?
- How well must the skill be performed?
- What are the important conditions or constraints under which the performance must occur?

Final Report Development

Salary Administrative Policies and Presentation of Final Report

- Recommendations and survey results will be finalized
- Movement through the SBP System will be reviewed and recommendations for maintenance will be made
- Formal presentation

Flowchart:
- Organizational Readiness? → Acceptable Environment? → Yes → Set up skill-based pay committees with SMEs → Develop Skill Hierarchies → Develop and price skill blocks → Design Training & Certification Programs → Prepare skill inventory for each employee
- No → Do not use Skill-based Pay

Level of Employee Involvement

What level of employee involvement will the organization allow in the development of the Skill-based Pay System?

- Management will serve to guide the employees in the development of the system
- Employee input and involvement are very important to the success of the new system
- SMEs – Subject Matter Experts

Subject Matter Expert (SME) Teams

1. Include employees from all levels
2. Provide time and support for SME Team meetings
3. SME Teams will be heavily involved in the SBP Development process
4. Provide organizational review of SME Team deliverables

Job Analysis Questionnaire

A. Identification / General Information

Employee Name:	Joe Sample
If more than one Employee participated in completing this questionnaire, put "Multiple Employees" and attach a list of all participants to this form	
Current Job Title:	Utility Technician II
Department Name:	Water Resources
Immediate Supervisor's Name:	John Director
Immediate Supervisor's Title:	Water Resources Director
Length of Service with the Organization: ___ Years ___ Months	
Length of Service in Current Job: ___ Years ___ Months	
Describe you normal work schedule	
Monday – Friday 7:00 a.m. to 4:00 p.m.	

Completing the JAQ (continued)

B. Brief Description of the Job

The purpose of this position is to: *provide multi-skilled services in operation and maintenance of the associated assets of the Water System.*

This is accomplished by: *installing, monitoring, repairing and maintaining water systems and treatment plant systems equipment and facilities. Additionally responsible for monitoring and recording water usage.*

Other duties include: *providing emergency services on an as needed basis and performing various administrative duties as necessary.*

Completing the JAQ (continued)

C. Essential Functions

Sample Function: *Provides multi-skilled services for the operation and maintenance of the Water System*	Percentage of Time: *35%*
	Physical Strength Code: *M*

Tasks performed to accomplish this function:
1. *Conducting routine installation, monitoring, maintenance and emergency repair*
2. *Monitors and services water systems by investigating/locating repair sites*
3. *Manages work requirements & inventory by assessing equipment/supply needs*

Completing the JAQ (continued)

D. Equipment, Certifications & Other Requirements

Machines, Tools, Equipment and Work Aids: List machines, tools and equipment required for this job (not Computer Equipment and Software): *Light and Heavy Equipment; Various Meters, Testing & Precision*

Computer Equipment and Software: List all computer equipment and software that is required for this job: *Personal computer, printer, scanner*

Primary Work Location: Please check the type of location where the primary job duties are performed.
- ❏ Office Environment
- ❏ Warehouse
- ❏ Shop
- ❏ Vehicle
- ❏ Recreation Centers/Neighborhood Centers
- ❏ Outdoors (Specify) _____
- ❏ Other (Specify) _____

Completing the JAQ (continued)

D. Equipment, Certifications & Other Requirements

Protective Equipment Required: List protective equipment, if any, which is required for this job.

Safety glasses, gloves, hard hat, steel toe boots

Certification and Other Requirements: (List any licenses, certifications, statutory requirements, or registrations required for this position. This does not necessarily mean the license you have, but what is required to hire or promote someone into this position, either internally or from the outside. Use exact name of license, certification, etc.).

1. *Certified Hydrostatic Technician*
2.

Completing the JAQ (continued)

E. Career Path Definition

Please indicate other Organization jobs that are related to this position as part of a career family.

Other jobs in the Organization to which those that hold my current position might be promoted.	Supervisor or Manager
My Current Job	
Other jobs in the Organization that would prepare applicants for my current position.	Assistant or Seasonal Employee

---

Completing the JAQ (continued)

F. Supervisory & Management Responsibilities

Supervisory Responsibility: Yes or No, does this position involve directing the work of others?

If Yes, please list the job titles (not working titles) and # of employees you supervise.

Assistant	One
Seasonal Employee	Three

Nature of Work Direction: If you answered "Yes" to the question above, please indicate the nature of work direction provided by the job by placing an "X" next to it.

	Work requires the occasional direction of helpers, assistants, seasonal employees, interns, volunteers or temporary employees.
X	Work requires functioning as a lead worker performing essentially the same work as those directed and includes overseeing work quality, training, instructing, and scheduling work.
	Work requires supervising and monitoring performance for a regular group of employees or a work unit including providing input on hiring/disciplinary actions and work objectives/effectiveness and realigning work as needed.
	Work requires managing and monitoring work performance by directing subordinate supervisors or administrators including making final decisions on hiring and disciplinary actions, evaluating program/work objectives and effectiveness, and realigning work and staffing assignments, as needed.
	Work requires managing and monitoring work performance of senior department managers including evaluating program/work objectives and effectiveness, establishing broad organizational goals and realigning work and staffing for the department.

Appendix Q ©Copyright 2003, 2004 - All rights reserved - The Waters Consulting Group, Inc

Completing the JAQ (continued)

- Complete and accurate answers, take your time.
- Describe the job, not your personal qualifications.
- Collaborate with co-workers in the same job. As an option, complete one questionnaire for employees in the same job and have all employees in that job sign the JAQ.
- Review and proofread your completed questionnaire before you turn it in.
- JAQ is due to supervisors/managers by June 30th.

Manager/Supervisor Role

Your assistance is important

- Encourage employees to participate in groups or individually
- Allow employees time to ask questions and provide ideas relating to the SBP system
- Supervisor support and assistance is important
- Timelines are important to completion of the project

Organizational Readiness Survey

Survey distributed to Employees to assess organizational readiness to implement a Skill-based Pay Program as it relates to areas of:

1. Current performance management and reward practices
2. Training and development
3. Management practices
4. Coworker relations
5. Employee practices and viewpoints

Your Assistance is Important

The Survey serves to…

- Allow an opportunity for all employees to anonymously and confidentially give feedback regarding the SBP system
- Explore general trends in feelings and actions surrounding the SBP system
- Determine those areas where the system is progressing effectively
- Determine those areas where the system needs further assistance and focus

---

Introducing Skill-based Pay

Employee Presentation
-END OF PRESENTATION-

Presented by: **THE WATERS CONSULTING GROUP, INC.**
2695 Villa Creek Drive • Suite 104 • Dallas • Texas • 75234 • www.watersconsulting.com